STAR WARS®
EMPIRE

VOLUME THREE: THE IMPERIAL PERSPECTIVE

THIS STORY TAKES PLACE DURING
AND SHORTLY AFTER THE EVENTS
IN STAR WARS: A NEW HOPE.

STAR WARS: EMPIRE VOLUME 3

THIS VOLUME COLLECTS ISSUES #13, 14 AND #16-
19 OF THE COMIC-BOOK SERIES STAR WARS: EMPIRE.

PUBLISHED BY
DARK HORSE BOOKS
A DIVISION OF DARK HORSE COMICS, INC.
10956 SE MAIN STREET
MILWAUKIE, OR 97222

WWW.DARKHORSE.COM
WWW.STARWARS.COM

TO FIND A COMICS SHOP IN YOUR
AREA, CALL THE COMIC SHOP
LOCATOR SERVICE TOLL-FREE
AT 1-888-266-4226

FIRST EDITION: OCTOBER 2004
ISBN: 1-59307-128-0

3 5 7 9 10 8 6 4 2

PRINTED IN CHINA

VOLUME THREE:
THE IMPERIAL PERSPECTIVE

WRITERS PAUL ALDEN
JEREMY BARLOW
WELLES HARTLEY
RON MARZ

ARTISTS PATRICK BLAINE
BRIAN CHING
DAVIDÉ FABBRI
& CHRISTIAN DALLA VECCHIA
RAUL TREVINO

COLORISTS MICHAEL ATIYEH
DAVIDÉ FABBRI
RAUL TREVINO
STUDIO F

LETTERERS SNO CONE STUDIOS
MICHAEL DAVID THOMAS

FRONT COVER ART BY DOUG WHEATLEY

CK COVER ART BY DAVID MICHAEL BECK
& BRAD ANDERSON

PUBLISHER
MIKE RICHARDSON

COLLECTION DESIGNER
LANI SCHREIBSTEIN

ART DIRECTOR
LIA RIBACCHI

ASSOCIATE EDITOR
JEREMY BARLOW

EDITOR
RANDY STRADLEY

SPECIAL THANKS TO
SUE ROSTONI, AMY GARY,
CHRIS CERASI, AND LUCY AUTREY WILSON
AT LUCAS LICENSING

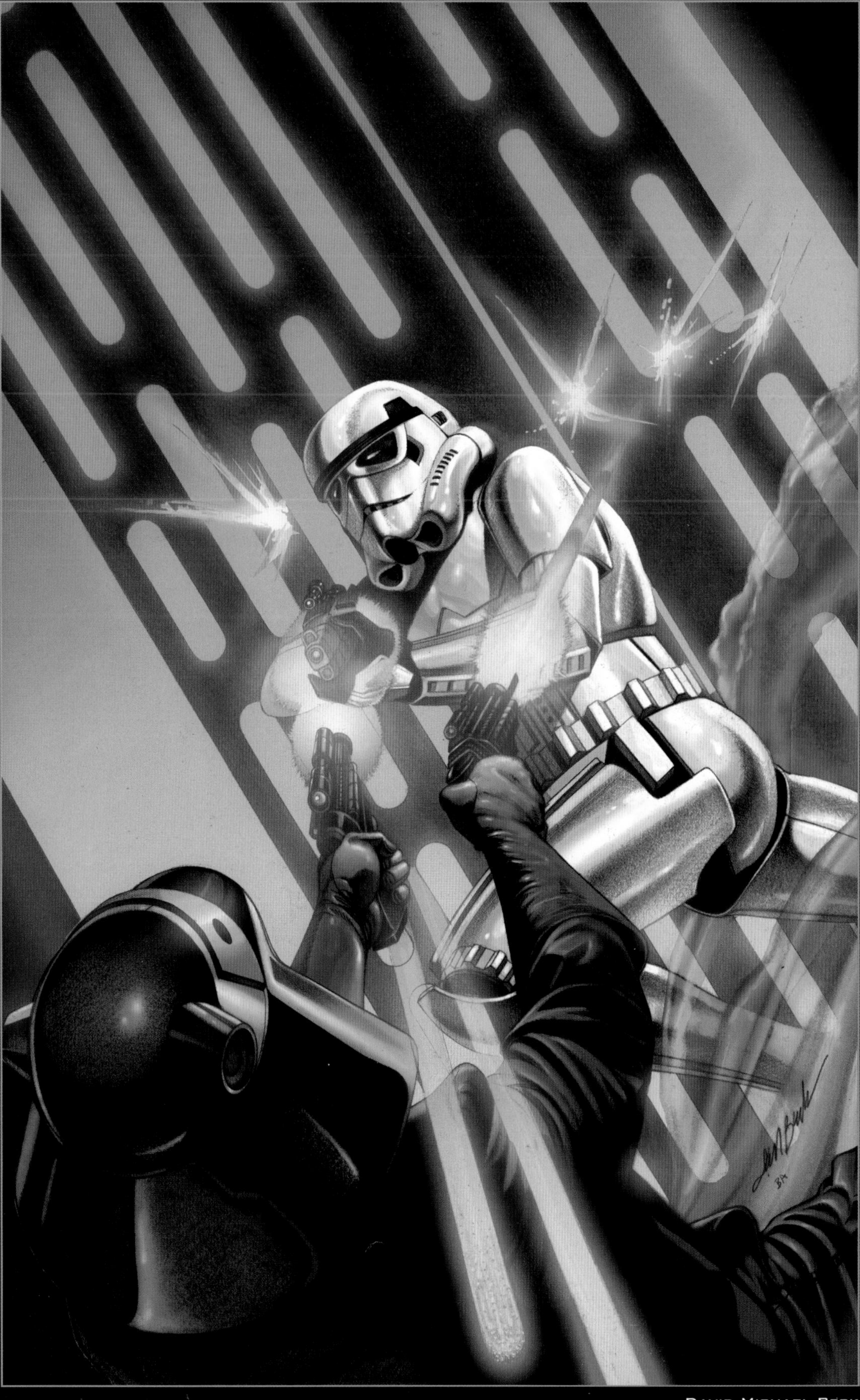

DAVID MICHAEL BECK
COLORS BRAD ANDERSON

WHAT SIN LOYALTY?

Script JEREMY BARLOW
Art PATRICK BLAINE
Colors STUDIO F

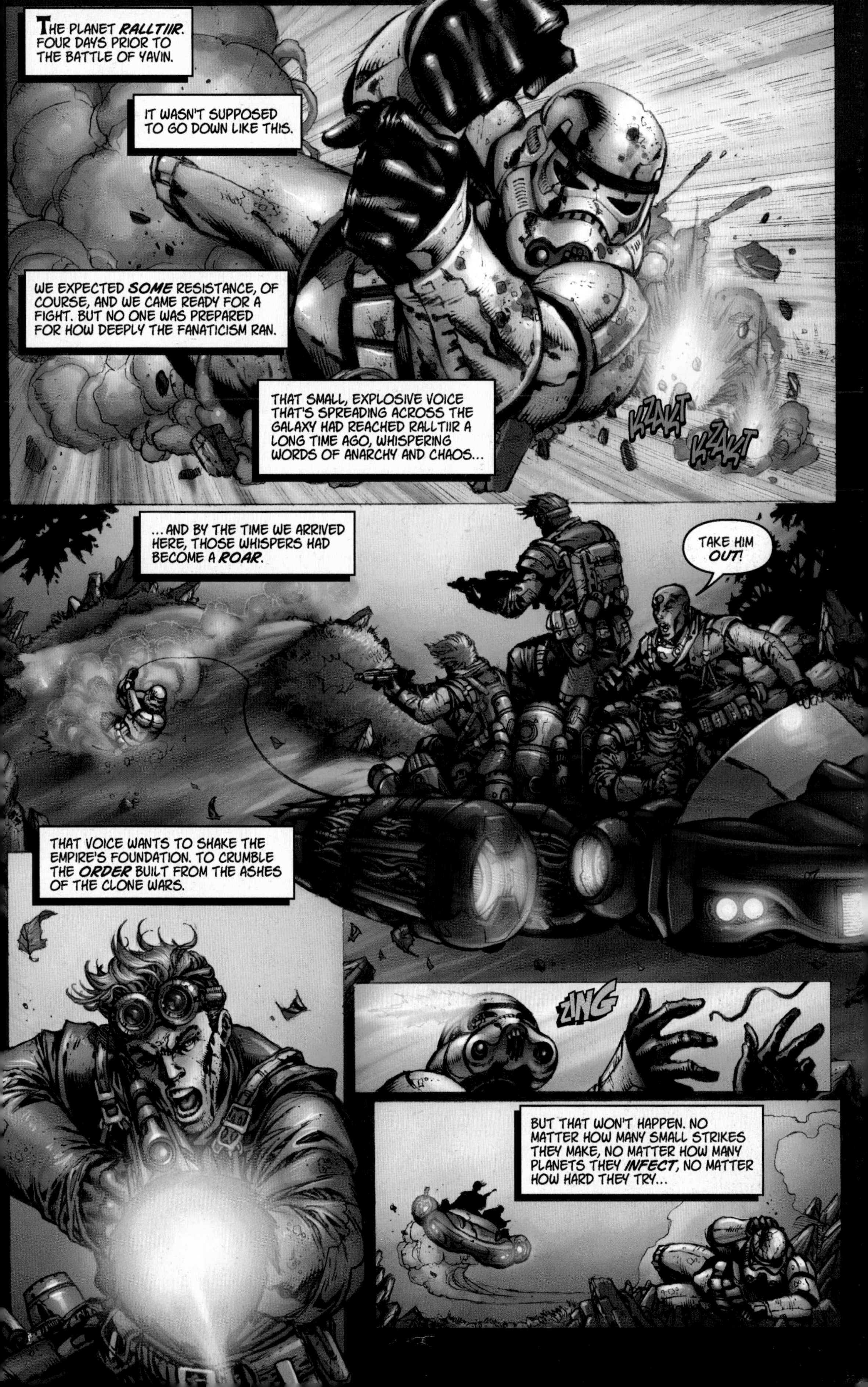

THE PLANET RALLTIIR. FOUR DAYS PRIOR TO THE BATTLE OF YAVIN.
IT WASN'T SUPPOSED TO GO DOWN LIKE THIS.
WE EXPECTED SOME RESISTANCE, OF COURSE, AND WE CAME READY FOR A FIGHT. BUT NO ONE WAS PREPARED FOR HOW DEEPLY THE FANATICISM RAN.
THAT SMALL, EXPLOSIVE VOICE THAT'S SPREADING ACROSS THE GALAXY HAD REACHED RALLTIIR A LONG TIME AGO, WHISPERING WORDS OF ANARCHY AND CHAOS...
KZAKT
KZAKT
...AND BY THE TIME WE ARRIVED HERE, THOSE WHISPERS HAD BECOME A ROAR.
TAKE HIM OUT!
THAT VOICE WANTS TO SHAKE THE EMPIRE'S FOUNDATION. TO CRUMBLE THE ORDER BUILT FROM THE ASHES OF THE CLONE WARS.
ZING
BUT THAT WON'T HAPPEN. NO MATTER HOW MANY SMALL STRIKES THEY MAKE, NO MATTER HOW MANY PLANETS THEY INFECT, NO MATTER HOW HARD THEY TRY...

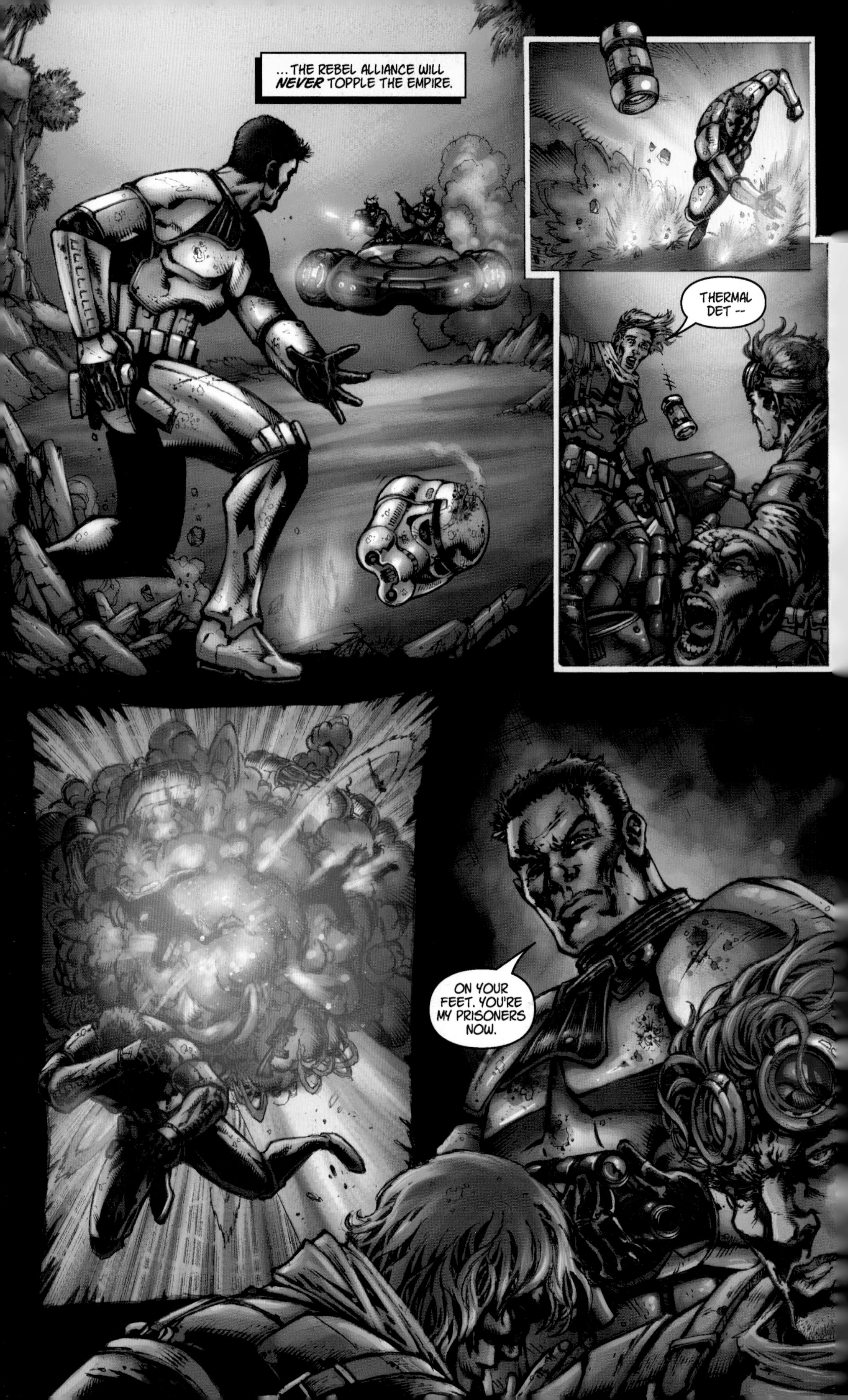

...THE REBEL ALLIANCE WILL NEVER TOPPLE THE EMPIRE.
THERMAL DET --
ON YOUR FEET. YOU'RE MY PRISONERS NOW.

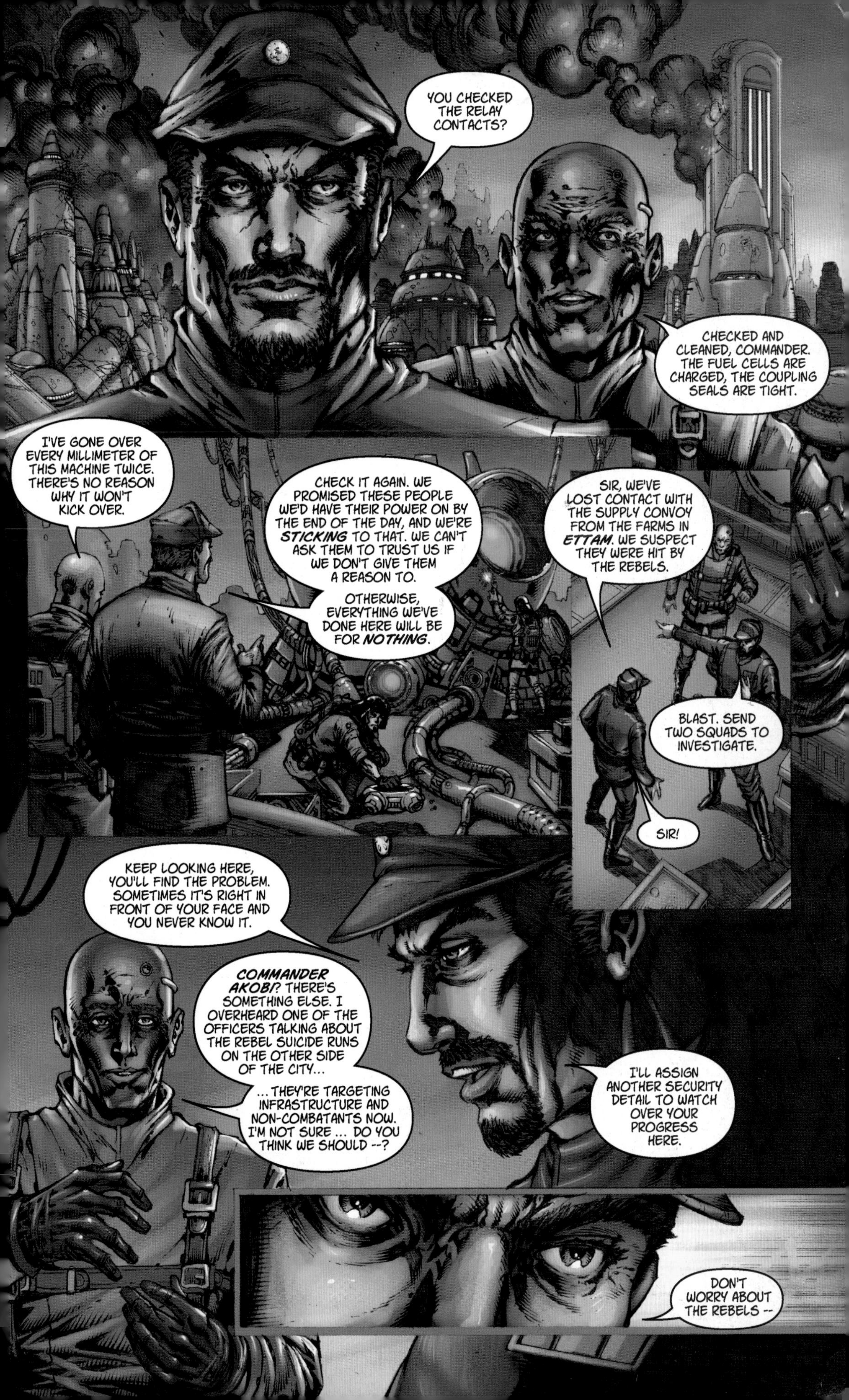
YOU CHECKED THE RELAY CONTACTS?
CHECKED AND CLEANED, COMMANDER. THE FUEL CELLS ARE CHARGED, THE COUPLING SEALS ARE TIGHT.
I'VE GONE OVER EVERY MILLIMETER OF THIS MACHINE TWICE. THERE'S NO REASON WHY IT WON'T KICK OVER.
CHECK IT AGAIN. WE PROMISED THESE PEOPLE WE'D HAVE THEIR POWER ON BY THE END OF THE DAY, AND WE'RE *STICKING* TO THAT. WE CAN'T ASK THEM TO TRUST US IF WE DON'T GIVE THEM A REASON TO.
OTHERWISE, EVERYTHING WE'VE DONE HERE WILL BE FOR *NOTHING*.
SIR, WE'VE LOST CONTACT WITH THE SUPPLY CONVOY FROM THE FARMS IN *ETTAM*. WE SUSPECT THEY WERE HIT BY THE REBELS.
BLAST. SEND TWO SQUADS TO INVESTIGATE.
SIR!
KEEP LOOKING HERE, YOU'LL FIND THE PROBLEM. SOMETIMES IT'S RIGHT IN FRONT OF YOUR FACE AND YOU NEVER KNOW IT.
COMMANDER AKOBI? THERE'S SOMETHING ELSE. I OVERHEARD ONE OF THE OFFICERS TALKING ABOUT THE REBEL SUICIDE RUNS ON THE OTHER SIDE OF THE CITY...
... THEY'RE TARGETING INFRASTRUCTURE AND NON-COMBATANTS NOW. I'M NOT SURE ... DO YOU THINK WE SHOULD --?
I'LL ASSIGN ANOTHER SECURITY DETAIL TO WATCH OVER YOUR PROGRESS HERE.
DON'T WORRY ABOUT THE REBELS --

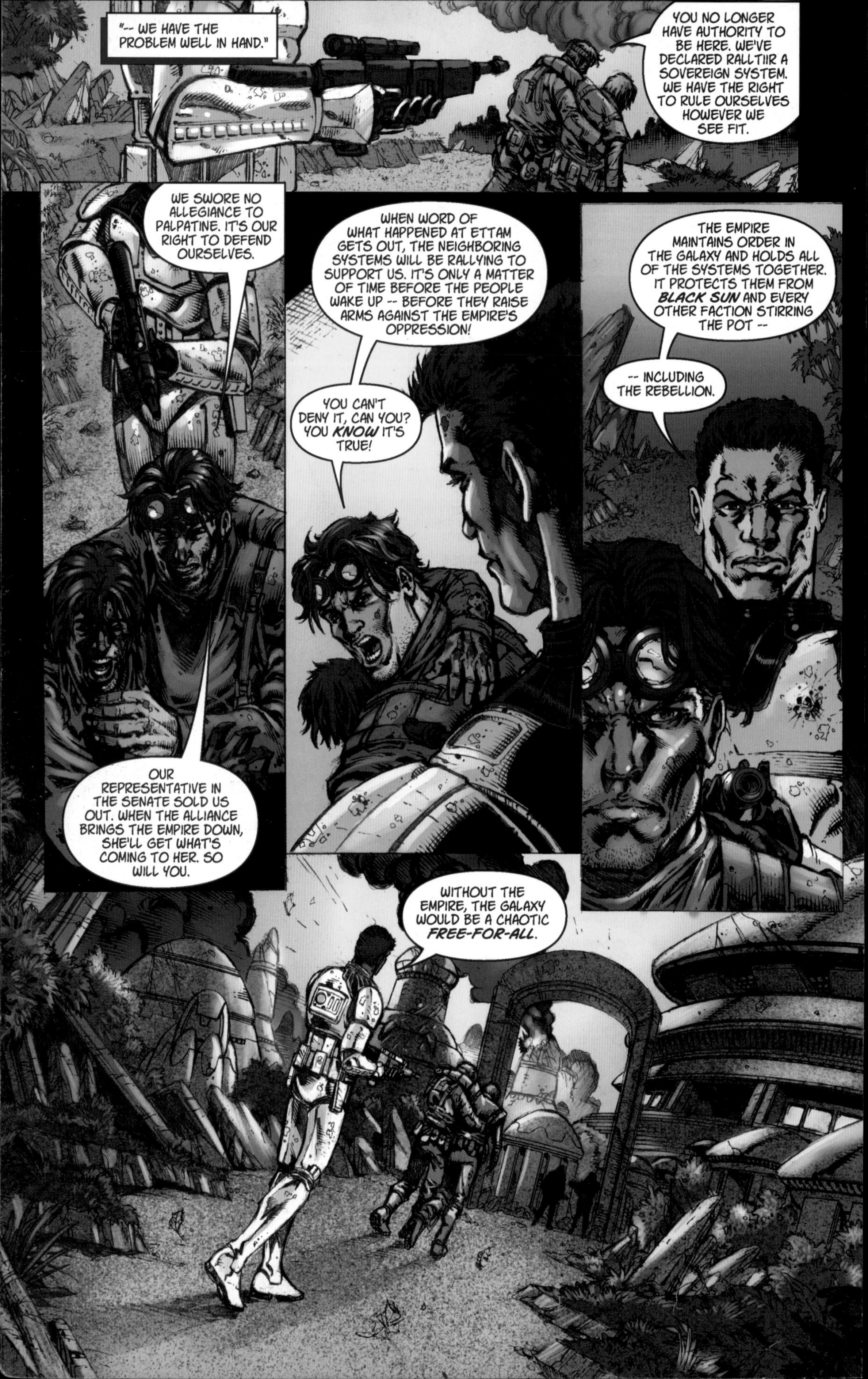
"-- WE HAVE THE PROBLEM WELL IN HAND."
YOU NO LONGER HAVE AUTHORITY TO BE HERE. WE'VE DECLARED RALLTIIR A SOVEREIGN SYSTEM. WE HAVE THE RIGHT TO RULE OURSELVES HOWEVER WE SEE FIT.
WE SWORE NO ALLEGIANCE TO PALPATINE. IT'S OUR RIGHT TO DEFEND OURSELVES.
OUR REPRESENTATIVE IN THE SENATE SOLD US OUT. WHEN THE ALLIANCE BRINGS THE EMPIRE DOWN, SHE'LL GET WHAT'S COMING TO HER. SO WILL YOU.
WHEN WORD OF WHAT HAPPENED AT ETTAM GETS OUT, THE NEIGHBORING SYSTEMS WILL BE RALLYING TO SUPPORT US. IT'S ONLY A MATTER OF TIME BEFORE THE PEOPLE WAKE UP -- BEFORE THEY RAISE ARMS AGAINST THE EMPIRE'S OPPRESSION!
YOU CAN'T DENY IT, CAN YOU? YOU ***KNOW*** IT'S TRUE!
THE EMPIRE MAINTAINS ORDER IN THE GALAXY AND HOLDS ALL OF THE SYSTEMS TOGETHER. IT PROTECTS THEM FROM ***BLACK SUN*** AND EVERY OTHER FACTION STIRRING THE POT --
-- INCLUDING THE REBELLION.
WITHOUT THE EMPIRE, THE GALAXY WOULD BE A CHAOTIC ***FREE-FOR-ALL***.

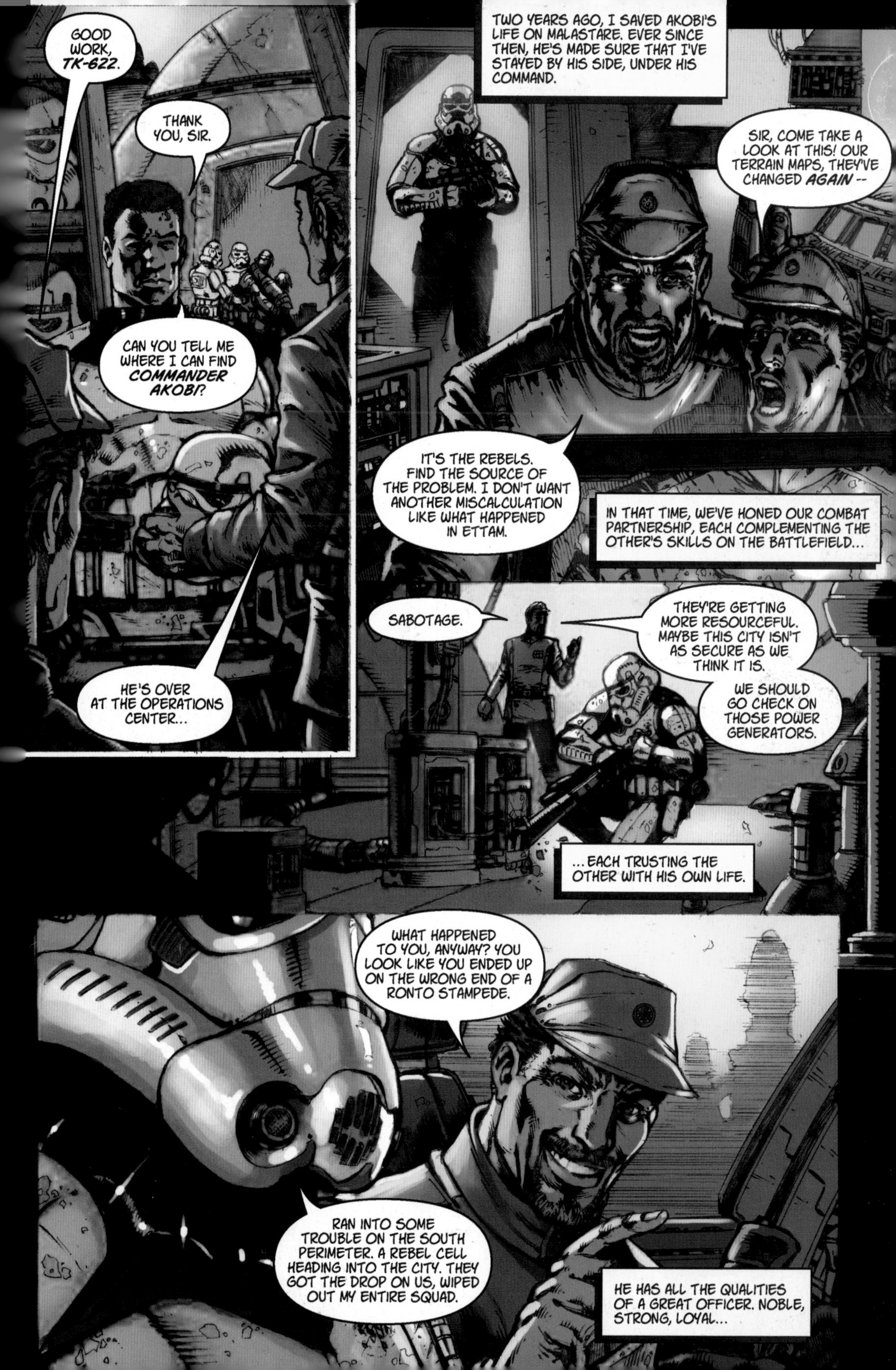
GOOD WORK, TK-622.
THANK YOU, SIR.
CAN YOU TELL ME WHERE I CAN FIND COMMANDER AKOBI?
HE'S OVER AT THE OPERATIONS CENTER...
TWO YEARS AGO, I SAVED AKOBI'S LIFE ON MALASTARE. EVER SINCE THEN, HE'S MADE SURE THAT I'VE STAYED BY HIS SIDE, UNDER HIS COMMAND.
SIR, COME TAKE A LOOK AT THIS! OUR TERRAIN MAPS, THEY'VE CHANGED AGAIN --
IT'S THE REBELS. FIND THE SOURCE OF THE PROBLEM. I DON'T WANT ANOTHER MISCALCULATION LIKE WHAT HAPPENED IN ETTAM.
IN THAT TIME, WE'VE HONED OUR COMBAT PARTNERSHIP, EACH COMPLEMENTING THE OTHER'S SKILLS ON THE BATTLEFIELD...
SABOTAGE.
THEY'RE GETTING MORE RESOURCEFUL. MAYBE THIS CITY ISN'T AS SECURE AS WE THINK IT IS.
WE SHOULD GO CHECK ON THOSE POWER GENERATORS.
...EACH TRUSTING THE OTHER WITH HIS OWN LIFE.
WHAT HAPPENED TO YOU, ANYWAY? YOU LOOK LIKE YOU ENDED UP ON THE WRONG END OF A RONTO STAMPEDE.
RAN INTO SOME TROUBLE ON THE SOUTH PERIMETER. A REBEL CELL HEADING INTO THE CITY. THEY GOT THE DROP ON US, WIPED OUT MY ENTIRE SQUAD.
HE HAS ALL THE QUALITIES OF A GREAT OFFICER. NOBLE, STRONG, LOYAL...

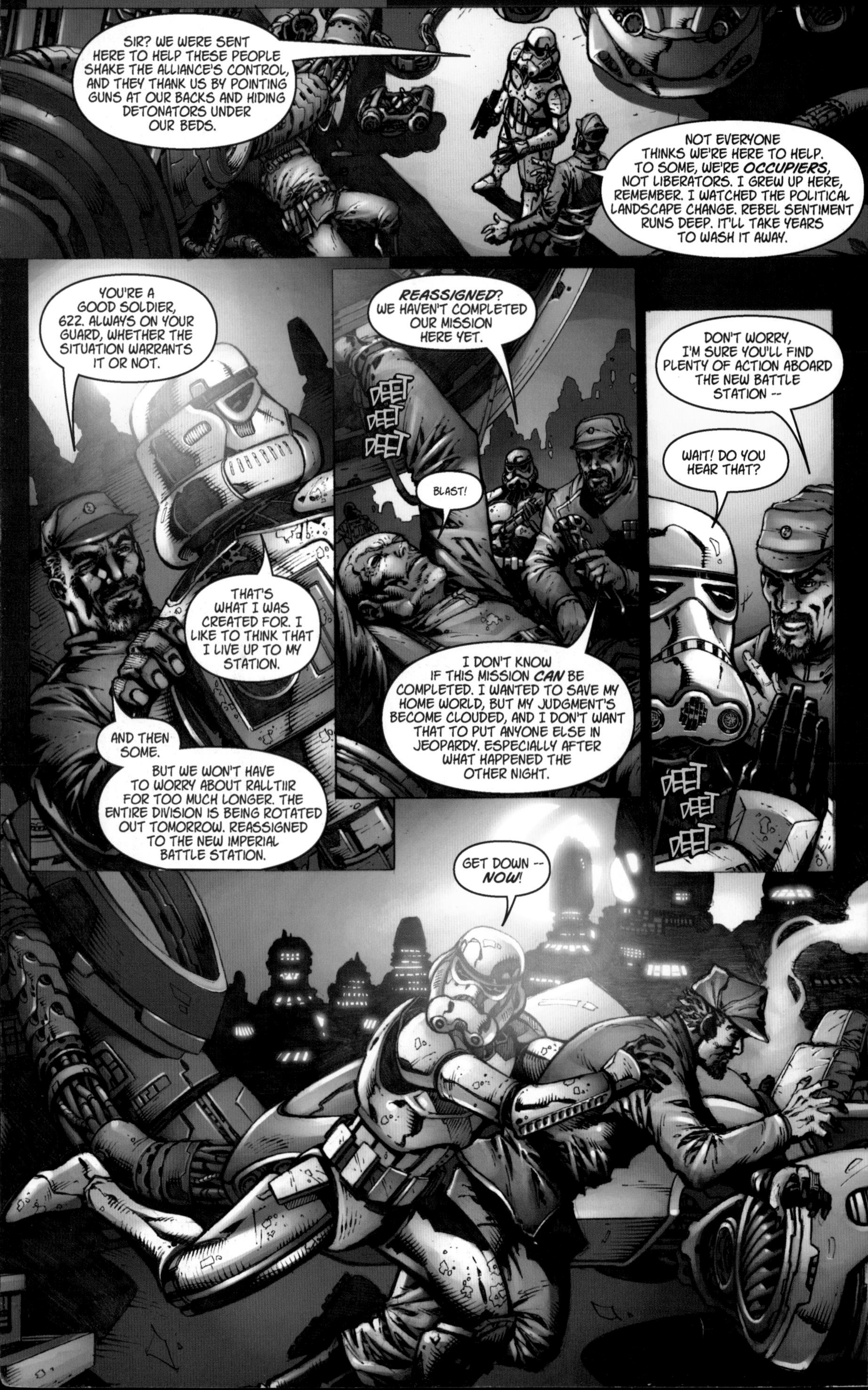
SIR? WE WERE SENT HERE TO HELP THESE PEOPLE SHAKE THE ALLIANCE'S CONTROL, AND THEY THANK US BY POINTING GUNS AT OUR BACKS AND HIDING DETONATORS UNDER OUR BEDS.
NOT EVERYONE THINKS WE'RE HERE TO HELP. TO SOME, WE'RE OCCUPIERS, NOT LIBERATORS. I GREW UP HERE, REMEMBER. I WATCHED THE POLITICAL LANDSCAPE CHANGE. REBEL SENTIMENT RUNS DEEP. IT'LL TAKE YEARS TO WASH IT AWAY.
YOU'RE A GOOD SOLDIER, 622. ALWAYS ON YOUR GUARD, WHETHER THE SITUATION WARRANTS IT OR NOT.
THAT'S WHAT I WAS CREATED FOR. I LIKE TO THINK THAT I LIVE UP TO MY STATION.
AND THEN SOME.
BUT WE WON'T HAVE TO WORRY ABOUT RALLTIIR FOR TOO MUCH LONGER. THE ENTIRE DIVISION IS BEING ROTATED OUT TOMORROW. REASSIGNED TO THE NEW IMPERIAL BATTLE STATION.
REASSIGNED? WE HAVEN'T COMPLETED OUR MISSION HERE YET.
DEET DEET DEET
BLAST!
I DON'T KNOW IF THIS MISSION CAN BE COMPLETED. I WANTED TO SAVE MY HOME WORLD, BUT MY JUDGMENT'S BECOME CLOUDED, AND I DON'T WANT THAT TO PUT ANYONE ELSE IN JEOPARDY. ESPECIALLY AFTER WHAT HAPPENED THE OTHER NIGHT.
DON'T WORRY, I'M SURE YOU'LL FIND PLENTY OF ACTION ABOARD THE NEW BATTLE STATION --
WAIT! DO YOU HEAR THAT?
DEET DEET DEET
GET DOWN -- NOW!

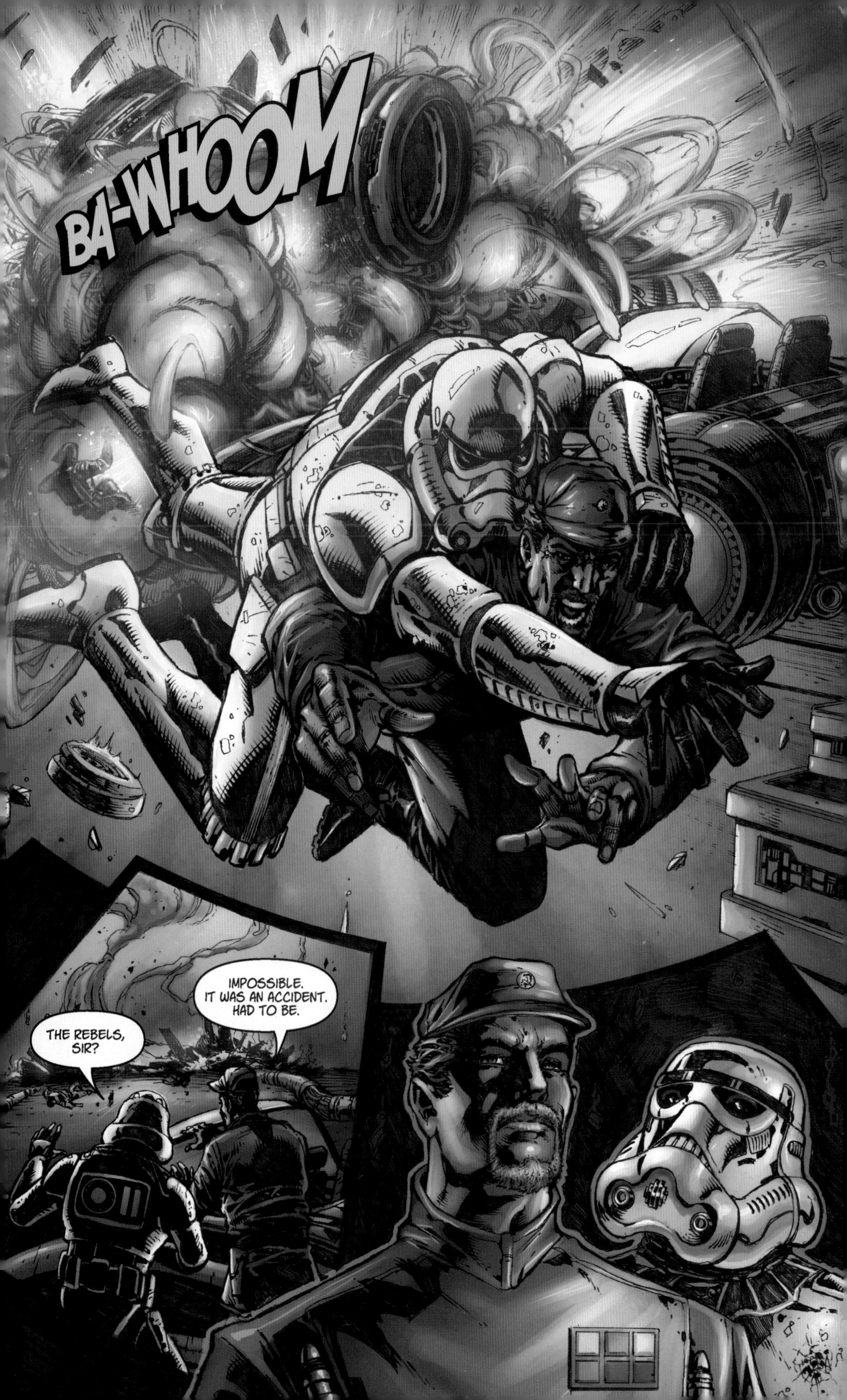
BA-WHOOM
THE REBELS, SIR?
IMPOSSIBLE. IT WAS AN ACCIDENT. HAD TO BE.

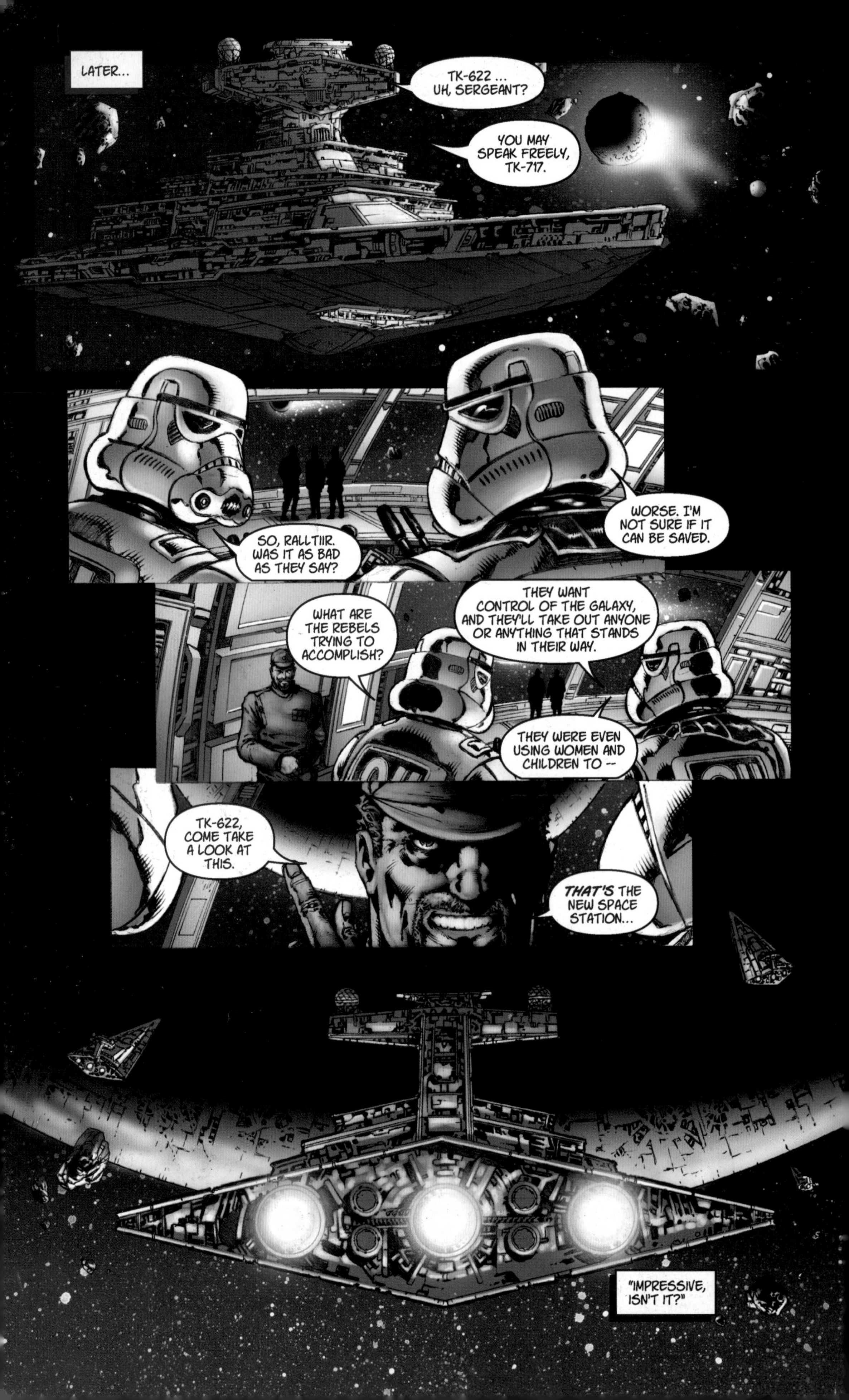
LATER...
TK-622 ... UH, SERGEANT?
YOU MAY SPEAK FREELY, TK-717.
SO, RALLTIIR. WAS IT AS BAD AS THEY SAY?
WORSE. I'M NOT SURE IF IT CAN BE SAVED.
WHAT ARE THE REBELS TRYING TO ACCOMPLISH?
THEY WANT CONTROL OF THE GALAXY, AND THEY'LL TAKE OUT ANYONE OR ANYTHING THAT STANDS IN THEIR WAY.
THEY WERE EVEN USING WOMEN AND CHILDREN TO --
TK-622, COME TAKE A LOOK AT THIS.
THAT'S THE NEW SPACE STATION...
"IMPRESSIVE, ISN'T IT?"

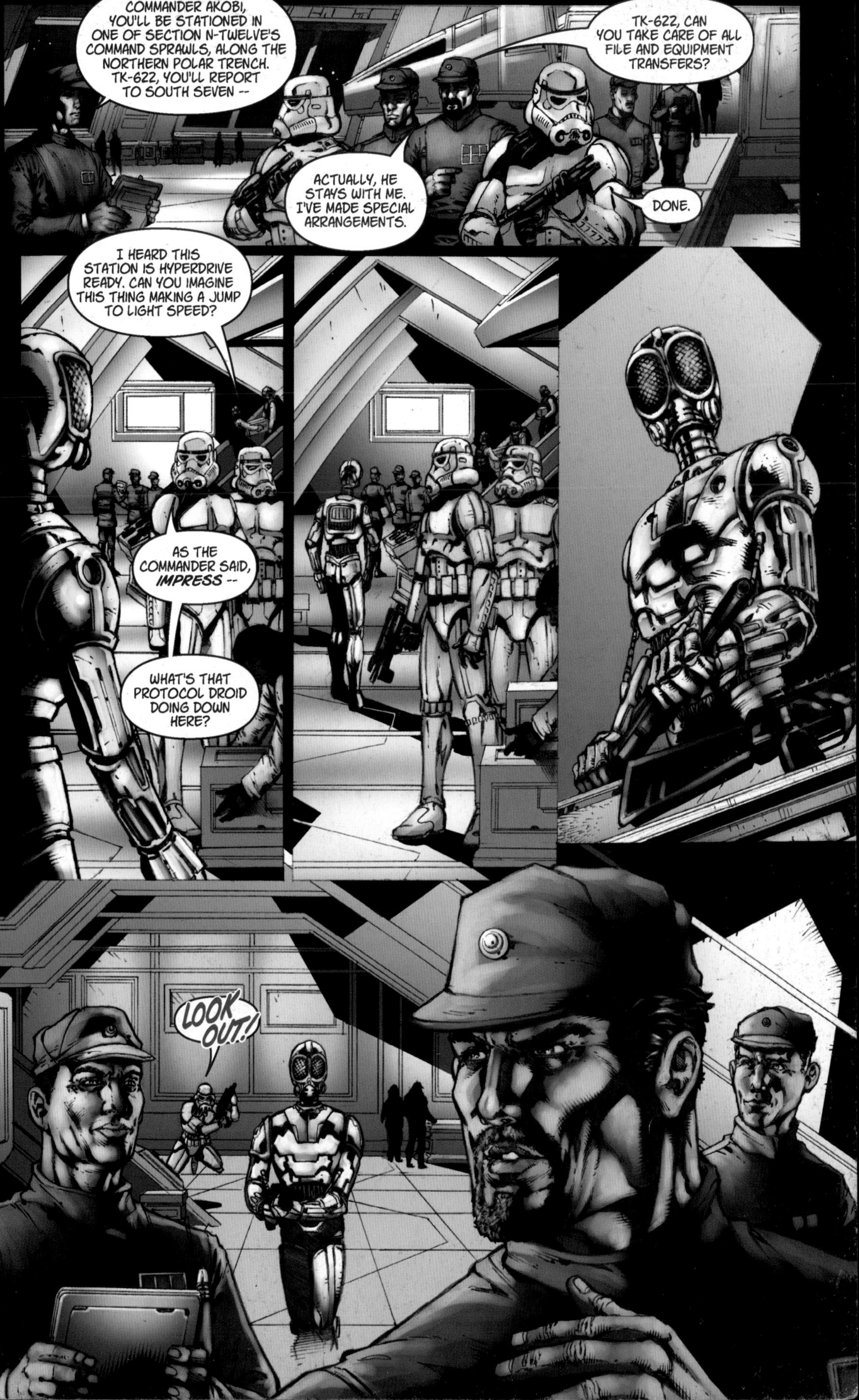
COMMANDER AKOBI, YOU'LL BE STATIONED IN ONE OF SECTION N-TWELVE'S COMMAND SPRAWLS, ALONG THE NORTHERN POLAR TRENCH. TK-622, YOU'LL REPORT TO SOUTH SEVEN --
ACTUALLY, HE STAYS WITH ME. I'VE MADE SPECIAL ARRANGEMENTS.
TK-622, CAN YOU TAKE CARE OF ALL FILE AND EQUIPMENT TRANSFERS?
DONE.
I HEARD THIS STATION IS HYPERDRIVE READY. CAN YOU IMAGINE THIS THING MAKING A JUMP TO LIGHT SPEED?
AS THE COMMANDER SAID, *IMPRESS* --
WHAT'S THAT PROTOCOL DROID DOING DOWN HERE?
LOOK OUT!

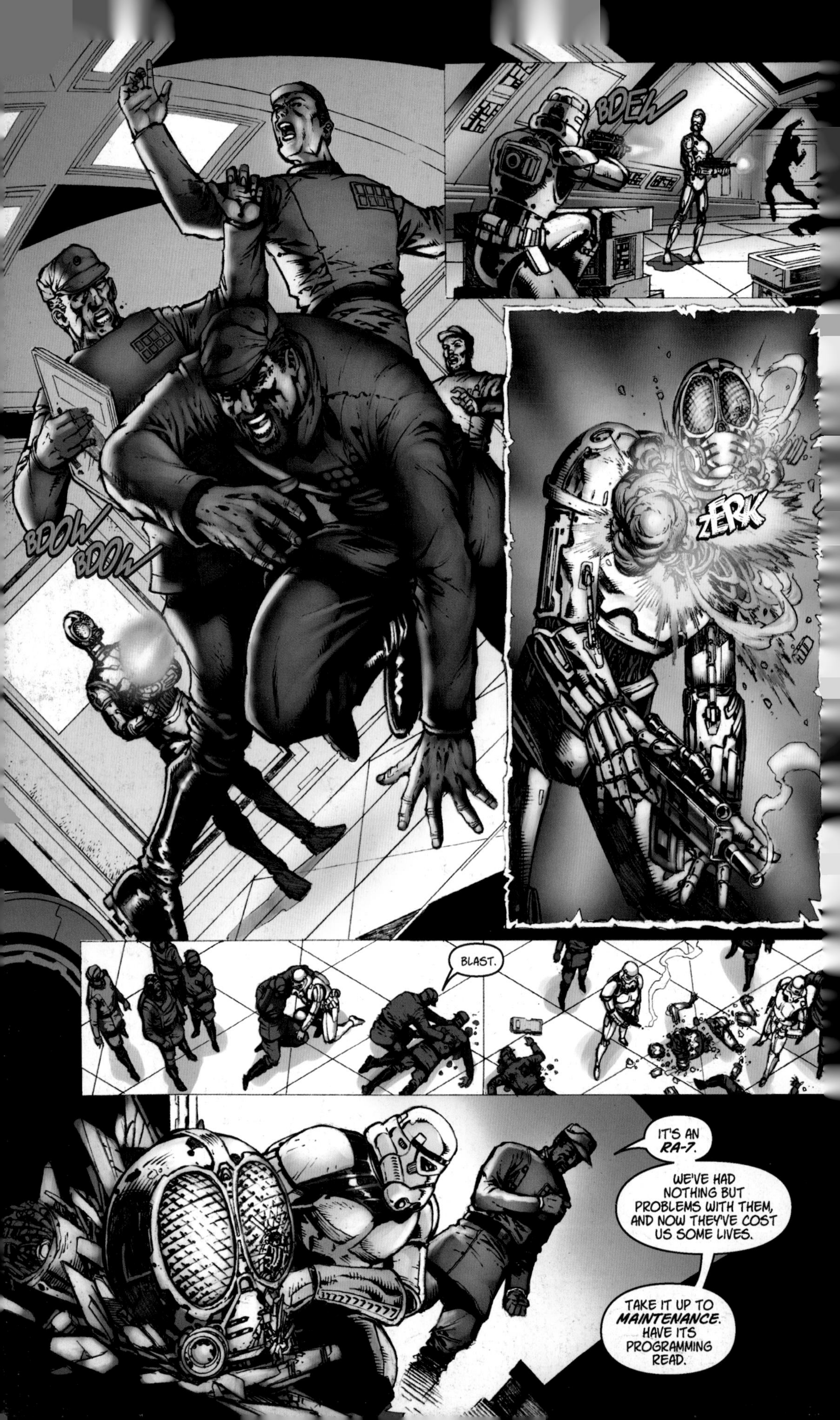
BDEW
BDOW BDOW
ZERK
BLAST.
IT'S AN *RA-7*.
WE'VE HAD NOTHING BUT PROBLEMS WITH THEM, AND NOW THEY'VE COST US SOME LIVES.
TAKE IT UP TO *MAINTENANCE*. HAVE ITS PROGRAMMING READ.

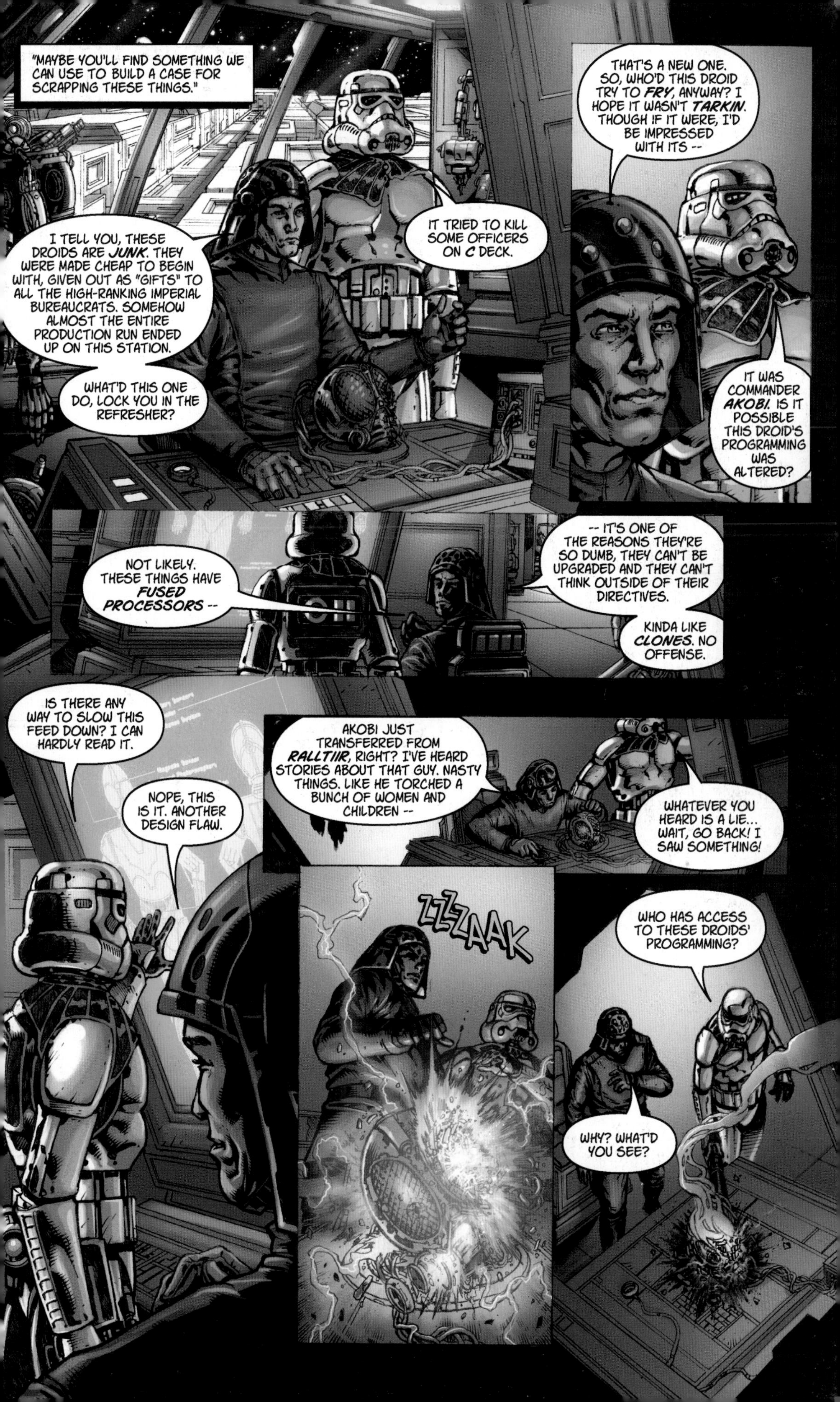
"MAYBE YOU'LL FIND SOMETHING WE CAN USE TO BUILD A CASE FOR SCRAPPING THESE THINGS."
I TELL YOU, THESE DROIDS ARE JUNK. THEY WERE MADE CHEAP TO BEGIN WITH, GIVEN OUT AS "GIFTS" TO ALL THE HIGH-RANKING IMPERIAL BUREAUCRATS. SOMEHOW ALMOST THE ENTIRE PRODUCTION RUN ENDED UP ON THIS STATION.
WHAT'D THIS ONE DO, LOCK YOU IN THE REFRESHER?
IT TRIED TO KILL SOME OFFICERS ON C DECK.
THAT'S A NEW ONE. SO, WHO'D THIS DROID TRY TO FRY, ANYWAY? I HOPE IT WASN'T TARKIN. THOUGH IF IT WERE, I'D BE IMPRESSED WITH ITS --
IT WAS COMMANDER AKOBI. IS IT POSSIBLE THIS DROID'S PROGRAMMING WAS ALTERED?
NOT LIKELY. THESE THINGS HAVE FUSED PROCESSORS --
-- IT'S ONE OF THE REASONS THEY'RE SO DUMB, THEY CAN'T BE UPGRADED AND THEY CAN'T THINK OUTSIDE OF THEIR DIRECTIVES.
KINDA LIKE CLONES. NO OFFENSE.
IS THERE ANY WAY TO SLOW THIS FEED DOWN? I CAN HARDLY READ IT.
NOPE, THIS IS IT. ANOTHER DESIGN FLAW.
AKOBI JUST TRANSFERRED FROM RALLTIIR, RIGHT? I'VE HEARD STORIES ABOUT THAT GUY. NASTY THINGS. LIKE HE TORCHED A BUNCH OF WOMEN AND CHILDREN --
WHATEVER YOU HEARD IS A LIE... WAIT, GO BACK! I SAW SOMETHING!
ZZZZAAK
WHO HAS ACCESS TO THESE DROIDS' PROGRAMMING?
WHY? WHAT'D YOU SEE?

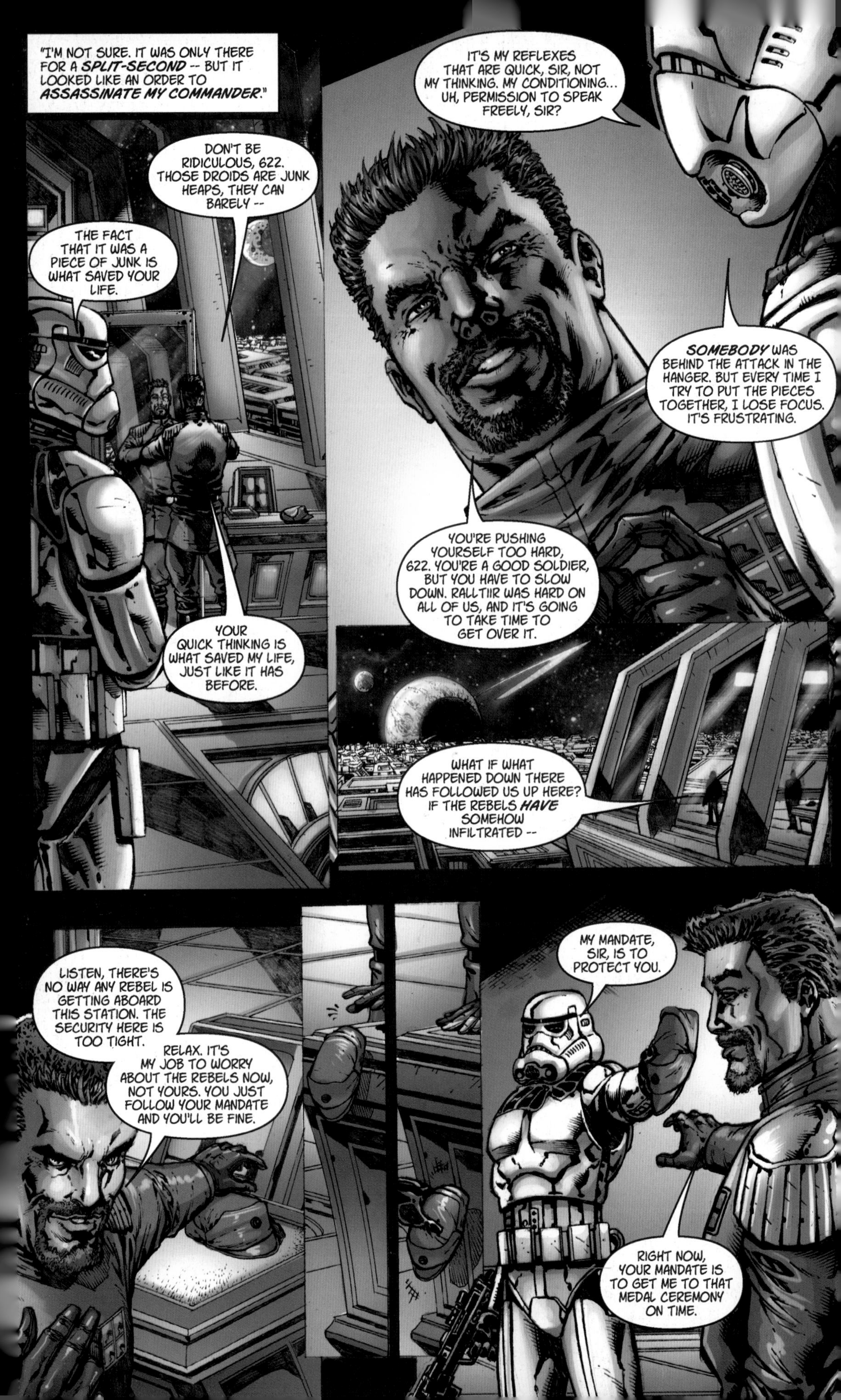
"I'M NOT SURE. IT WAS ONLY THERE FOR A SPLIT-SECOND -- BUT IT LOOKED LIKE AN ORDER TO ASSASSINATE MY COMMANDER."
DON'T BE RIDICULOUS, 622. THOSE DROIDS ARE JUNK HEAPS, THEY CAN BARELY --
THE FACT THAT IT WAS A PIECE OF JUNK IS WHAT SAVED YOUR LIFE.
YOUR QUICK THINKING IS WHAT SAVED MY LIFE, JUST LIKE IT HAS BEFORE.
IT'S MY REFLEXES THAT ARE QUICK, SIR, NOT MY THINKING. MY CONDITIONING... UH, PERMISSION TO SPEAK FREELY, SIR?
SOMEBODY WAS BEHIND THE ATTACK IN THE HANGER. BUT EVERY TIME I TRY TO PUT THE PIECES TOGETHER, I LOSE FOCUS. IT'S FRUSTRATING.
YOU'RE PUSHING YOURSELF TOO HARD, 622. YOU'RE A GOOD SOLDIER, BUT YOU HAVE TO SLOW DOWN. RALLTIIR WAS HARD ON ALL OF US, AND IT'S GOING TO TAKE TIME TO GET OVER IT.
WHAT IF WHAT HAPPENED DOWN THERE HAS FOLLOWED US UP HERE? IF THE REBELS HAVE SOMEHOW INFILTRATED --
LISTEN, THERE'S NO WAY ANY REBEL IS GETTING ABOARD THIS STATION. THE SECURITY HERE IS TOO TIGHT.
RELAX. IT'S MY JOB TO WORRY ABOUT THE REBELS NOW, NOT YOURS. YOU JUST FOLLOW YOUR MANDATE AND YOU'LL BE FINE.
MY MANDATE, SIR, IS TO PROTECT YOU.
RIGHT NOW, YOUR MANDATE IS TO GET ME TO THAT MEDAL CEREMONY ON TIME.

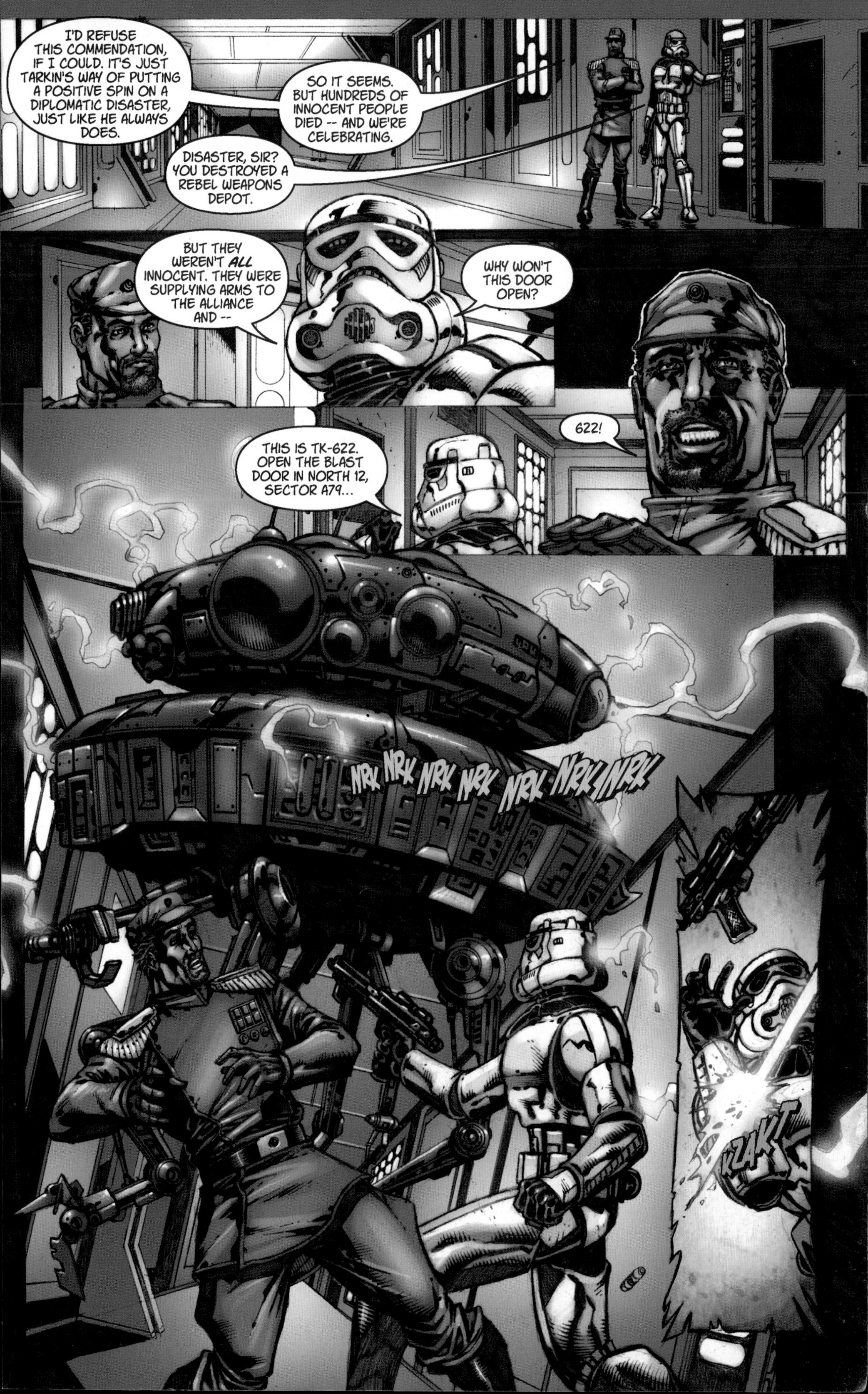
I'D REFUSE THIS COMMENDATION, IF I COULD. IT'S JUST TARKIN'S WAY OF PUTTING A POSITIVE SPIN ON A DIPLOMATIC DISASTER, JUST LIKE HE ALWAYS DOES.
DISASTER, SIR? YOU DESTROYED A REBEL WEAPONS DEPOT.
SO IT SEEMS. BUT HUNDREDS OF INNOCENT PEOPLE DIED -- AND WE'RE CELEBRATING.
BUT THEY WEREN'T ALL INNOCENT. THEY WERE SUPPLYING ARMS TO THE ALLIANCE AND --
WHY WON'T THIS DOOR OPEN?
THIS IS TK-622. OPEN THE BLAST DOOR IN NORTH 12, SECTOR A79...
622!
NRK NRK NRK NRK NRK NRK NRK
KZAKT

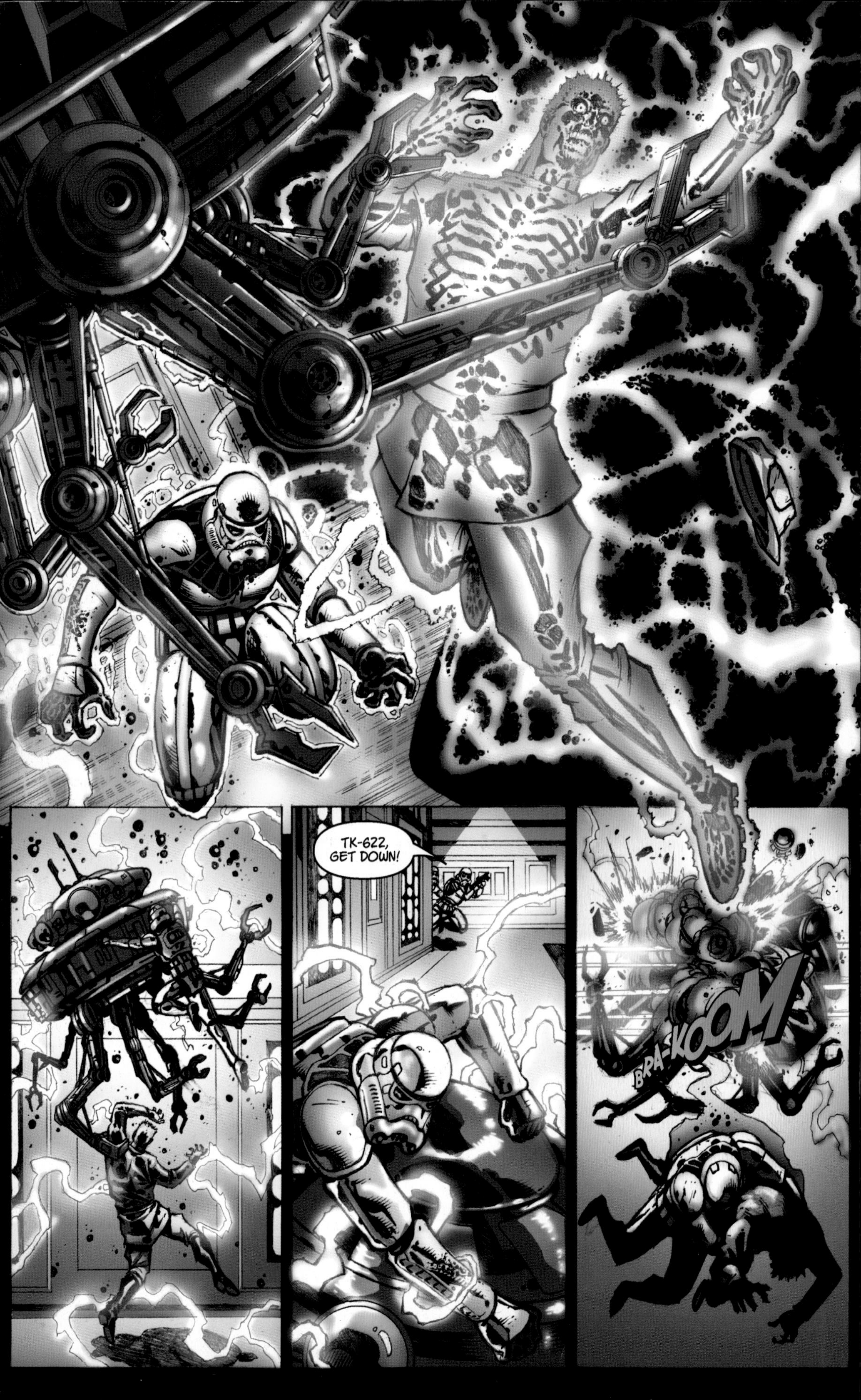
TK-622, GET DOWN!
BRA-KOOM

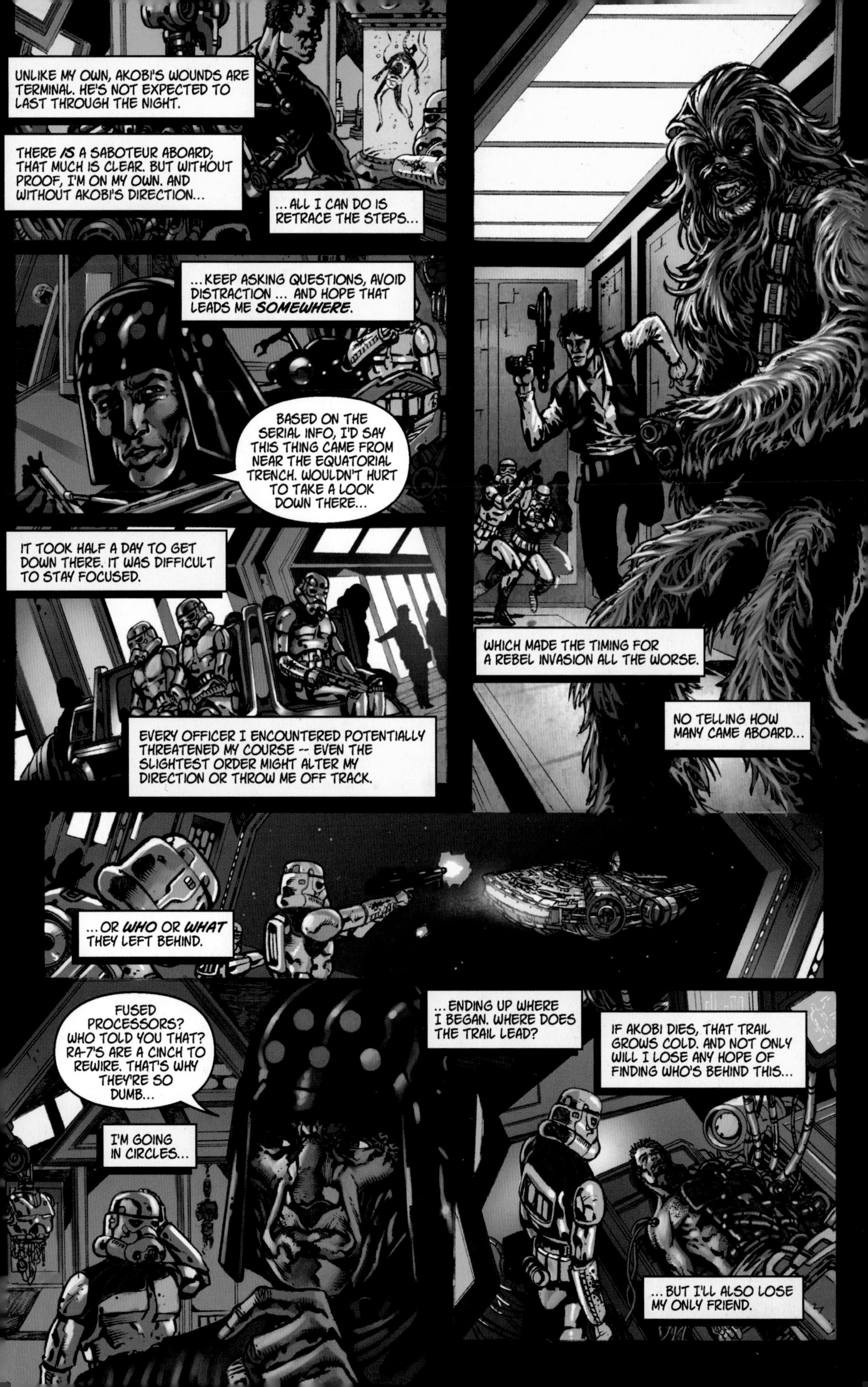
UNLIKE MY OWN, AKOBI'S WOUNDS ARE TERMINAL. HE'S NOT EXPECTED TO LAST THROUGH THE NIGHT.
THERE *IS* A SABOTEUR ABOARD; THAT MUCH IS CLEAR. BUT WITHOUT PROOF, I'M ON MY OWN. AND WITHOUT AKOBI'S DIRECTION...
...ALL I CAN DO IS RETRACE THE STEPS...
...KEEP ASKING QUESTIONS, AVOID DISTRACTION ... AND HOPE THAT LEADS ME *SOMEWHERE*.
BASED ON THE SERIAL INFO, I'D SAY THIS THING CAME FROM NEAR THE EQUATORIAL TRENCH. WOULDN'T HURT TO TAKE A LOOK DOWN THERE...
IT TOOK HALF A DAY TO GET DOWN THERE. IT WAS DIFFICULT TO STAY FOCUSED.
EVERY OFFICER I ENCOUNTERED POTENTIALLY THREATENED MY COURSE -- EVEN THE SLIGHTEST ORDER MIGHT ALTER MY DIRECTION OR THROW ME OFF TRACK.
WHICH MADE THE TIMING FOR A REBEL INVASION ALL THE WORSE.
NO TELLING HOW MANY CAME ABOARD...
...OR *WHO* OR *WHAT* THEY LEFT BEHIND.
FUSED PROCESSORS? WHO TOLD YOU THAT? RA-7'S ARE A CINCH TO REWIRE. THAT'S WHY THEY'RE SO DUMB...
I'M GOING IN CIRCLES...
...ENDING UP WHERE I BEGAN. WHERE DOES THE TRAIL LEAD?
IF AKOBI DIES, THAT TRAIL GROWS COLD. AND NOT ONLY WILL I LOSE ANY HOPE OF FINDING WHO'S BEHIND THIS...
...BUT I'LL ALSO LOSE MY ONLY FRIEND.

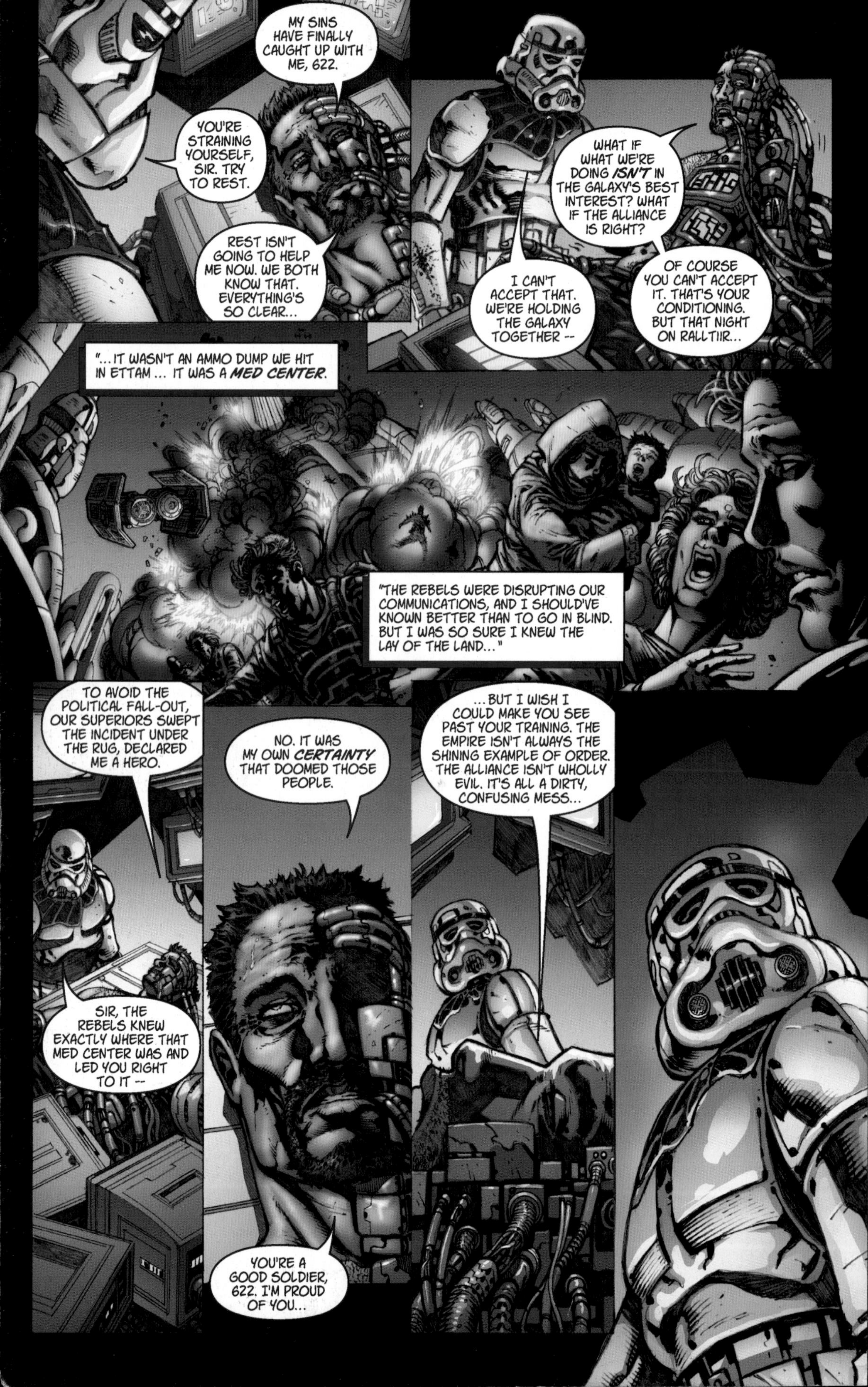
MY SINS HAVE FINALLY CAUGHT UP WITH ME, 622.
YOU'RE STRAINING YOURSELF, SIR. TRY TO REST.
REST ISN'T GOING TO HELP ME NOW. WE BOTH KNOW THAT. EVERYTHING'S SO CLEAR...
WHAT IF WHAT WE'RE DOING ISN'T IN THE GALAXY'S BEST INTEREST? WHAT IF THE ALLIANCE IS RIGHT?
I CAN'T ACCEPT THAT. WE'RE HOLDING THE GALAXY TOGETHER --
OF COURSE YOU CAN'T ACCEPT IT. THAT'S YOUR CONDITIONING. BUT THAT NIGHT ON RALLTIIR...
"...IT WASN'T AN AMMO DUMP WE HIT IN ETTAM ... IT WAS A MED CENTER.
"THE REBELS WERE DISRUPTING OUR COMMUNICATIONS, AND I SHOULD'VE KNOWN BETTER THAN TO GO IN BLIND. BUT I WAS SO SURE I KNEW THE LAY OF THE LAND..."
TO AVOID THE POLITICAL FALL-OUT, OUR SUPERIORS SWEPT THE INCIDENT UNDER THE RUG, DECLARED ME A HERO.
SIR, THE REBELS KNEW EXACTLY WHERE THAT MED CENTER WAS AND LED YOU RIGHT TO IT --
NO. IT WAS MY OWN CERTAINTY THAT DOOMED THOSE PEOPLE.
YOU'RE A GOOD SOLDIER, 622. I'M PROUD OF YOU...
...BUT I WISH I COULD MAKE YOU SEE PAST YOUR TRAINING. THE EMPIRE ISN'T ALWAYS THE SHINING EXAMPLE OF ORDER. THE ALLIANCE ISN'T WHOLLY EVIL. IT'S ALL A DIRTY, CONFUSING MESS...

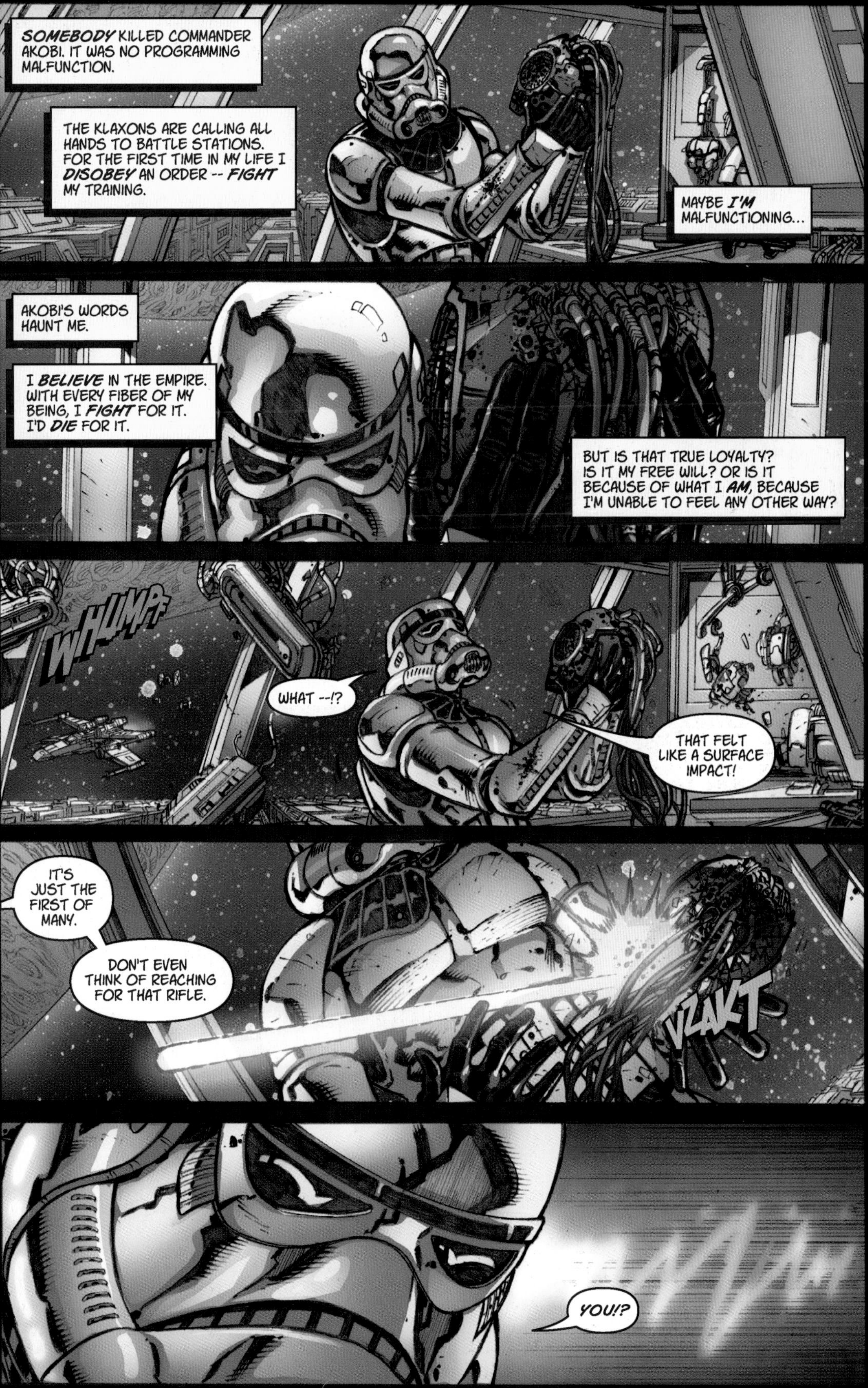
SOMEBODY KILLED COMMANDER AKOBI. IT WAS NO PROGRAMMING MALFUNCTION.
THE KLAXONS ARE CALLING ALL HANDS TO BATTLE STATIONS. FOR THE FIRST TIME IN MY LIFE I DISOBEY AN ORDER -- FIGHT MY TRAINING.
MAYBE I'M MALFUNCTIONING...
AKOBI'S WORDS HAUNT ME.
I BELIEVE IN THE EMPIRE. WITH EVERY FIBER OF MY BEING, I FIGHT FOR IT. I'D DIE FOR IT.
BUT IS THAT TRUE LOYALTY? IS IT MY FREE WILL? OR IS IT BECAUSE OF WHAT I AM, BECAUSE I'M UNABLE TO FEEL ANY OTHER WAY?
WHUMPF
WHAT --!?
THAT FELT LIKE A SURFACE IMPACT!
IT'S JUST THE FIRST OF MANY.
DON'T EVEN THINK OF REACHING FOR THAT RIFLE.
VZAKT
YOU!?

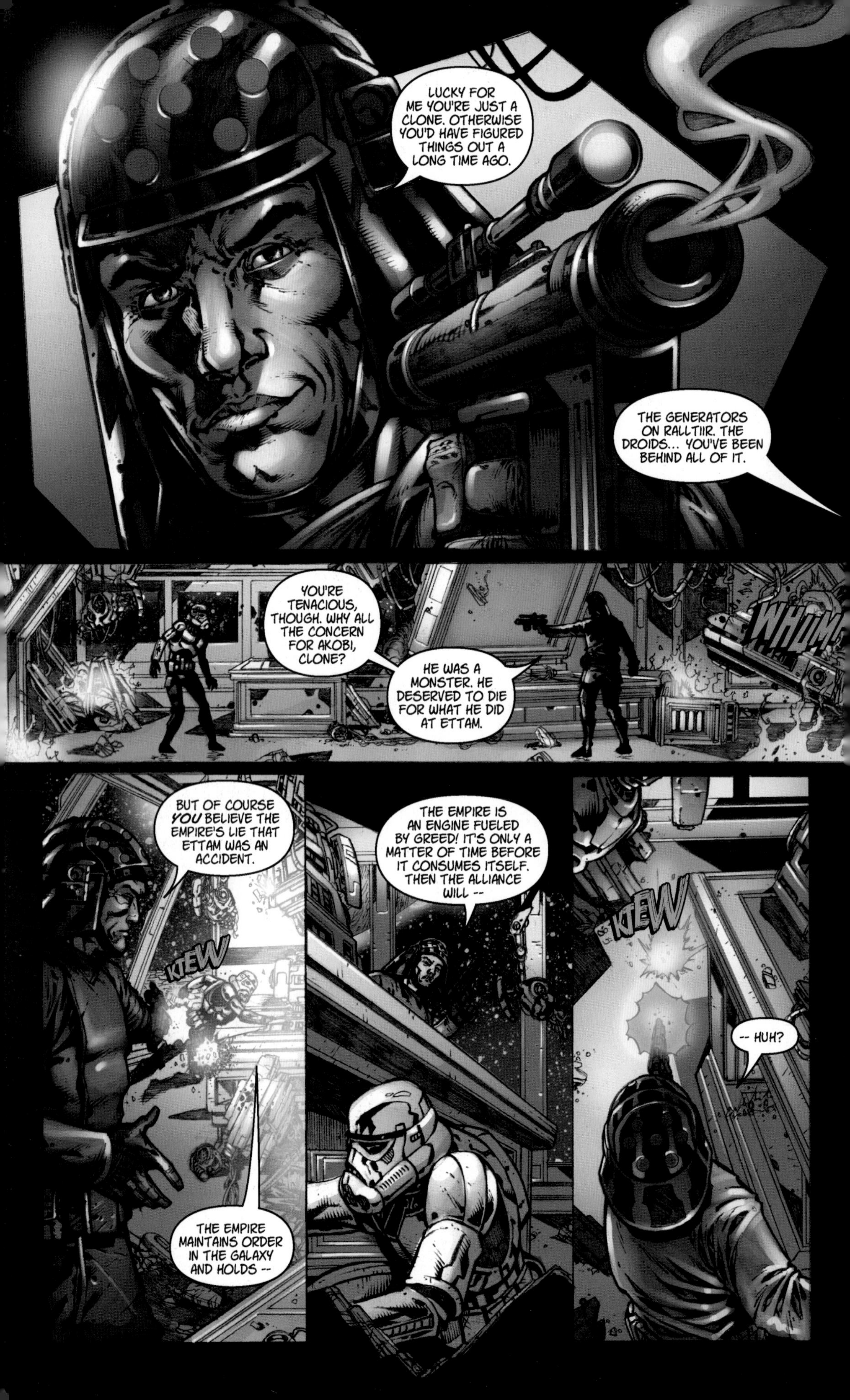
LUCKY FOR ME YOU'RE JUST A CLONE. OTHERWISE YOU'D HAVE FIGURED THINGS OUT A LONG TIME AGO.
THE GENERATORS ON RALLTIIR. THE DROIDS... YOU'VE BEEN BEHIND ALL OF IT.
YOU'RE TENACIOUS, THOUGH. WHY ALL THE CONCERN FOR AKOBI, CLONE?
HE WAS A MONSTER. HE DESERVED TO DIE FOR WHAT HE DID AT ETTAM.
WHUM
BUT OF COURSE *YOU* BELIEVE THE EMPIRE'S LIE THAT ETTAM WAS AN ACCIDENT.
KTEW
THE EMPIRE MAINTAINS ORDER IN THE GALAXY AND HOLDS --
THE EMPIRE IS AN ENGINE FUELED BY GREED! IT'S ONLY A MATTER OF TIME BEFORE IT CONSUMES ITSELF. THEN THE ALLIANCE WILL --
KTEW
-- HUH?

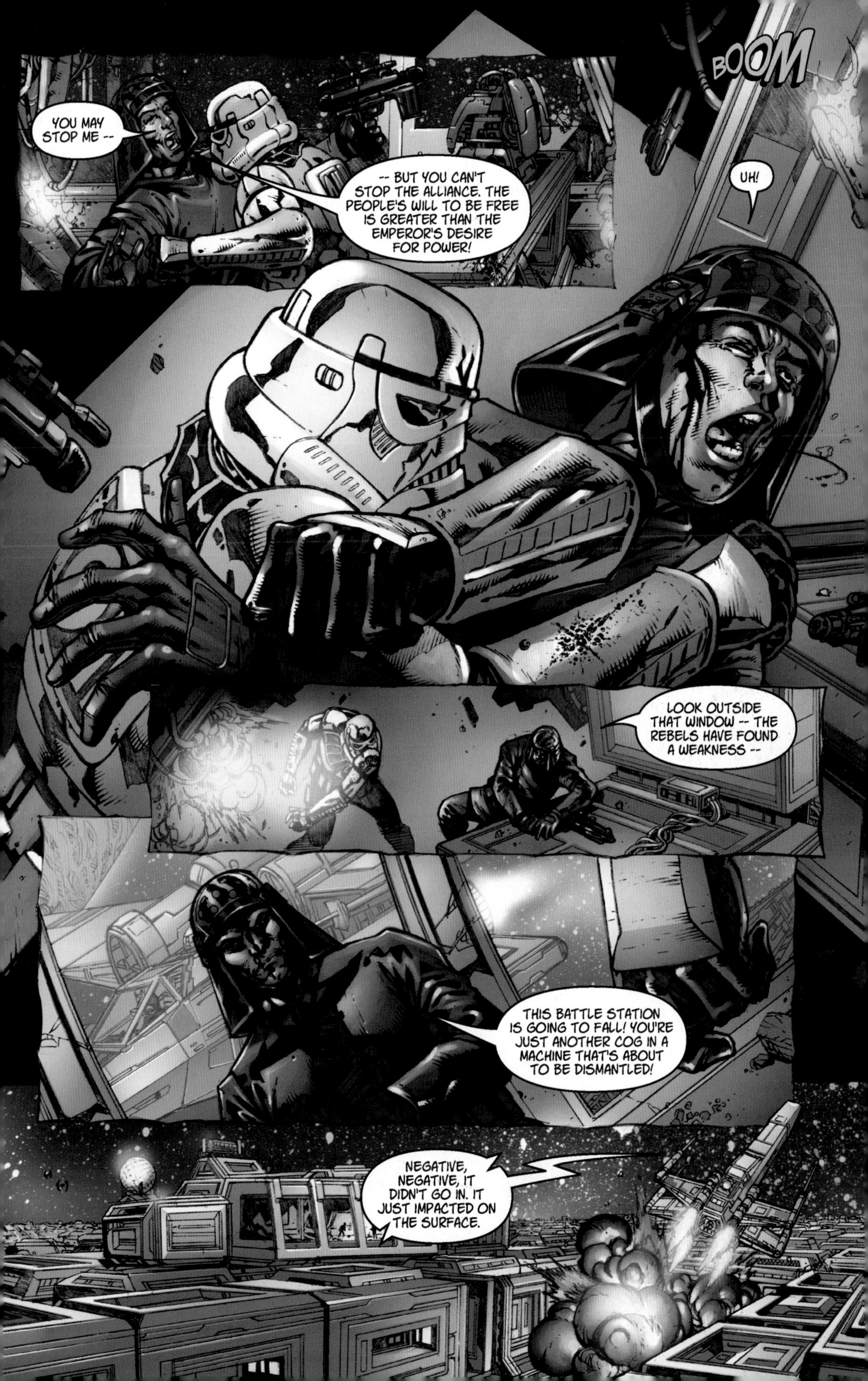
YOU MAY STOP ME --
-- BUT YOU CAN'T STOP THE ALLIANCE. THE PEOPLE'S WILL TO BE FREE IS GREATER THAN THE EMPEROR'S DESIRE FOR POWER!
BOOM
UH!
LOOK OUTSIDE THAT WINDOW -- THE REBELS HAVE FOUND A WEAKNESS --
THIS BATTLE STATION IS GOING TO FALL! YOU'RE JUST ANOTHER COG IN A MACHINE THAT'S ABOUT TO BE DISMANTLED!
NEGATIVE, NEGATIVE, IT DIDN'T GO IN. IT JUST IMPACTED ON THE SURFACE.

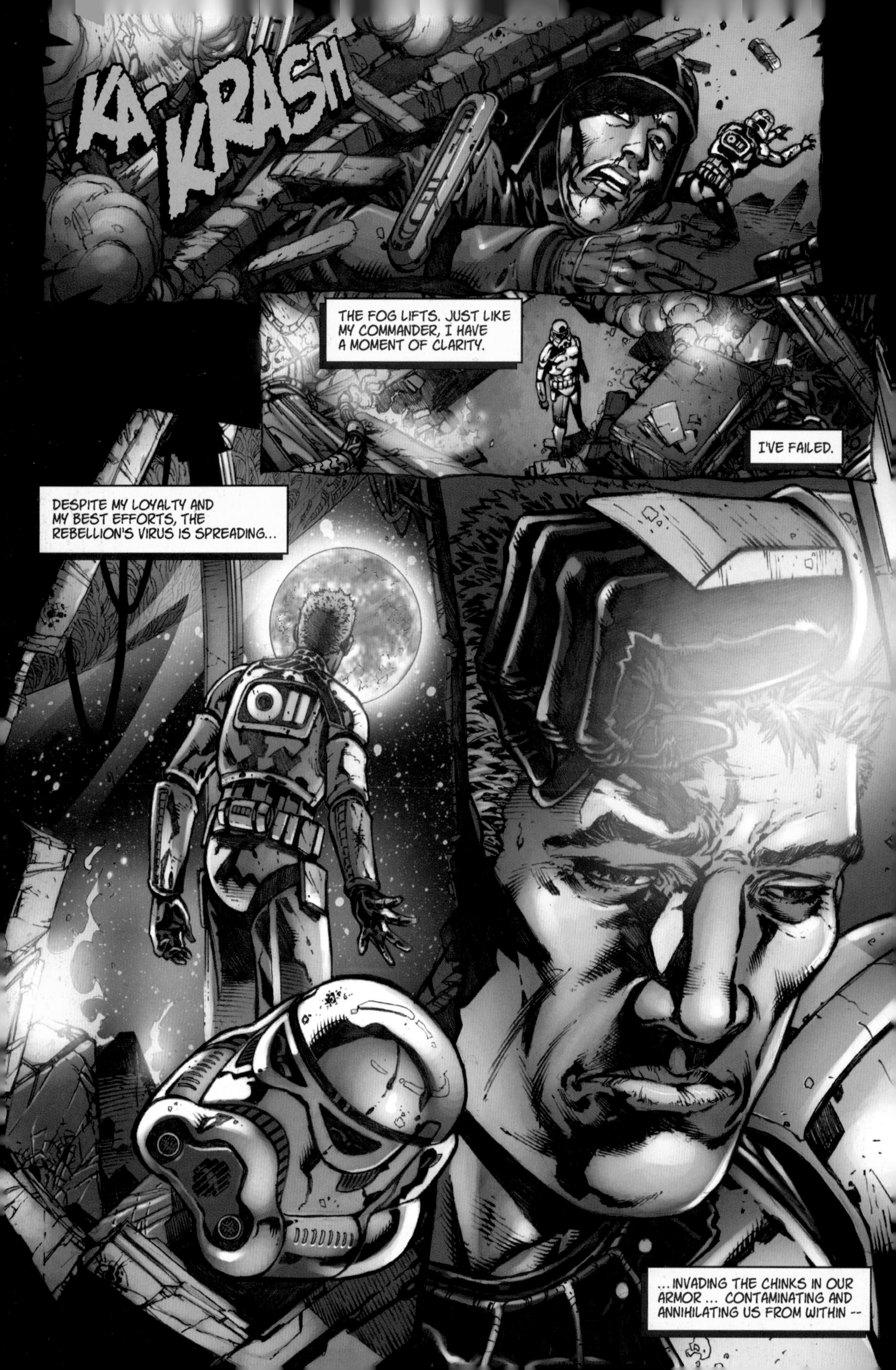
KA-KRASH
THE FOG LIFTS. JUST LIKE MY COMMANDER, I HAVE A MOMENT OF CLARITY.
I'VE FAILED.
DESPITE MY LOYALTY AND MY BEST EFFORTS, THE REBELLION'S VIRUS IS SPREADING...
...INVADING THE CHINKS IN OUR ARMOR... CONTAMINATING AND ANNIHILATING US FROM WITHIN --

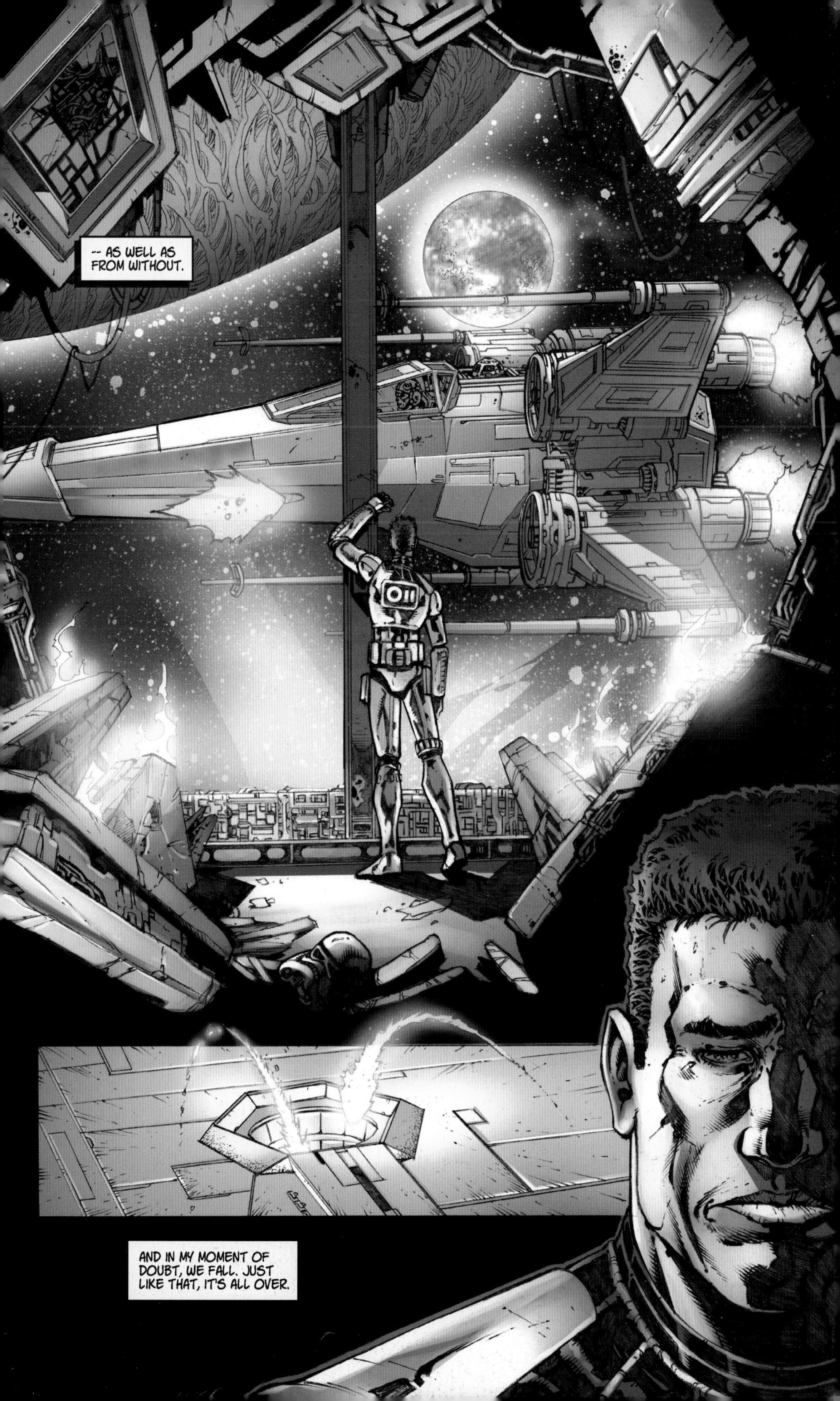

-- AS WELL AS FROM WITHOUT.
AND IN MY MOMENT OF DOUBT, WE FALL. JUST LIKE THAT, IT'S ALL OVER.

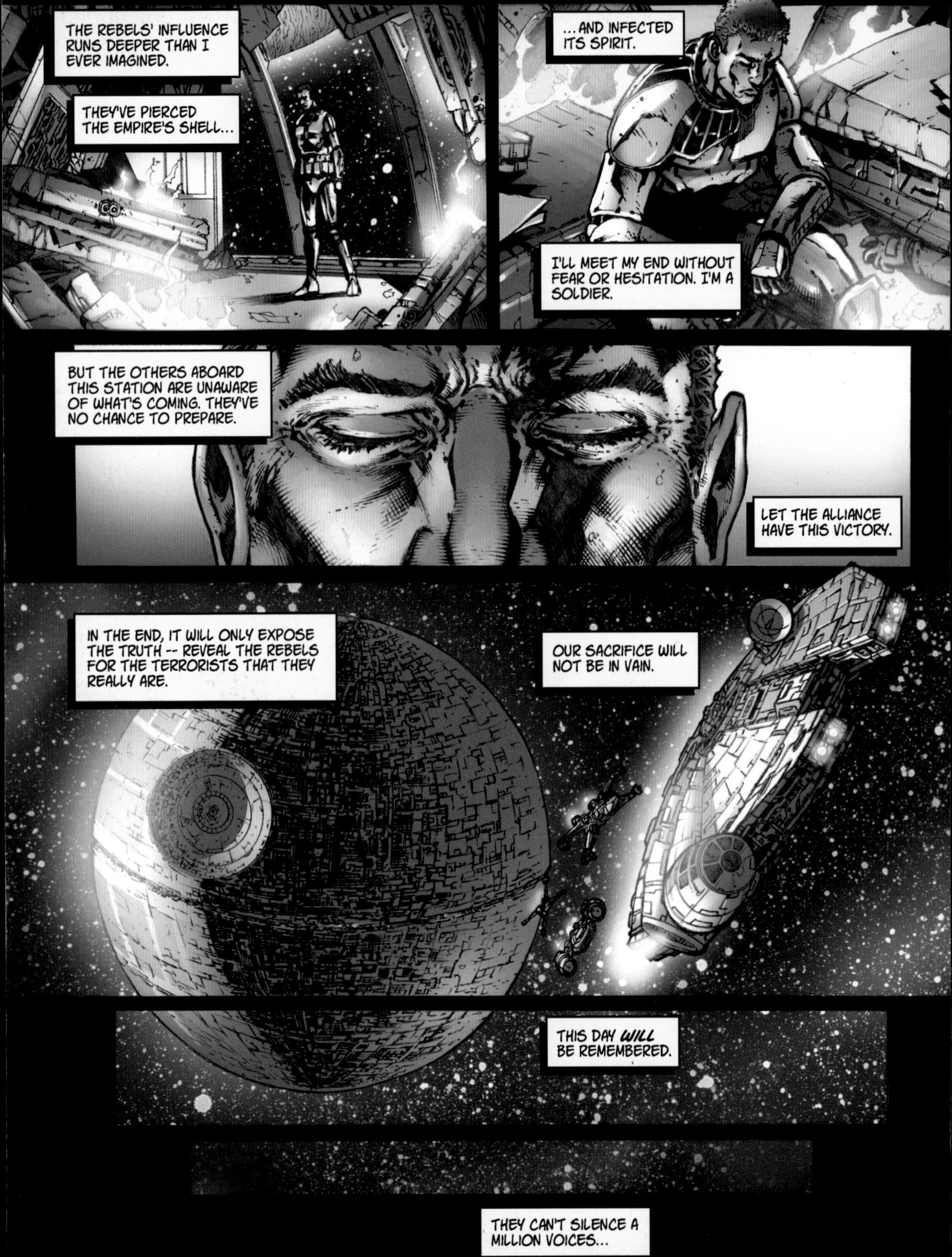
THE REBELS' INFLUENCE RUNS DEEPER THAN I EVER IMAGINED.
THEY'VE PIERCED THE EMPIRE'S SHELL...
...AND INFECTED ITS SPIRIT.
I'LL MEET MY END WITHOUT FEAR OR HESITATION. I'M A SOLDIER.
BUT THE OTHERS ABOARD THIS STATION ARE UNAWARE OF WHAT'S COMING. THEY'VE NO CHANCE TO PREPARE.
LET THE ALLIANCE HAVE THIS VICTORY.
IN THE END, IT WILL ONLY EXPOSE THE TRUTH -- REVEAL THE REBELS FOR THE TERRORISTS THAT THEY REALLY ARE.
OUR SACRIFICE WILL NOT BE IN VAIN.
THIS DAY *WILL* BE REMEMBERED.
THEY CAN'T SILENCE A MILLION VOICES...

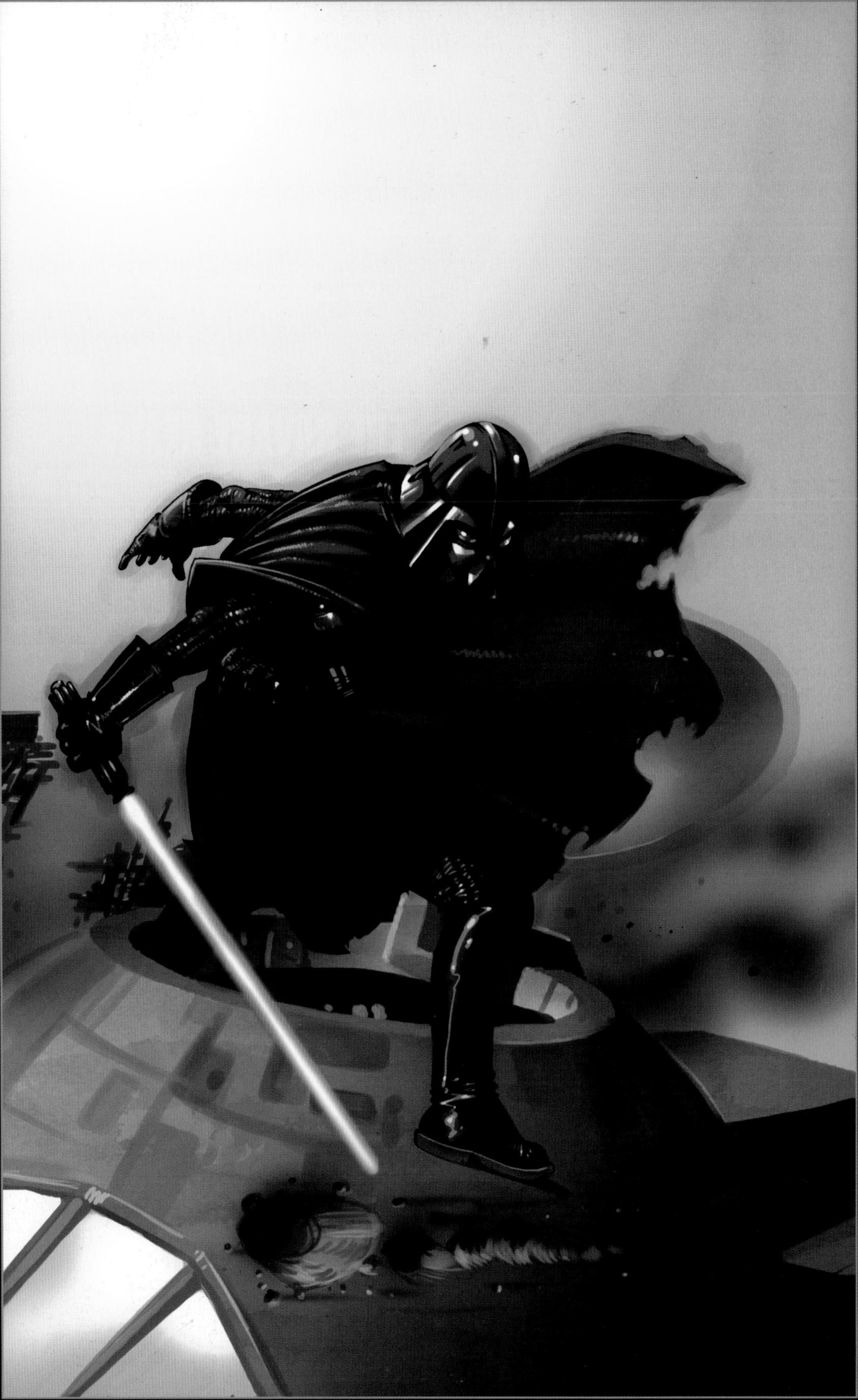

Francisco Ruiz Velasco

THE SAVAGE HEART

SCRIPT PAUL ALDEN
ART RAUL TREVINO

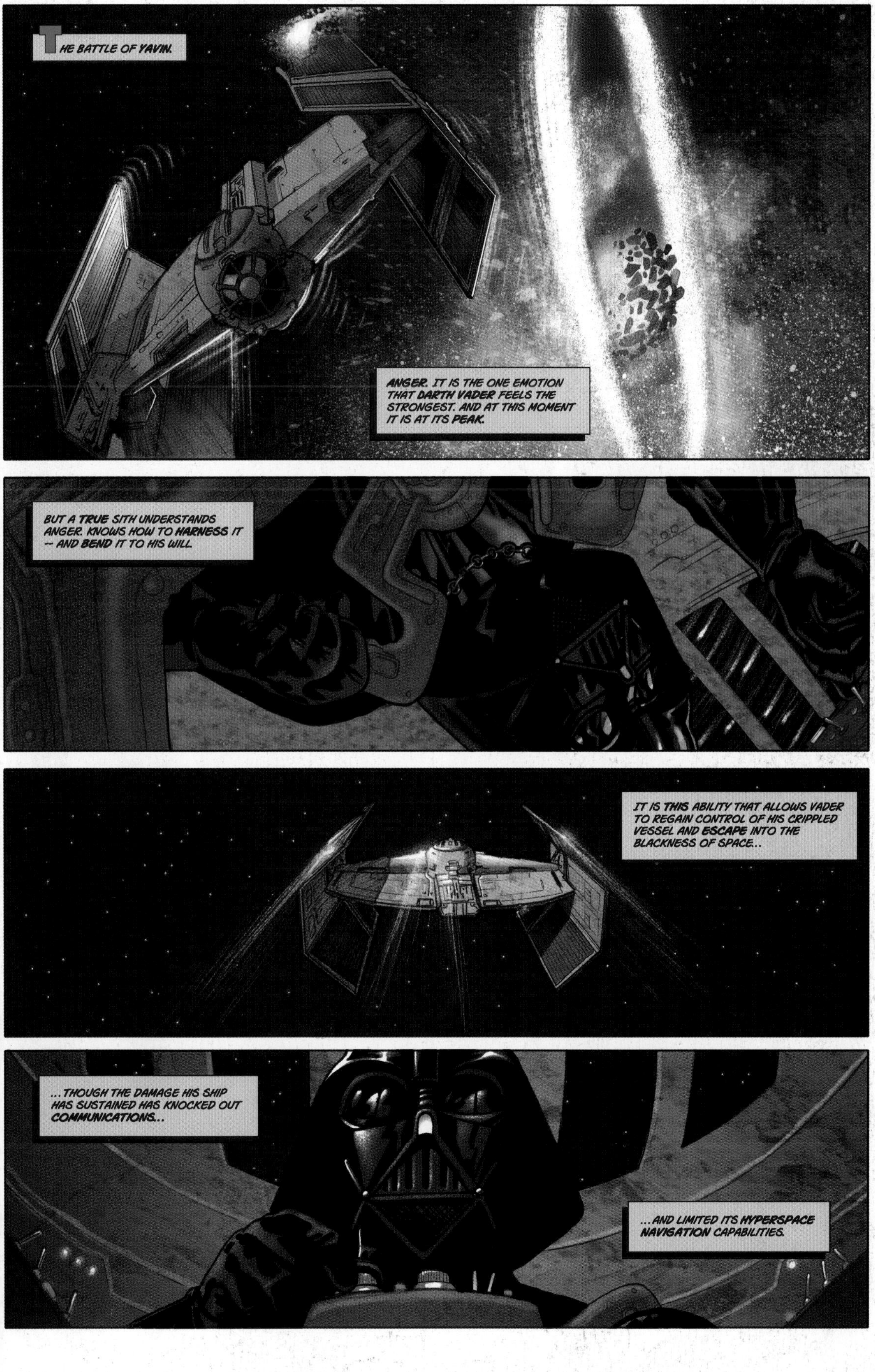
THE BATTLE OF YAVIN.
ANGER. IT IS THE ONE EMOTION THAT DARTH VADER FEELS THE STRONGEST. AND AT THIS MOMENT IT IS AT ITS PEAK.
BUT A TRUE SITH UNDERSTANDS ANGER. KNOWS HOW TO HARNESS IT -- AND BEND IT TO HIS WILL.
IT IS THIS ABILITY THAT ALLOWS VADER TO REGAIN CONTROL OF HIS CRIPPLED VESSEL AND ESCAPE INTO THE BLACKNESS OF SPACE...
...THOUGH THE DAMAGE HIS SHIP HAS SUSTAINED HAS KNOCKED OUT COMMUNICATIONS...
...AND LIMITED ITS HYPERSPACE NAVIGATION CAPABILITIES.

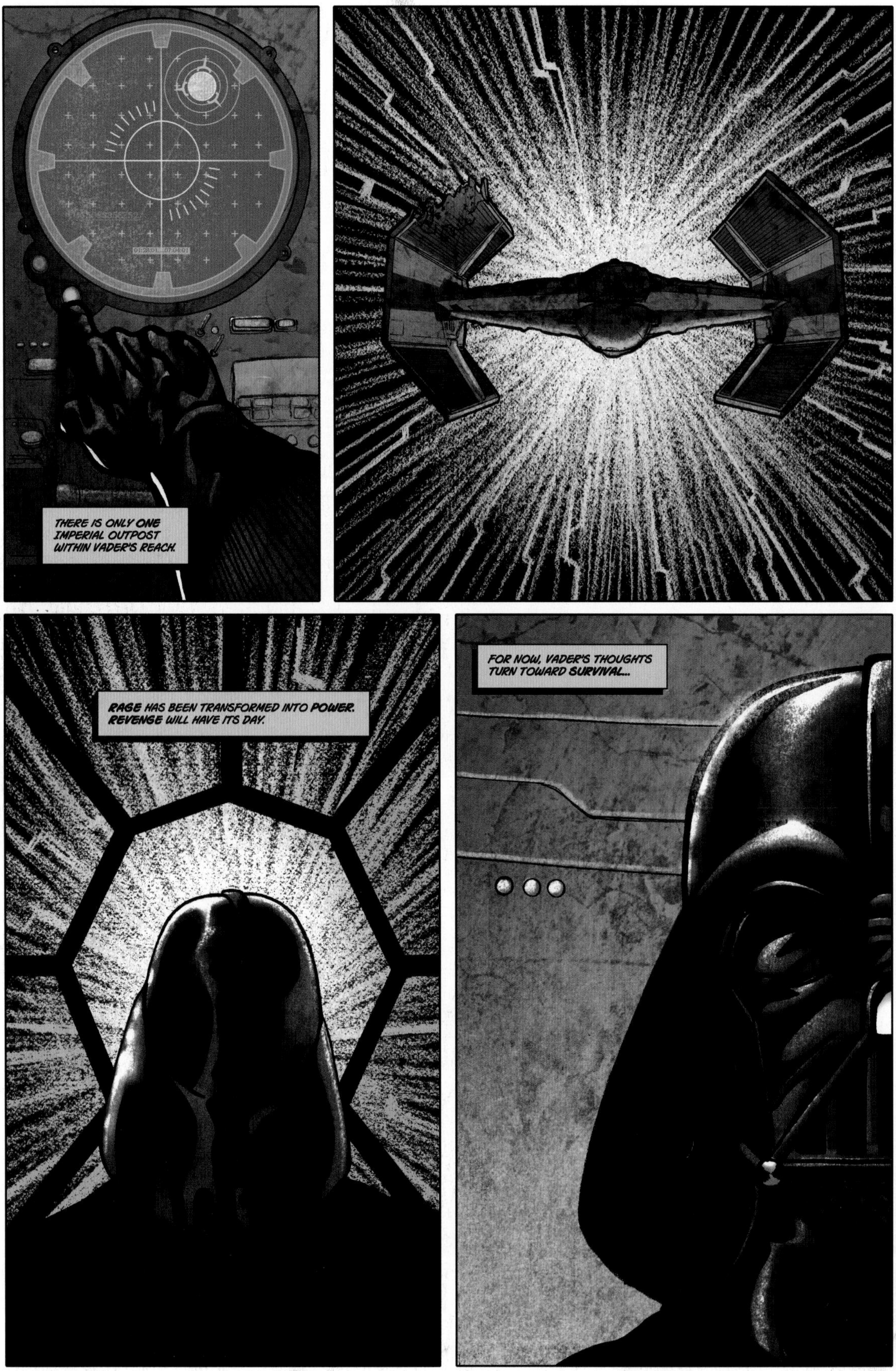
THERE IS ONLY ONE IMPERIAL OUTPOST WITHIN VADER'S REACH.
RAGE HAS BEEN TRANSFORMED INTO POWER. REVENGE WILL HAVE ITS DAY.
FOR NOW, VADER'S THOUGHTS TURN TOWARD SURVIVAL...

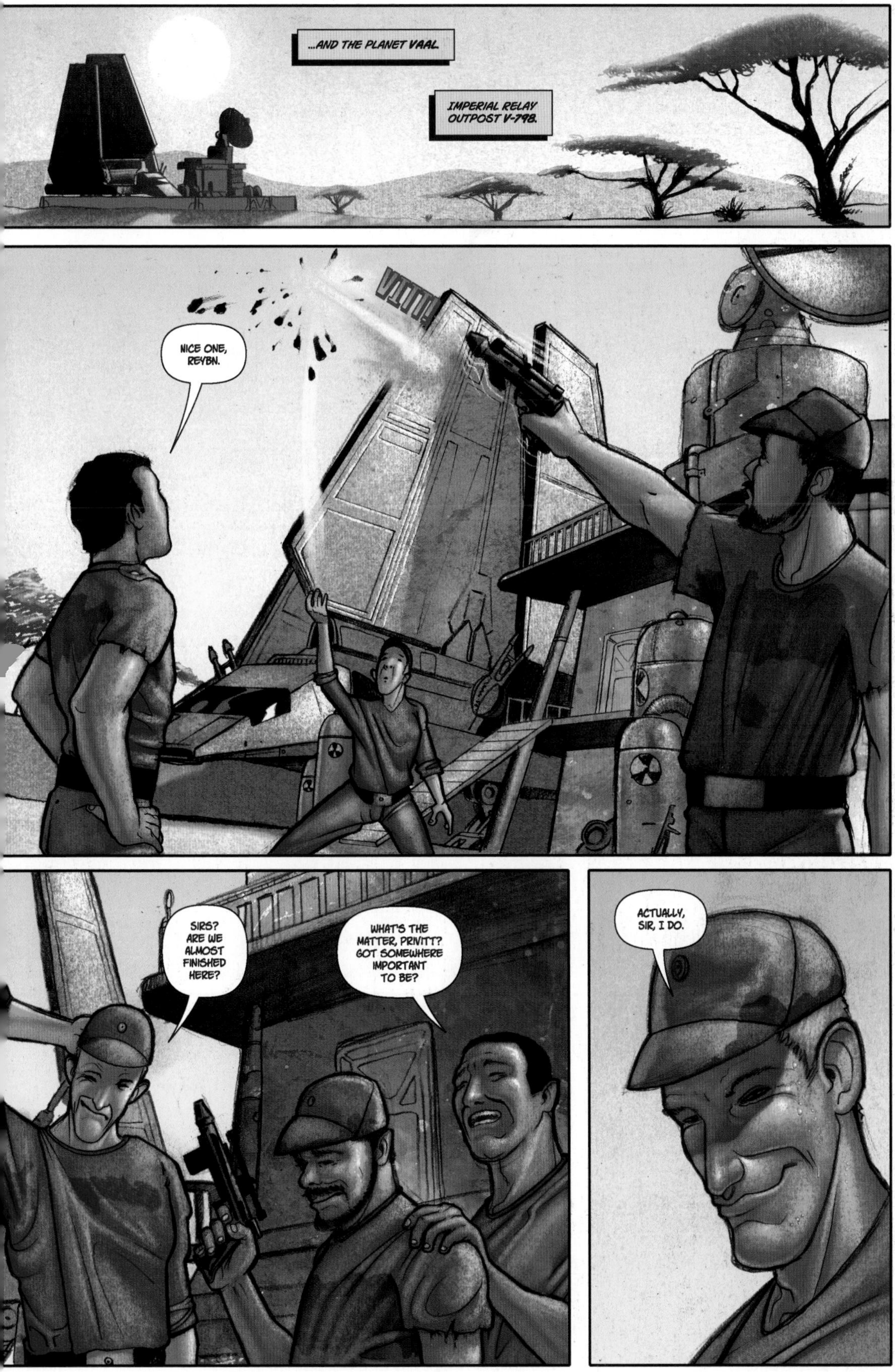
...AND THE PLANET VAAL.
IMPERIAL RELAY OUTPOST V-798.
NICE ONE, REYBN.
SIRS? ARE WE ALMOST FINISHED HERE?
WHAT'S THE MATTER, PRIVITT? GOT SOMEWHERE IMPORTANT TO BE?
ACTUALLY, SIR, I DO.

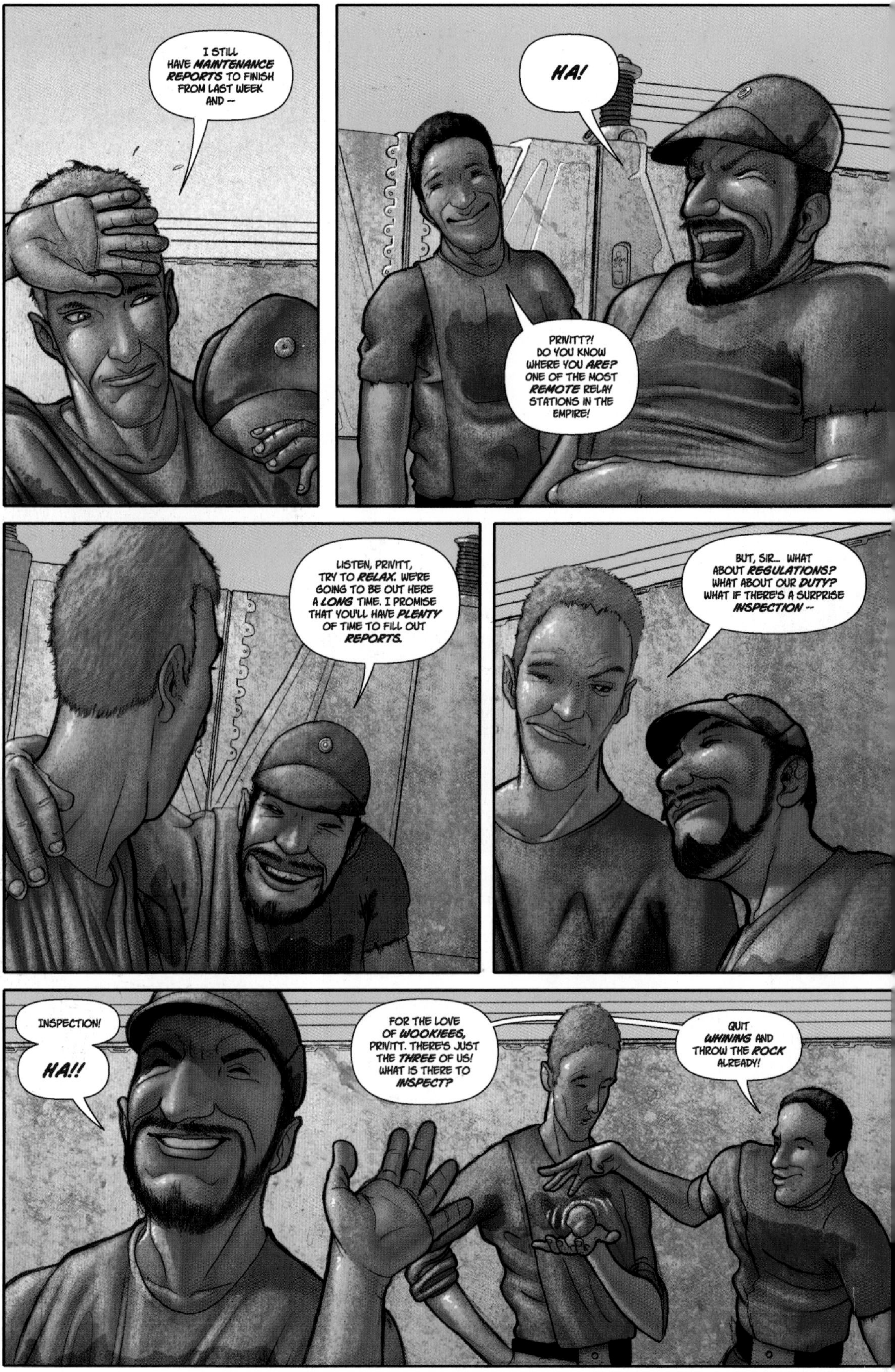
I STILL HAVE MAINTENANCE REPORTS TO FINISH FROM LAST WEEK AND --
HA!
PRIVITT?! DO YOU KNOW WHERE YOU ARE? ONE OF THE MOST REMOTE RELAY STATIONS IN THE EMPIRE!
LISTEN, PRIVITT, TRY TO RELAX. WE'RE GOING TO BE OUT HERE A LONG TIME. I PROMISE THAT YOU'LL HAVE PLENTY OF TIME TO FILL OUT REPORTS.
BUT, SIR... WHAT ABOUT REGULATIONS? WHAT ABOUT OUR DUTY? WHAT IF THERE'S A SURPRISE INSPECTION --
INSPECTION!
HA!!
FOR THE LOVE OF WOOKIEES, PRIVITT. THERE'S JUST THE THREE OF US! WHAT IS THERE TO INSPECT?
QUIT WHINING AND THROW THE ROCK ALREADY!

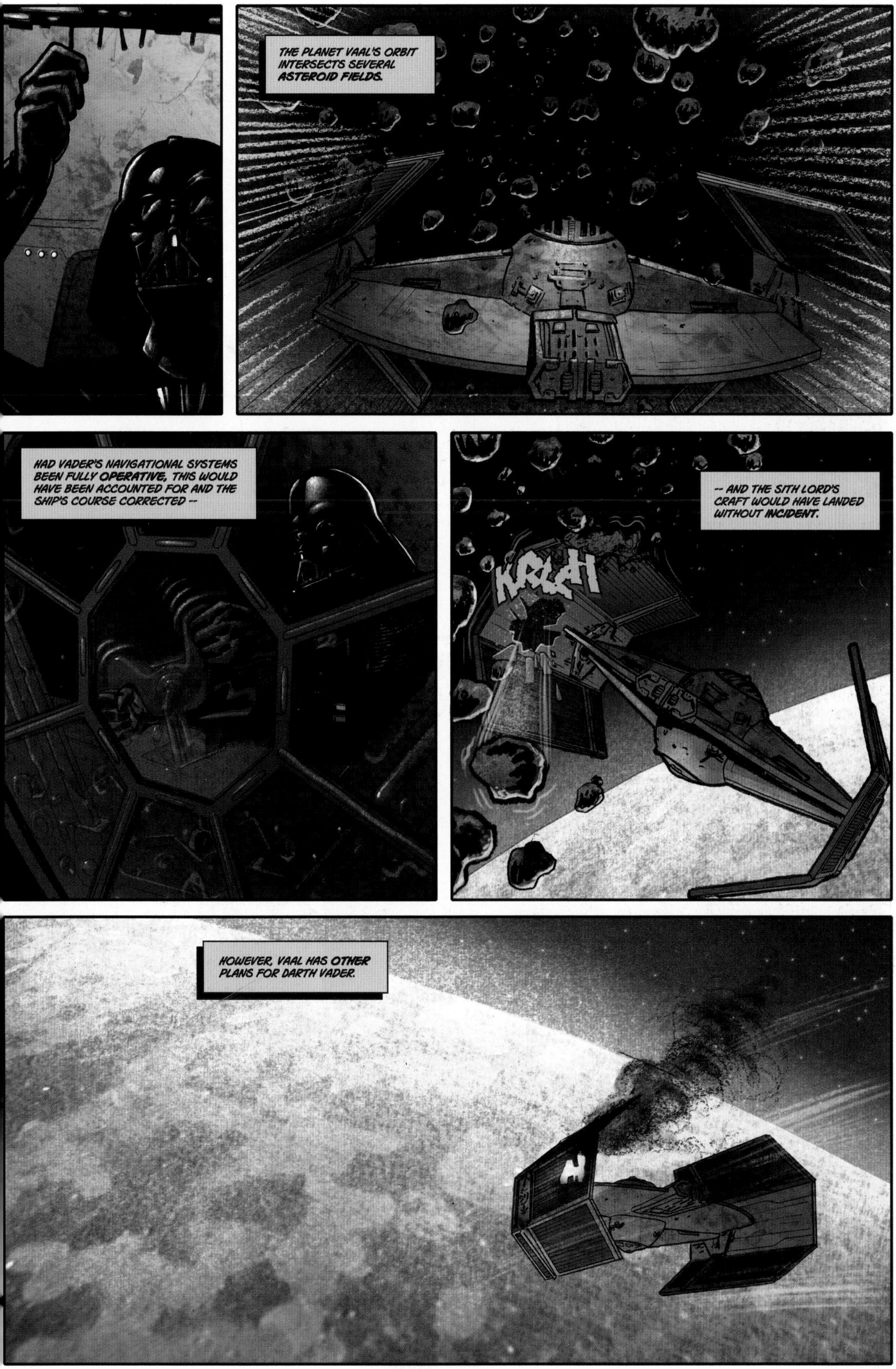
THE PLANET VAAL'S ORBIT INTERSECTS SEVERAL ASTEROID FIELDS.
HAD VADER'S NAVIGATIONAL SYSTEMS BEEN FULLY OPERATIVE, THIS WOULD HAVE BEEN ACCOUNTED FOR AND THE SHIP'S COURSE CORRECTED --
-- AND THE SITH LORD'S CRAFT WOULD HAVE LANDED WITHOUT INCIDENT.
HOWEVER, VAAL HAS OTHER PLANS FOR DARTH VADER.

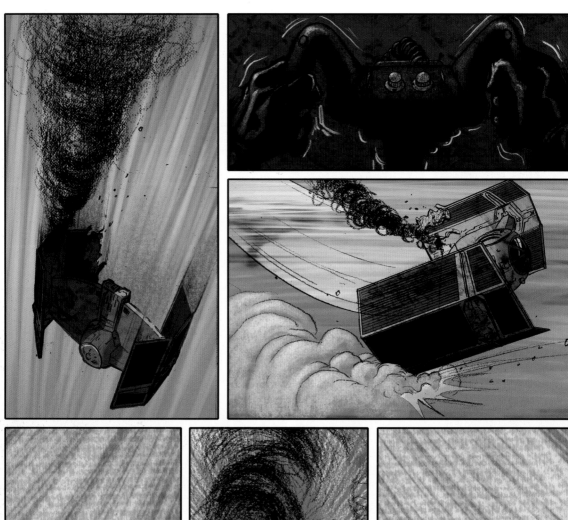

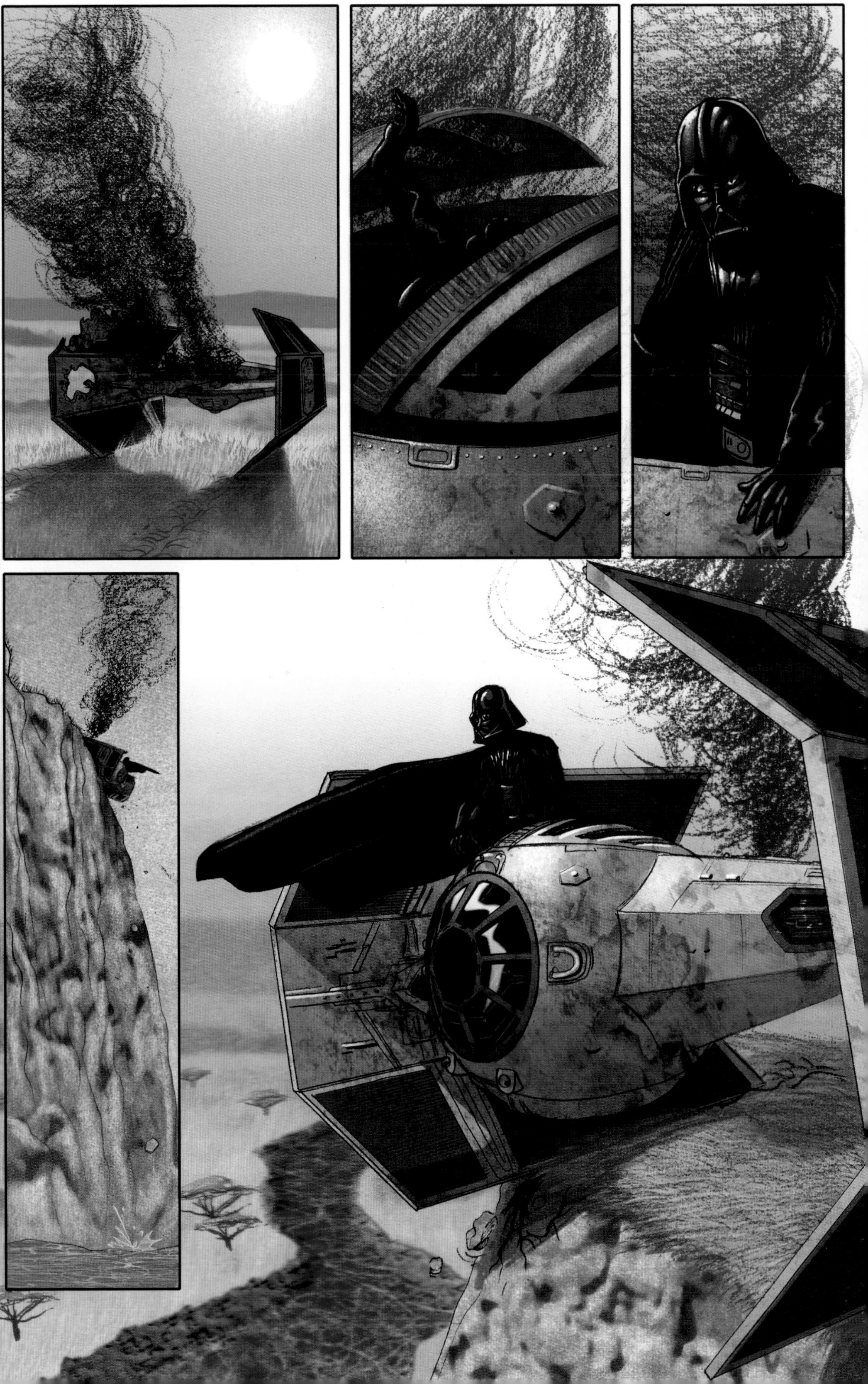

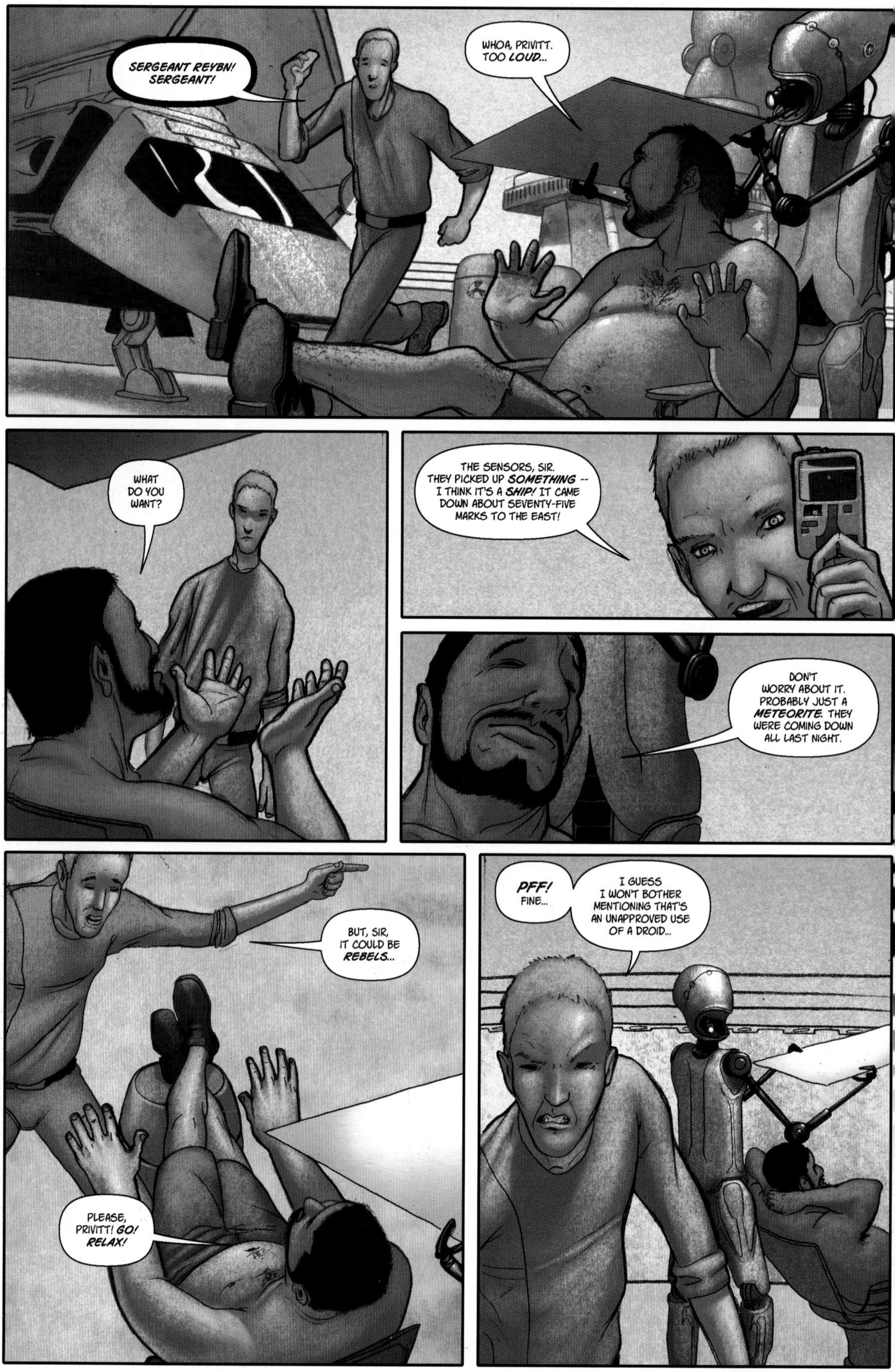
SERGEANT REYBN! SERGEANT!
WHOA, PRIVITT. TOO LOUD...
WHAT DO YOU WANT?
THE SENSORS, SIR. THEY PICKED UP SOMETHING -- I THINK IT'S A SHIP! IT CAME DOWN ABOUT SEVENTY-FIVE MARKS TO THE EAST!
DON'T WORRY ABOUT IT. PROBABLY JUST A METEORITE. THEY WERE COMING DOWN ALL LAST NIGHT.
BUT, SIR, IT COULD BE REBELS...
PLEASE, PRIVITT! GO! RELAX!
PFF! FINE...
I GUESS I WON'T BOTHER MENTIONING THAT'S AN UNAPPROVED USE OF A DROID...

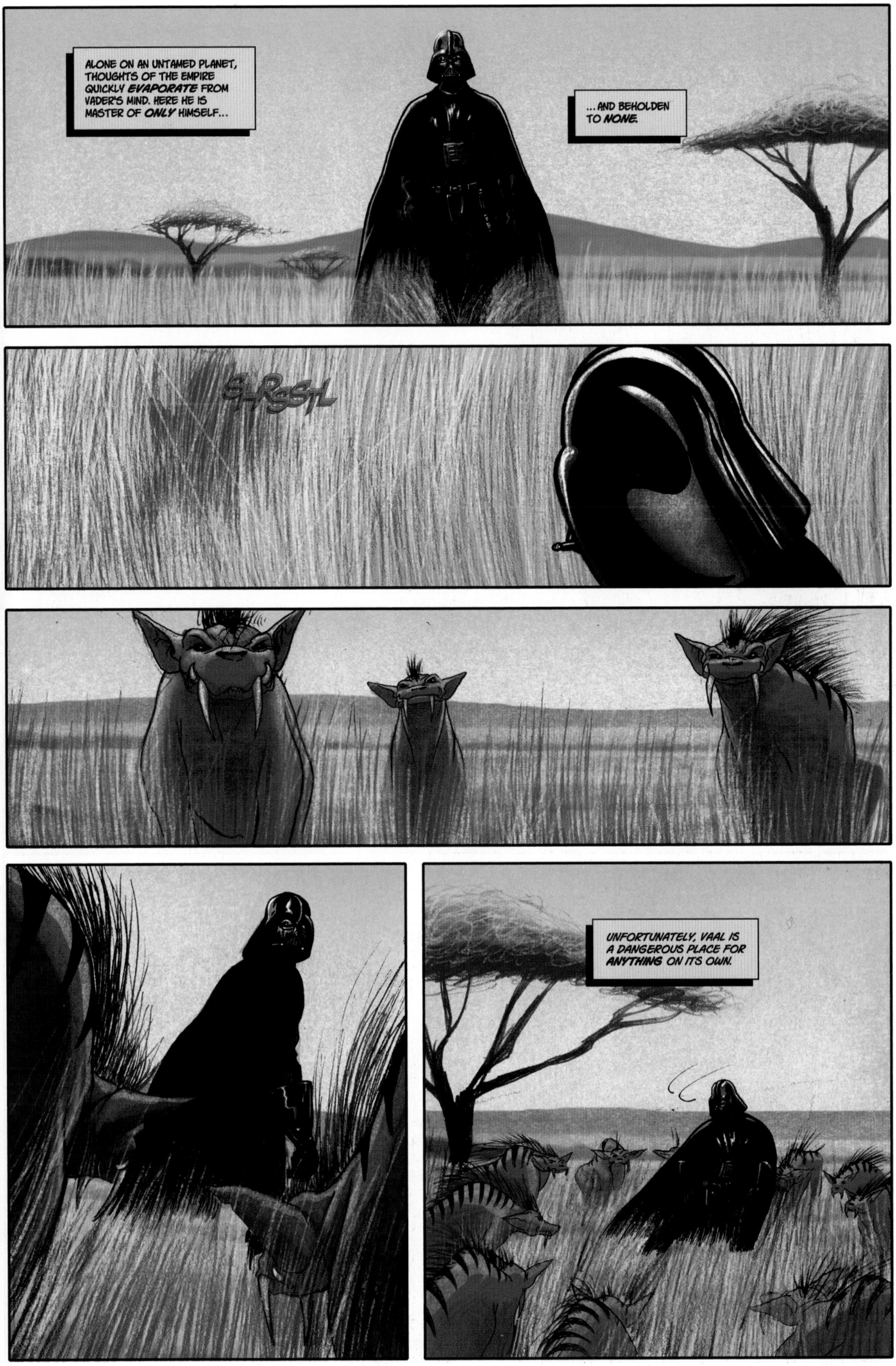
ALONE ON AN UNTAMED PLANET, THOUGHTS OF THE EMPIRE QUICKLY *EVAPORATE* FROM VADER'S MIND. HERE HE IS MASTER OF *ONLY* HIMSELF...
...AND BEHOLDEN TO *NONE*.
SHRSSHL
UNFORTUNATELY, VAAL IS A DANGEROUS PLACE FOR *ANYTHING* ON ITS OWN.

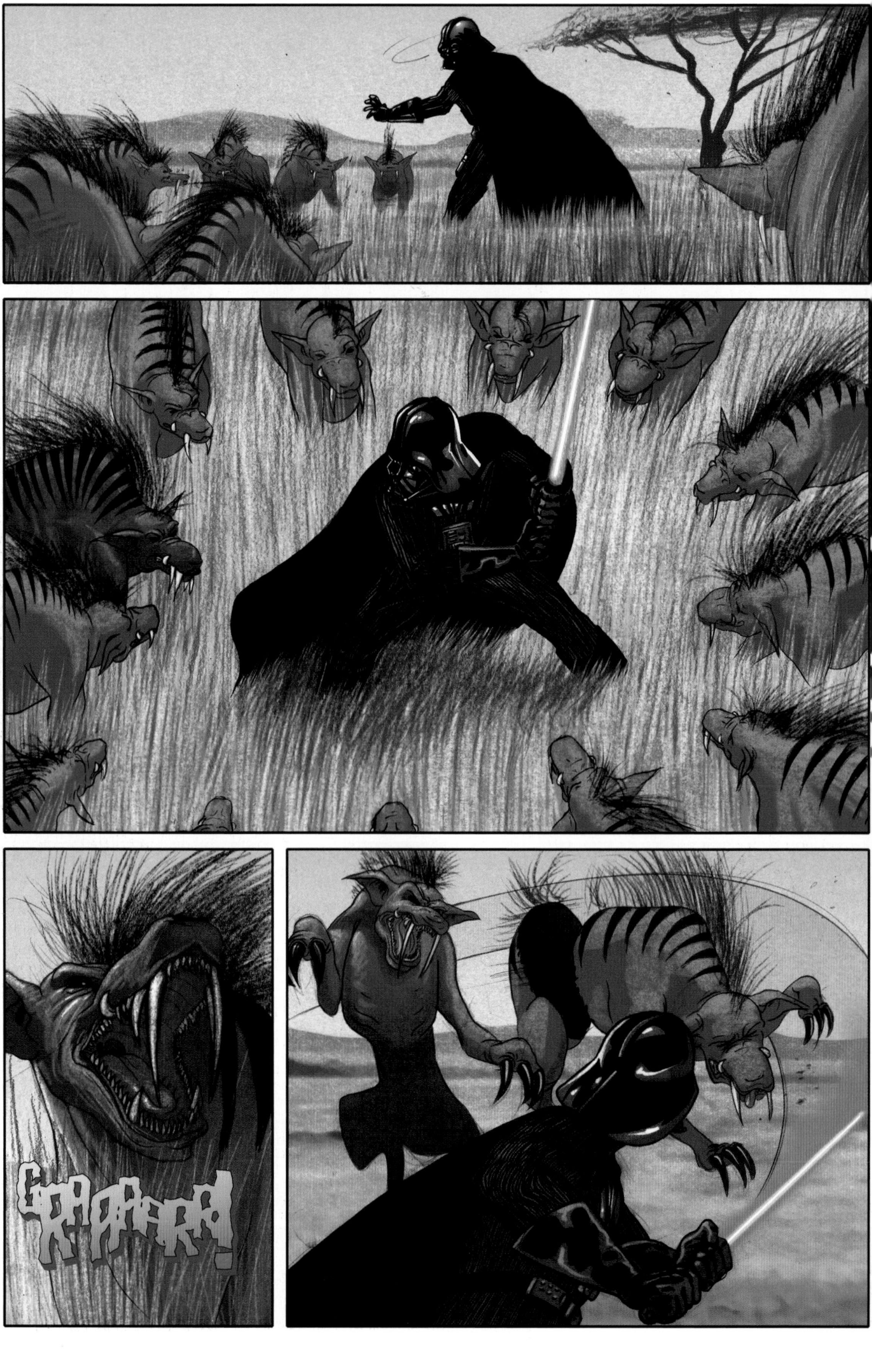
GRAAARR!

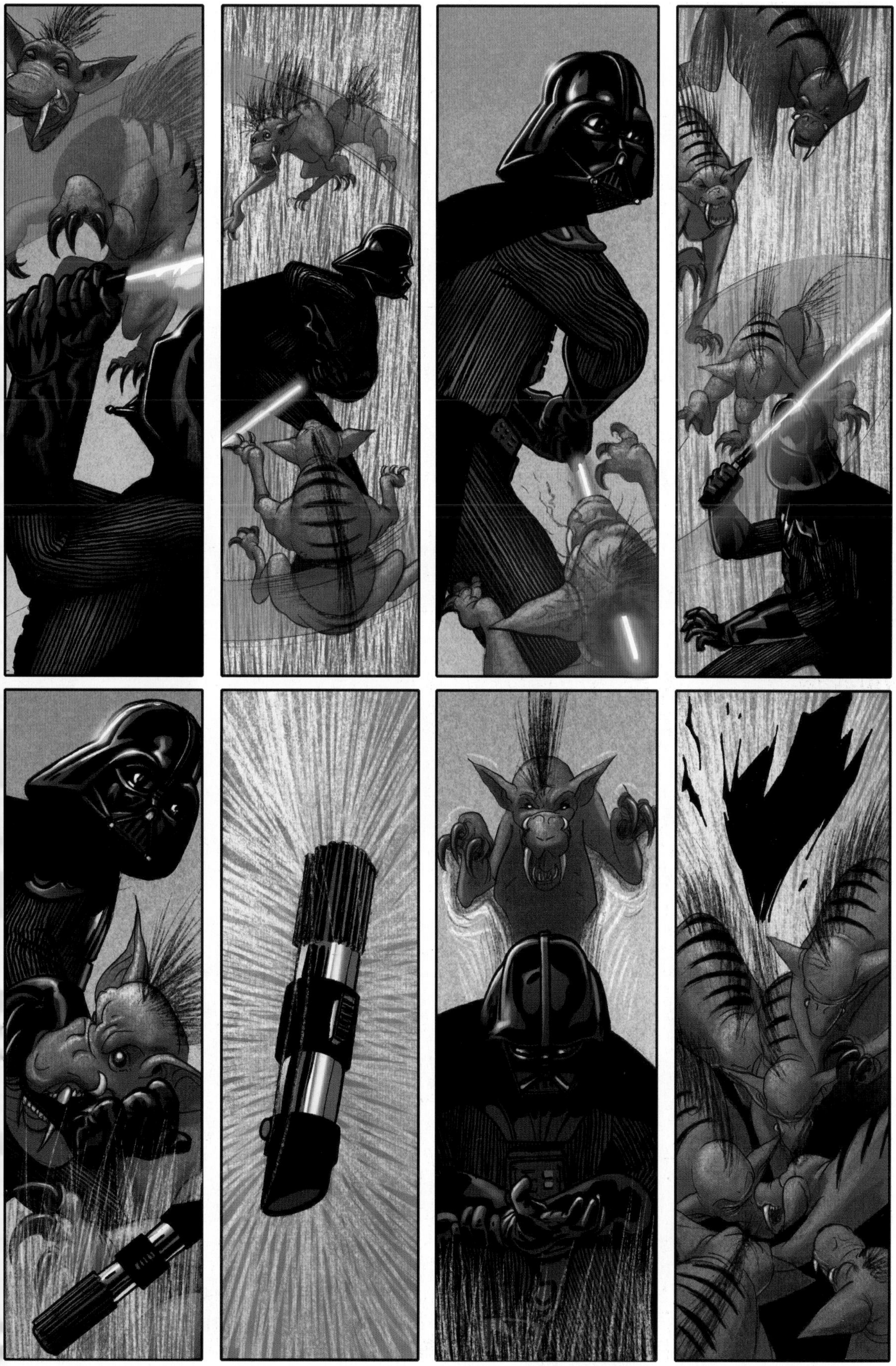

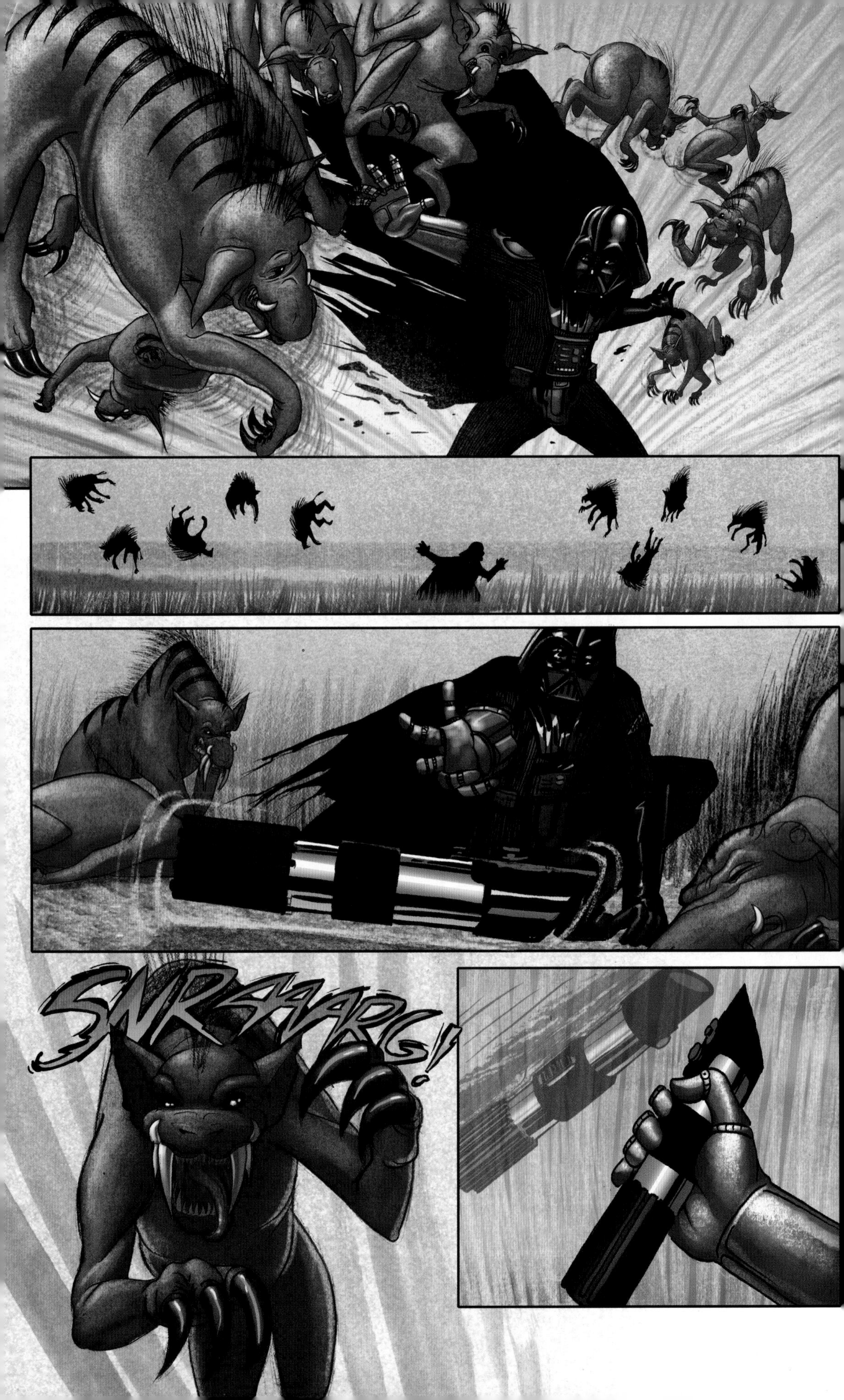
SNRAAARG!!

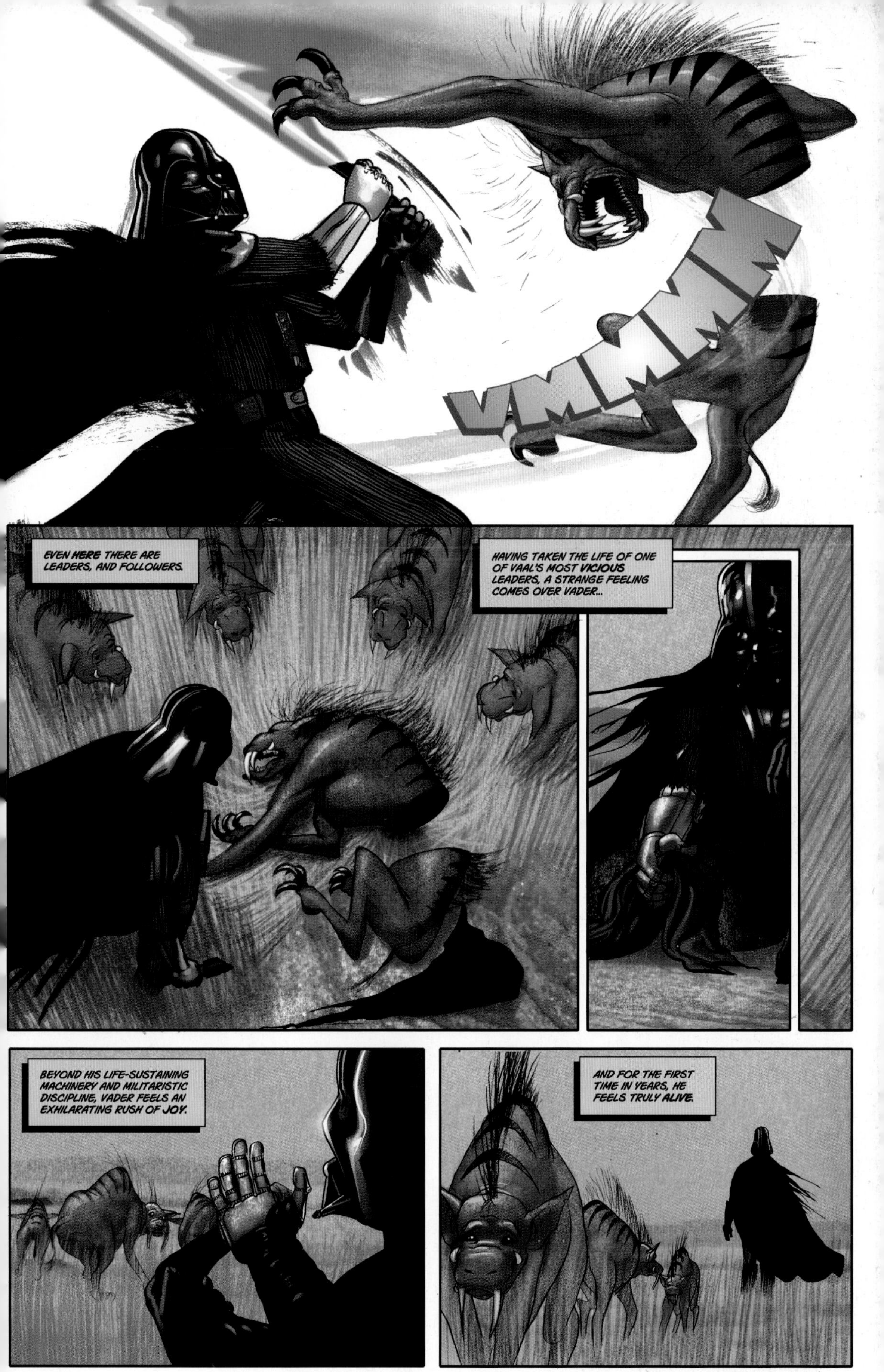
VMMMMM
EVEN HERE THERE ARE LEADERS, AND FOLLOWERS.
HAVING TAKEN THE LIFE OF ONE OF VAAL'S MOST VICIOUS LEADERS, A STRANGE FEELING COMES OVER VADER...
BEYOND HIS LIFE-SUSTAINING MACHINERY AND MILITARISTIC DISCIPLINE, VADER FEELS AN EXHILARATING RUSH OF JOY.
AND FOR THE FIRST TIME IN YEARS, HE FEELS TRULY ALIVE.

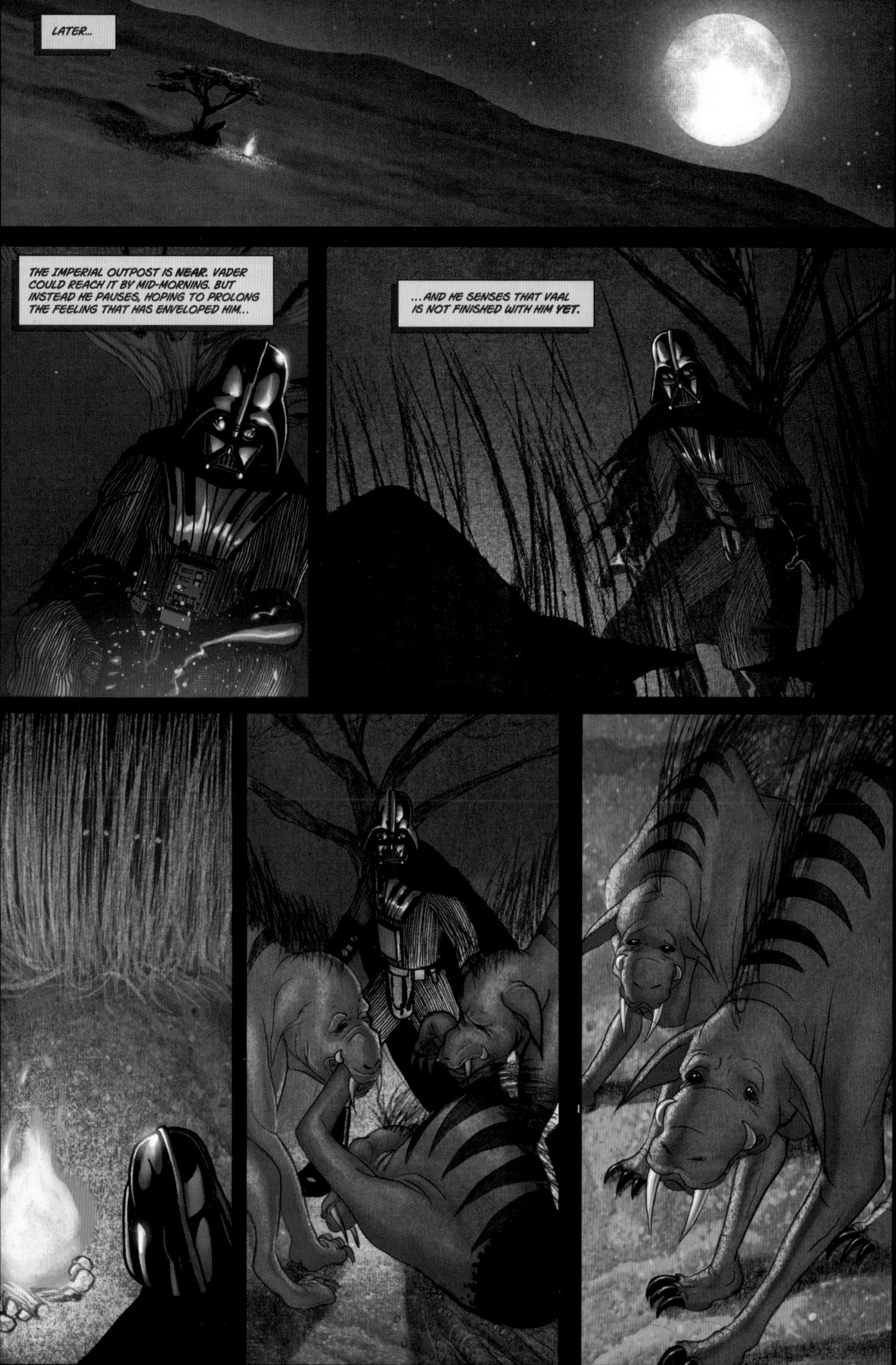
LATER...
THE IMPERIAL OUTPOST IS NEAR. VADER COULD REACH IT BY MID-MORNING. BUT INSTEAD HE PAUSES, HOPING TO PROLONG THE FEELING THAT HAS ENVELOPED HIM...
...AND HE SENSES THAT VAAL IS NOT FINISHED WITH HIM YET.

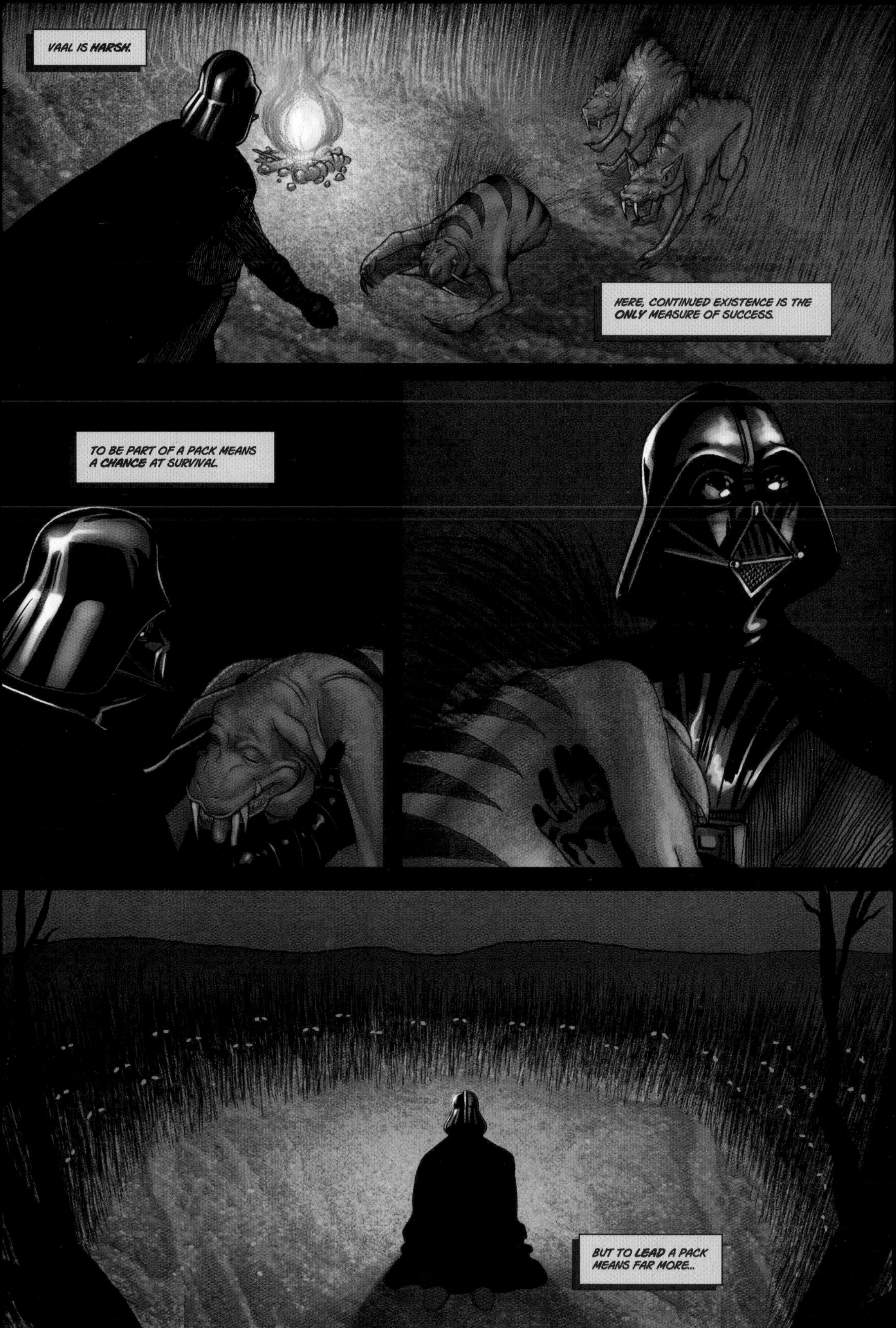
VAAL IS HARSH.
HERE, CONTINUED EXISTENCE IS THE ONLY MEASURE OF SUCCESS.
TO BE PART OF A PACK MEANS A CHANCE AT SURVIVAL.
BUT TO LEAD A PACK MEANS FAR MORE...

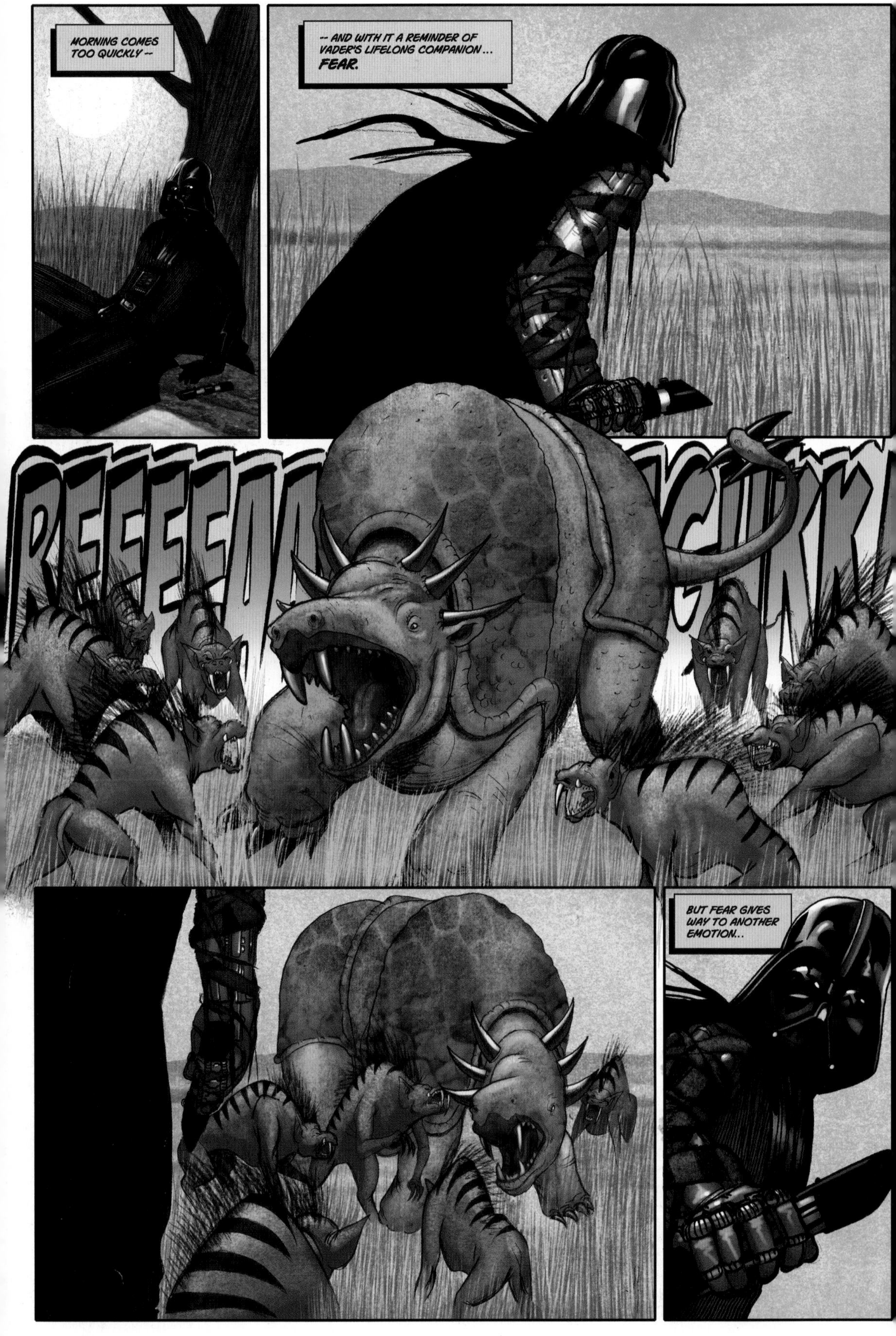
MORNING COMES TOO QUICKLY --
-- AND WITH IT A REMINDER OF VADER'S LIFELONG COMPANION... FEAR.
BUT FEAR GIVES WAY TO ANOTHER EMOTION...

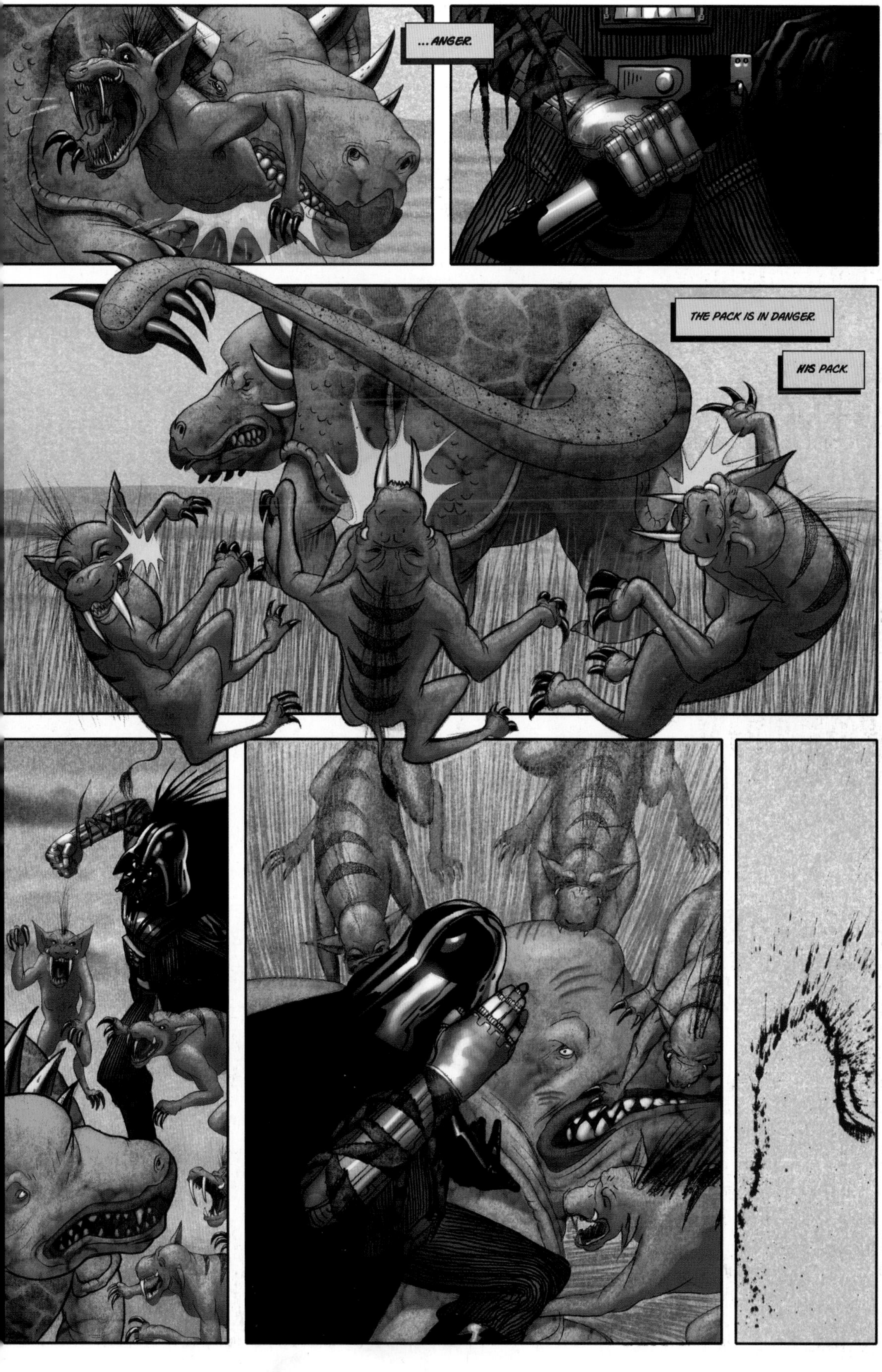
...ANGER.
THE PACK IS IN DANGER.
HIS PACK.

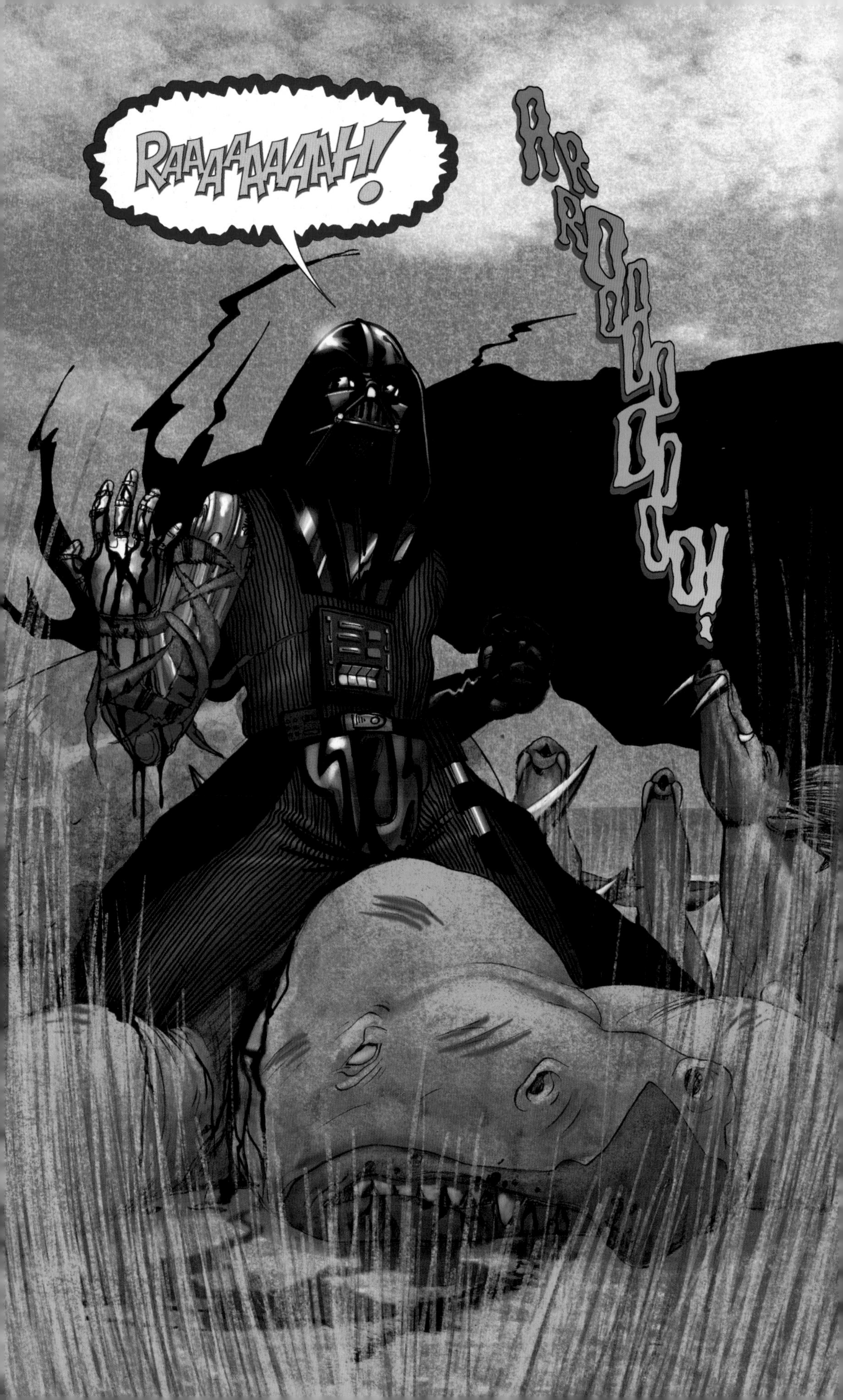
RAAAAAAAAH!
ARROOOOOOOO!

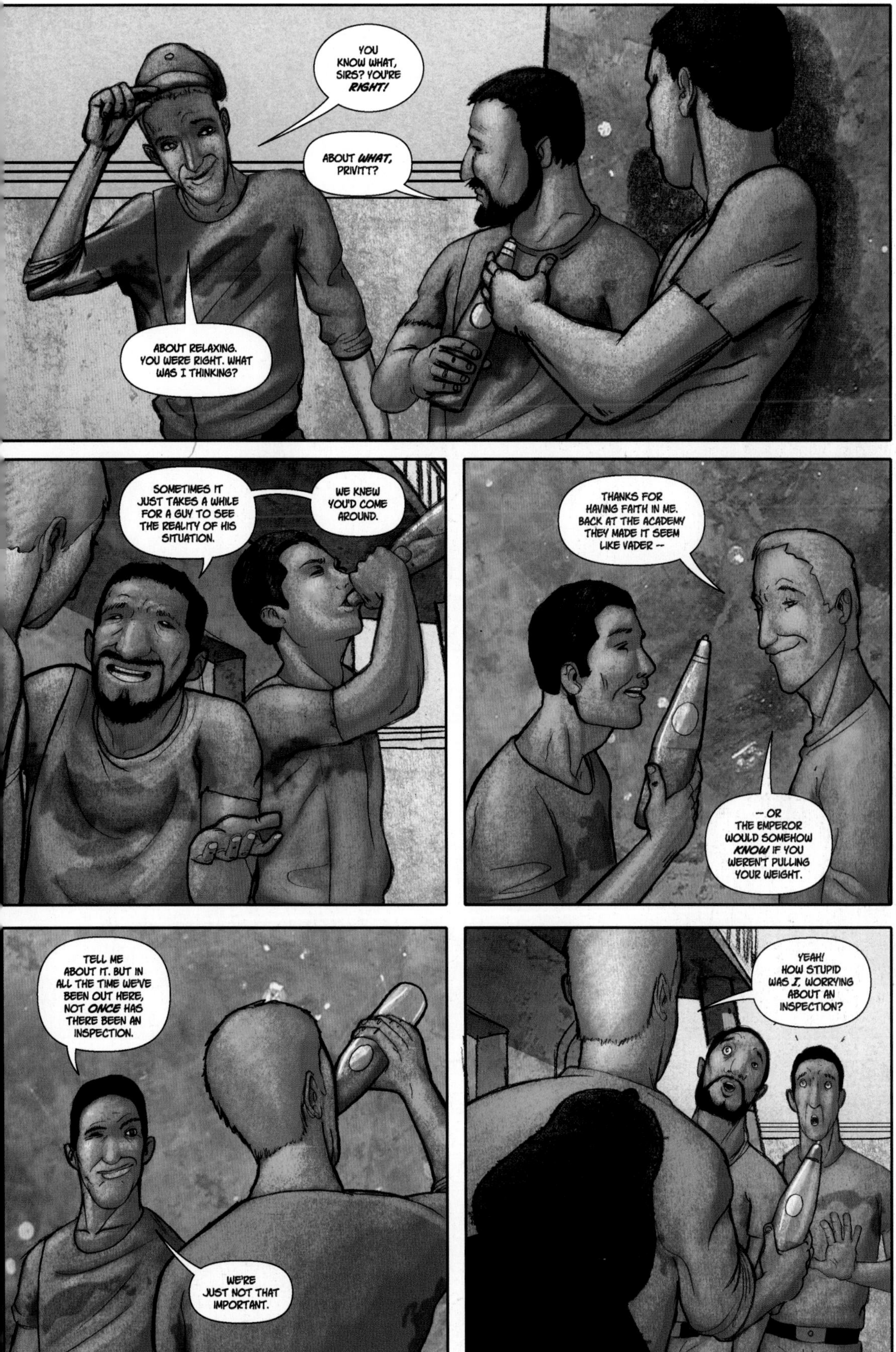
YOU KNOW WHAT, SIRS? YOU'RE *RIGHT!*
ABOUT *WHAT,* PRIVITT?
ABOUT RELAXING. YOU WERE RIGHT. WHAT WAS I THINKING?
SOMETIMES IT JUST TAKES A WHILE FOR A GUY TO SEE THE REALITY OF HIS SITUATION.
WE KNEW YOU'D COME AROUND.
THANKS FOR HAVING FAITH IN ME. BACK AT THE ACADEMY THEY MADE IT SEEM LIKE VADER --
-- OR THE EMPEROR WOULD SOMEHOW *KNOW* IF YOU WEREN'T PULLING YOUR WEIGHT.
TELL ME ABOUT IT. BUT IN ALL THE TIME WE'VE BEEN OUT HERE, NOT *ONCE* HAS THERE BEEN AN INSPECTION.
WE'RE JUST NOT THAT IMPORTANT.
YEAH! HOW STUPID WAS *I,* WORRYING ABOUT AN INSPECTION?

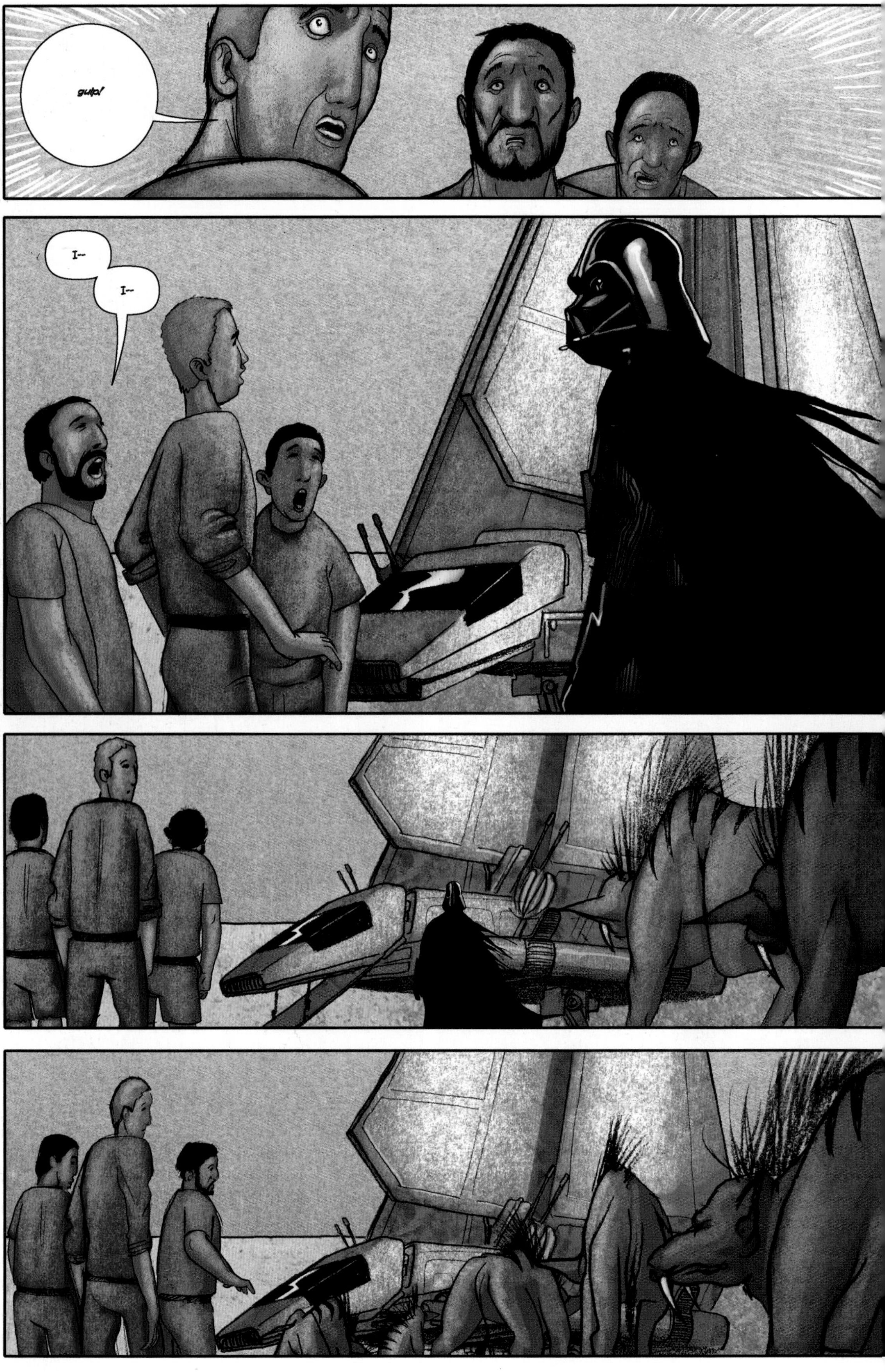
gulp!
I--
I--

CRRRRR

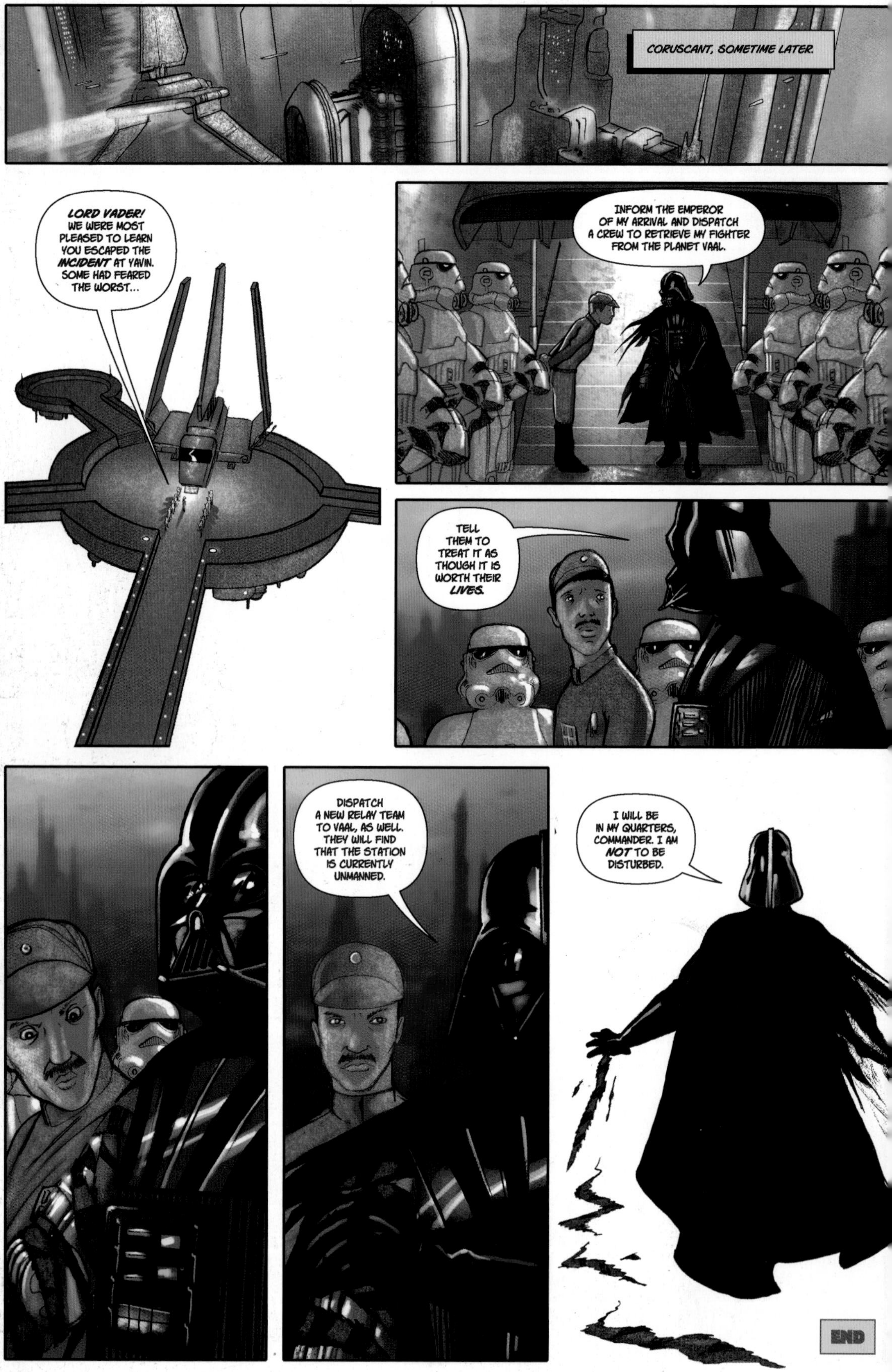
CORUSCANT, SOMETIME LATER.
LORD VADER! WE WERE MOST PLEASED TO LEARN YOU ESCAPED THE INCIDENT AT YAVIN. SOME HAD FEARED THE WORST...
INFORM THE EMPEROR OF MY ARRIVAL AND DISPATCH A CREW TO RETRIEVE MY FIGHTER FROM THE PLANET VAAL.
TELL THEM TO TREAT IT AS THOUGH IT IS WORTH THEIR LIVES.
DISPATCH A NEW RELAY TEAM TO VAAL, AS WELL. THEY WILL FIND THAT THE STATION IS CURRENTLY UNMANNED.
I WILL BE IN MY QUARTERS, COMMANDER. I AM NOT TO BE DISTURBED.
END

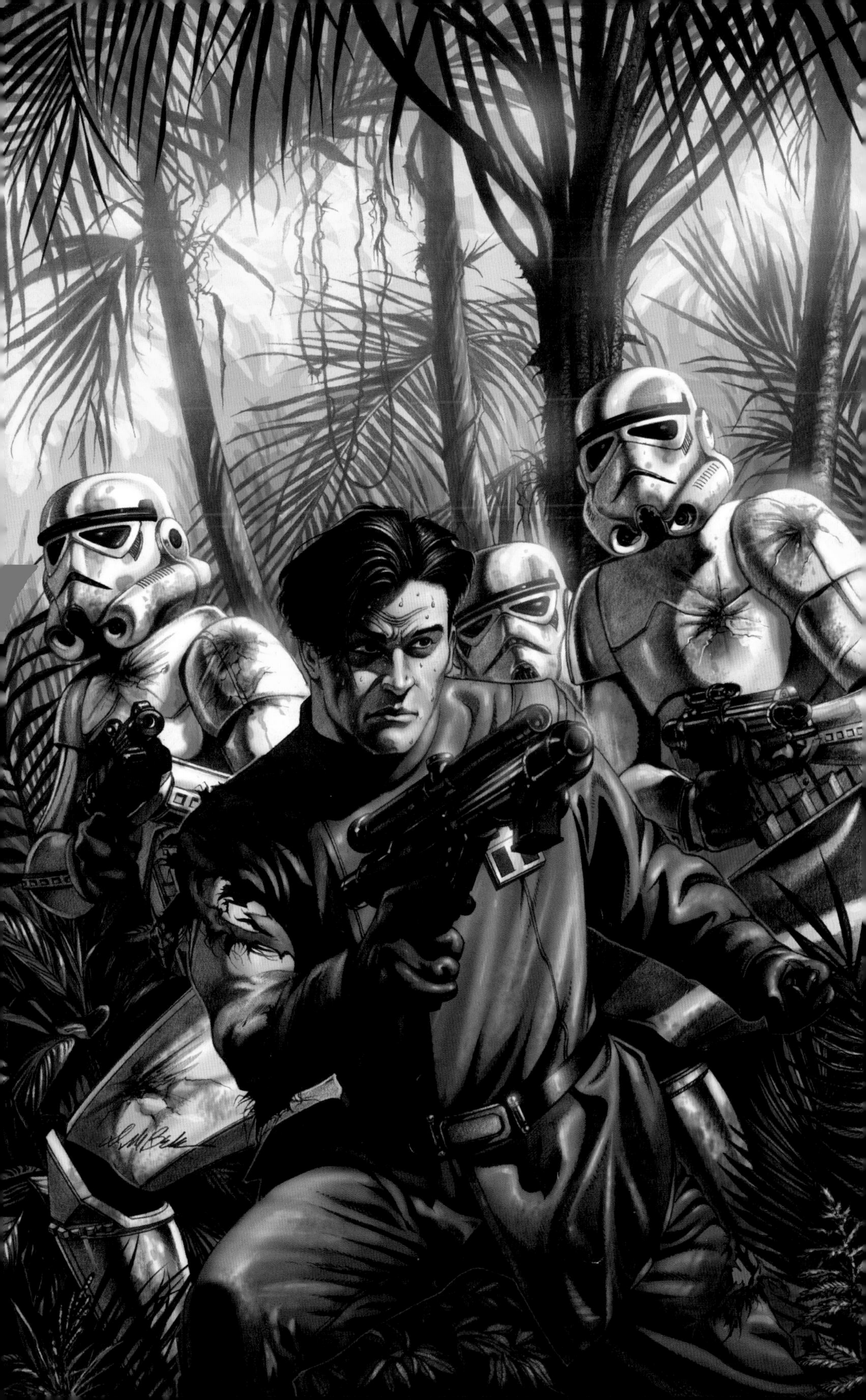

TO THE LAST MAN

Script WELLES HARTLEY
Pencils and colors DAVIDÉ FABBRI
Inks CHRISTIAN DALLA VECCHIA

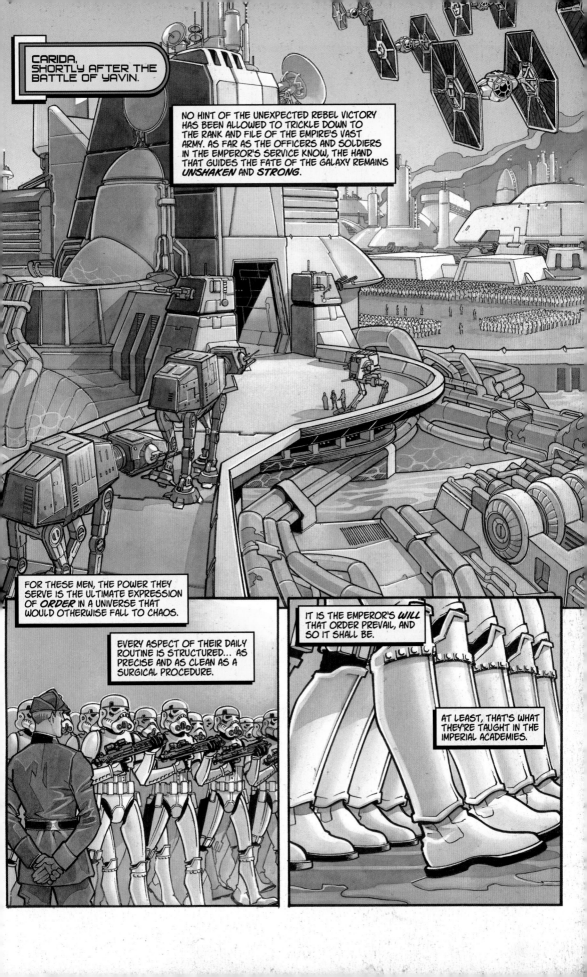

CARIDA, SHORTLY AFTER THE BATTLE OF YAVIN.

NO HINT OF THE UNEXPECTED REBEL VICTORY HAS BEEN ALLOWED TO TRICKLE DOWN TO THE RANK AND FILE OF THE EMPIRE'S VAST ARMY. AS FAR AS THE OFFICERS AND SOLDIERS IN THE EMPEROR'S SERVICE KNOW, THE HAND THAT GUIDES THE FATE OF THE GALAXY REMAINS *UNSHAKEN* AND *STRONG*.

FOR THESE MEN, THE POWER THEY SERVE IS THE ULTIMATE EXPRESSION OF *ORDER* IN A UNIVERSE THAT WOULD OTHERWISE FALL TO CHAOS.

EVERY ASPECT OF THEIR DAILY ROUTINE IS STRUCTURED... AS PRECISE AND AS CLEAN AS A SURGICAL PROCEDURE.

IT IS THE EMPEROR'S *WILL* THAT ORDER PREVAIL, AND SO IT SHALL BE.

AT LEAST, THAT'S WHAT THEY'RE TAUGHT IN THE IMPERIAL ACADEMIES.

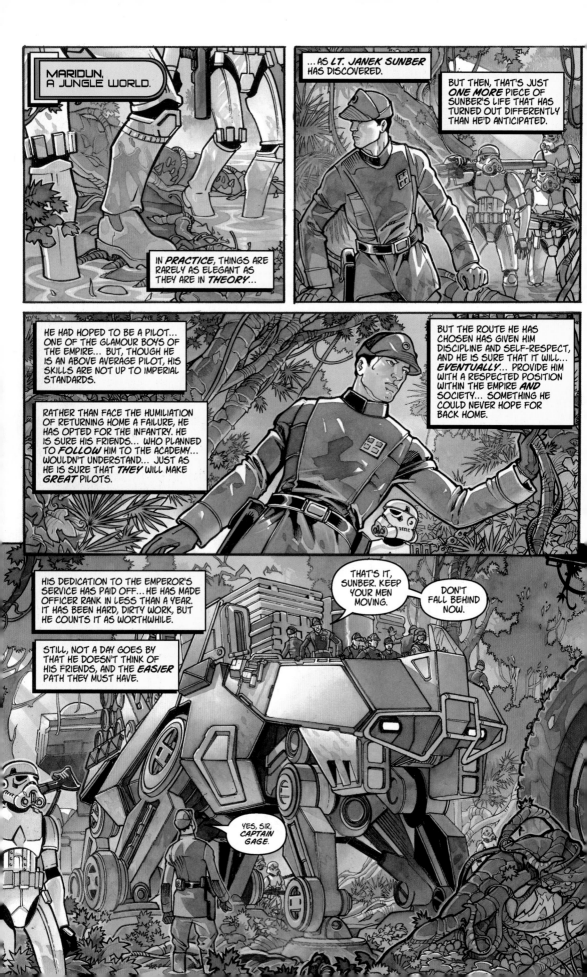

MARIDUN, A JUNGLE WORLD.

IN *PRACTICE*, THINGS ARE RARELY AS ELEGANT AS THEY ARE IN *THEORY*...

...AS *LT. JANEK SUNBER* HAS DISCOVERED.

BUT THEN, THAT'S JUST *ONE MORE* PIECE OF SUNBER'S LIFE THAT HAS TURNED OUT DIFFERENTLY THAN HE'D ANTICIPATED.

HE HAD HOPED TO BE A PILOT... ONE OF THE GLAMOUR BOYS OF THE EMPIRE... BUT, THOUGH HE IS AN ABOVE AVERAGE PILOT, HIS SKILLS ARE NOT UP TO IMPERIAL STANDARDS.

RATHER THAN FACE THE HUMILIATION OF RETURNING HOME A FAILURE, HE HAS OPTED FOR THE INFANTRY. HE IS SURE HIS FRIENDS... WHO PLANNED TO *FOLLOW* HIM TO THE ACADEMY... WOULDN'T UNDERSTAND... JUST AS HE IS SURE THAT *THEY* WILL MAKE *GREAT* PILOTS.

BUT THE ROUTE HE HAS CHOSEN HAS GIVEN HIM DISCIPLINE AND SELF-RESPECT, AND HE IS SURE THAT IT WILL... *EVENTUALLY*... PROVIDE HIM WITH A RESPECTED POSITION WITHIN THE EMPIRE *AND* SOCIETY... SOMETHING HE COULD NEVER HOPE FOR BACK HOME.

HIS DEDICATION TO THE EMPEROR'S SERVICE HAS PAID OFF... HE HAS MADE OFFICER RANK IN LESS THAN A YEAR. IT HAS BEEN HARD, DIRTY WORK, BUT HE COUNTS IT AS WORTHWHILE.

STILL, NOT A DAY GOES BY THAT HE DOESN'T THINK OF HIS FRIENDS, AND THE *EASIER* PATH THEY MUST HAVE.

THAT'S IT, SUNBER. KEEP YOUR MEN MOVING.

DON'T FALL BEHIND NOW.

YES, SIR, *CAPTAIN GAGE.*

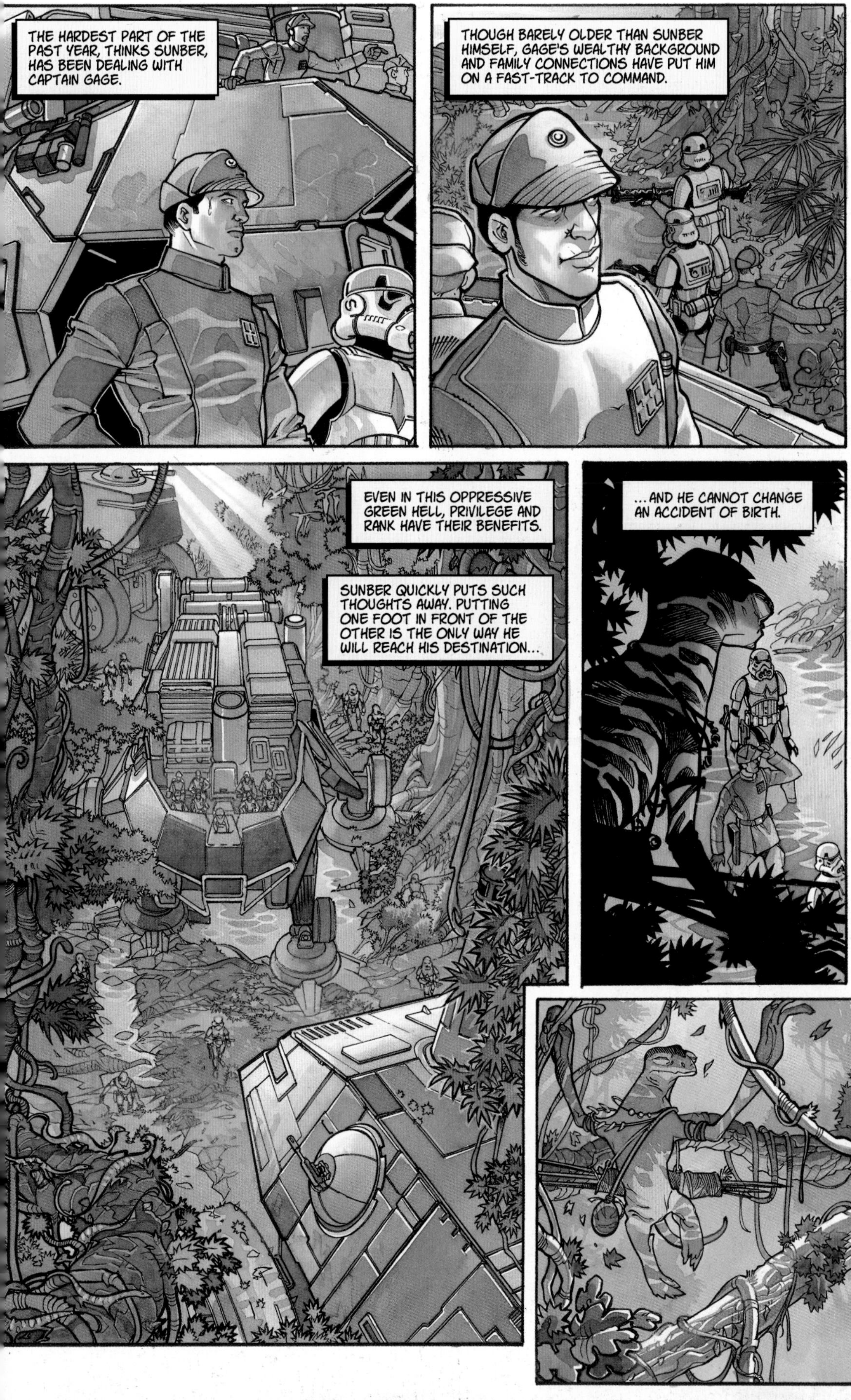
THE HARDEST PART OF THE PAST YEAR, THINKS SUNBER, HAS BEEN DEALING WITH CAPTAIN GAGE.
THOUGH BARELY OLDER THAN SUNBER HIMSELF, GAGE'S WEALTHY BACKGROUND AND FAMILY CONNECTIONS HAVE PUT HIM ON A FAST-TRACK TO COMMAND.
EVEN IN THIS OPPRESSIVE GREEN HELL, PRIVILEGE AND RANK HAVE THEIR BENEFITS.
SUNBER QUICKLY PUTS SUCH THOUGHTS AWAY. PUTTING ONE FOOT IN FRONT OF THE OTHER IS THE ONLY WAY HE WILL REACH HIS DESTINATION...
...AND HE CANNOT CHANGE AN ACCIDENT OF BIRTH.

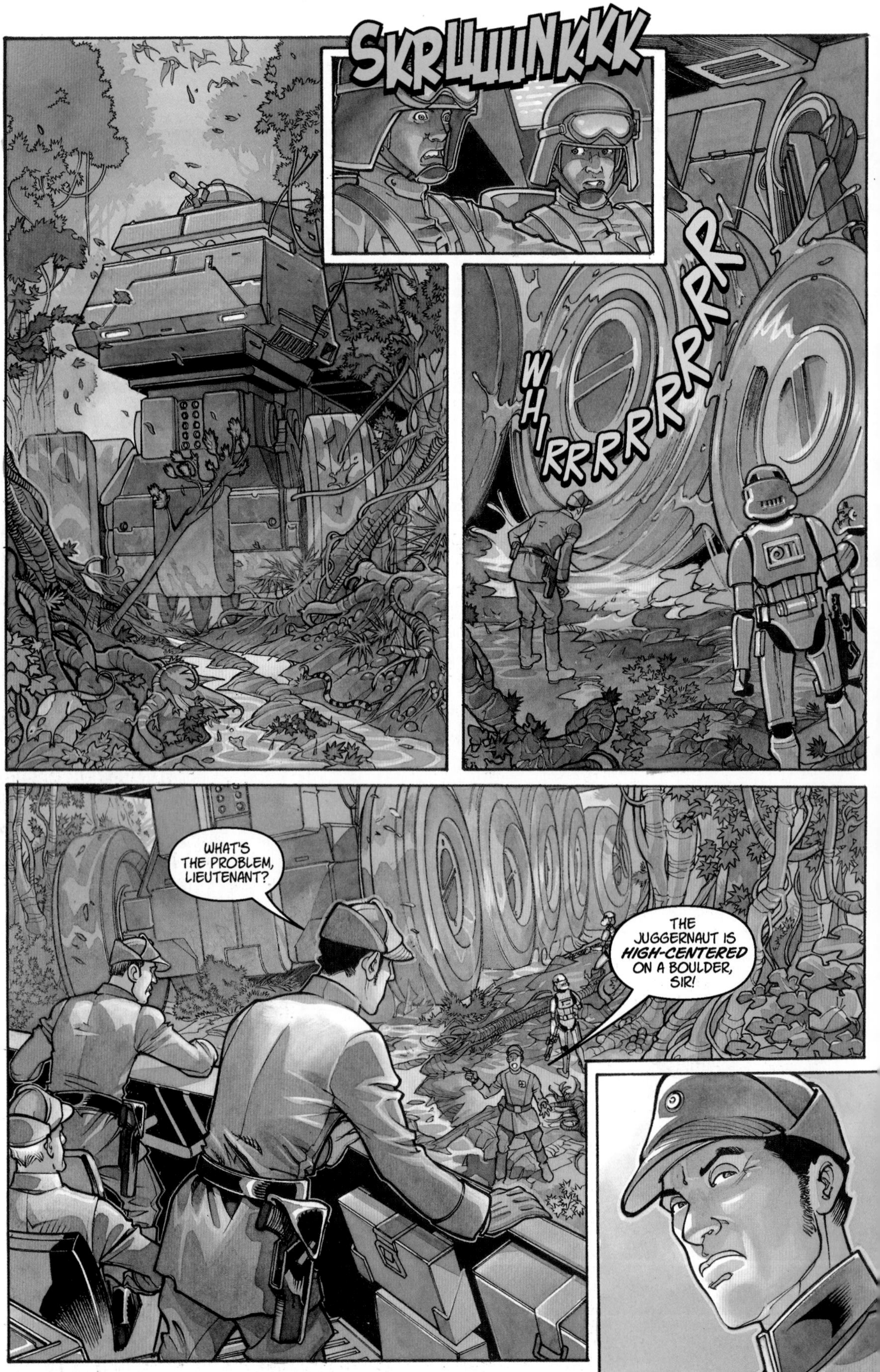
SKRUUUNKKK
WHIRRRRRRRR
WHAT'S THE PROBLEM, LIEUTENANT?
THE JUGGERNAUT IS HIGH-CENTERED ON A BOULDER, SIR!

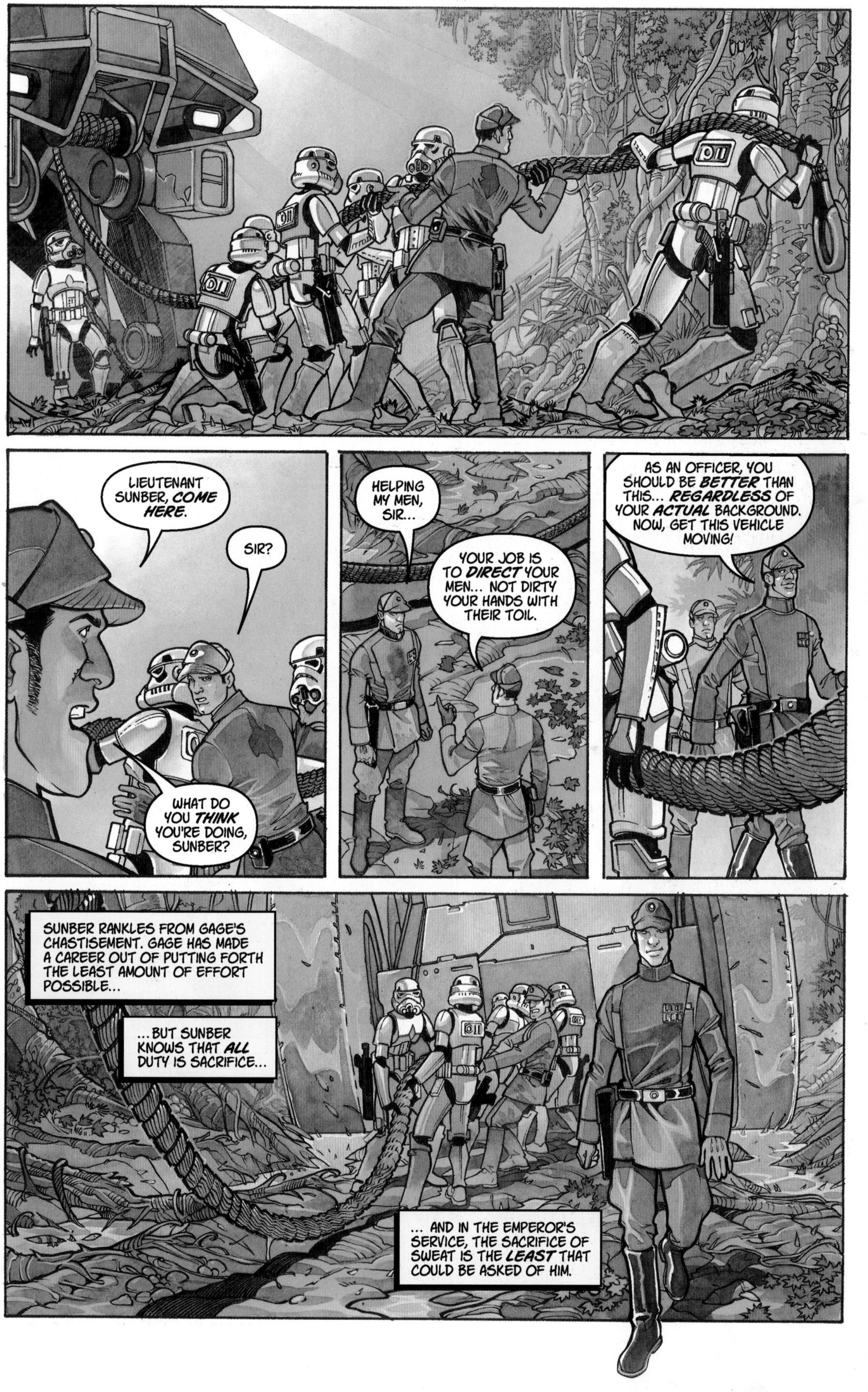
LIEUTENANT SUNBER, COME HERE.
SIR?
WHAT DO YOU THINK YOU'RE DOING, SUNBER?
HELPING MY MEN, SIR...
YOUR JOB IS TO DIRECT YOUR MEN... NOT DIRTY YOUR HANDS WITH THEIR TOIL.
AS AN OFFICER, YOU SHOULD BE BETTER THAN THIS... REGARDLESS OF YOUR ACTUAL BACKGROUND. NOW, GET THIS VEHICLE MOVING!
SUNBER RANKLES FROM GAGE'S CHASTISEMENT. GAGE HAS MADE A CAREER OUT OF PUTTING FORTH THE LEAST AMOUNT OF EFFORT POSSIBLE...
...BUT SUNBER KNOWS THAT ALL DUTY IS SACRIFICE...
... AND IN THE EMPEROR'S SERVICE, THE SACRIFICE OF SWEAT IS THE LEAST THAT COULD BE ASKED OF HIM.

DO **ALL** OF YOUR JUNIOR OFFICERS OBEY AS WELL AS SUNBER?

COMMANDER...?

WHA--? SUNBER...

I'VE SEEN IT BEFORE... A YOUNG OFFICER WILL DISREGARD PROTOCOL IN ORDER TO INGRATIATE HIMSELF TO HIS SUPERIORS. IT'S NOTHING BUT GRAND-STANDING...

REALLY?

I THINK LT. SUNBER'S EFFORTS ARE COMMENDABLE, **COMMANDER FRICKETT.**

HE HAS HIS PRIORITIES **STRAIGHT**... THE **MISSION** COMES FIRST.

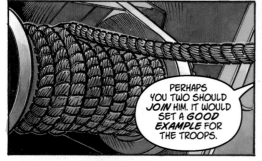

PERHAPS YOU TWO SHOULD **JOIN** HIM. IT WOULD SET A **GOOD EXAMPLE** FOR THE TROOPS.

UH, CERTAINLY, **GENERAL ZIERING,** SIR.

BUT THE TWO OFFICERS ARE RESCUED FROM EXERTION AND EMBARRASSMENT...

WHUNK

VRRRRRRR

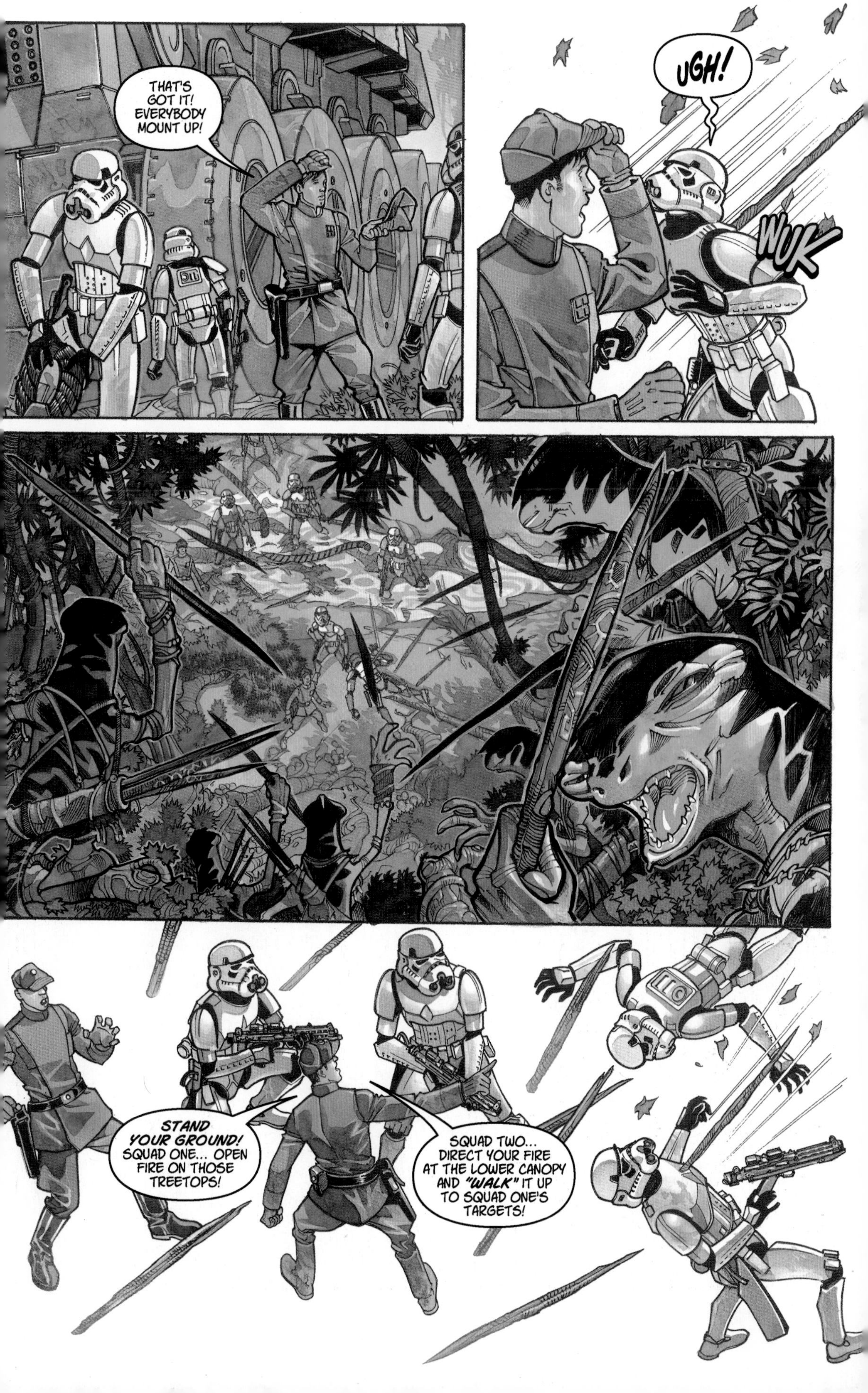
THAT'S GOT IT! EVERYBODY MOUNT UP!
UGH!
WUK
STAND YOUR GROUND! SQUAD ONE... OPEN FIRE ON THOSE TREETOPS!
SQUAD TWO... DIRECT YOUR FIRE AT THE LOWER CANOPY AND "WALK" IT UP TO SQUAD ONE'S TARGETS!

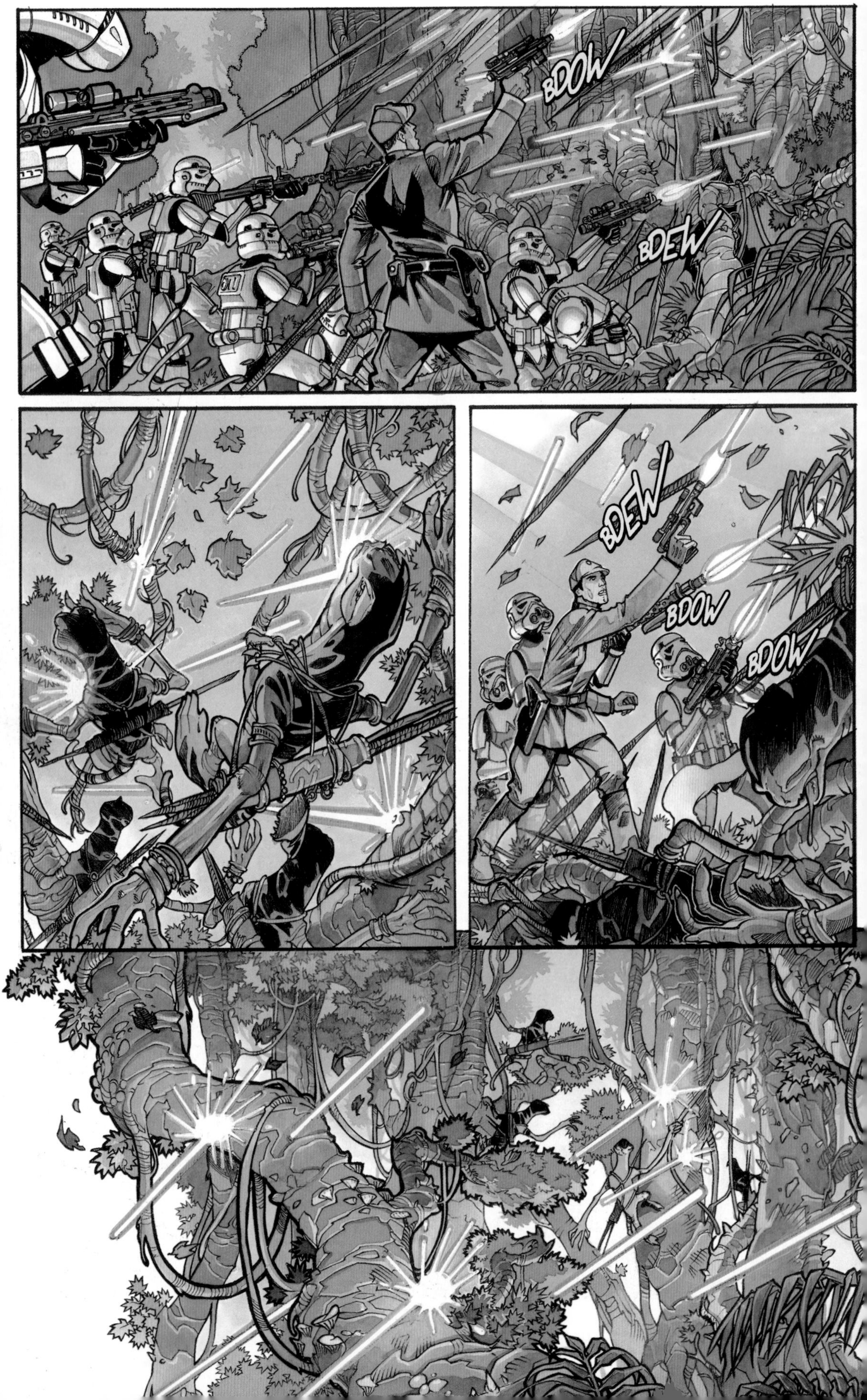

BDOW
BDEW
BDEW
BDOW
BDOW

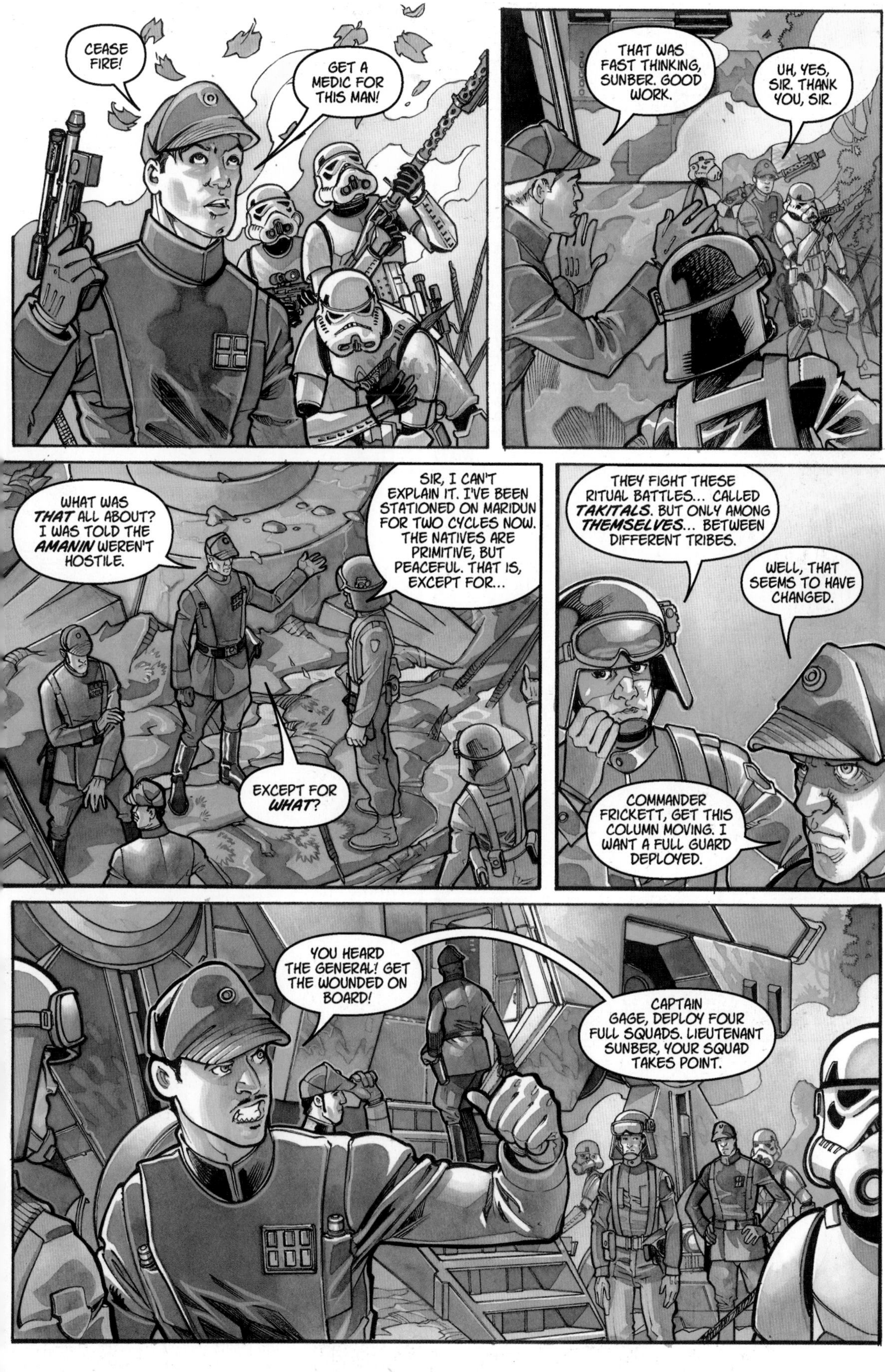
CEASE FIRE!
GET A MEDIC FOR THIS MAN!
THAT WAS FAST THINKING, SUNBER. GOOD WORK.
UH, YES, SIR. THANK YOU, SIR.
WHAT WAS *THAT* ALL ABOUT? I WAS TOLD THE *AMANIN* WEREN'T HOSTILE.
SIR, I CAN'T EXPLAIN IT. I'VE BEEN STATIONED ON MARIDUN FOR TWO CYCLES NOW. THE NATIVES ARE PRIMITIVE, BUT PEACEFUL. THAT IS, EXCEPT FOR...
EXCEPT FOR *WHAT*?
THEY FIGHT THESE RITUAL BATTLES... CALLED *TAKITALS*. BUT ONLY AMONG *THEMSELVES*... BETWEEN DIFFERENT TRIBES.
WELL, THAT SEEMS TO HAVE CHANGED.
COMMANDER FRICKETT, GET THIS COLUMN MOVING. I WANT A FULL GUARD DEPLOYED.
YOU HEARD THE GENERAL! GET THE WOUNDED ON BOARD!
CAPTAIN GAGE, DEPLOY FOUR FULL SQUADS. LIEUTENANT SUNBER, YOUR SQUAD TAKES POINT.

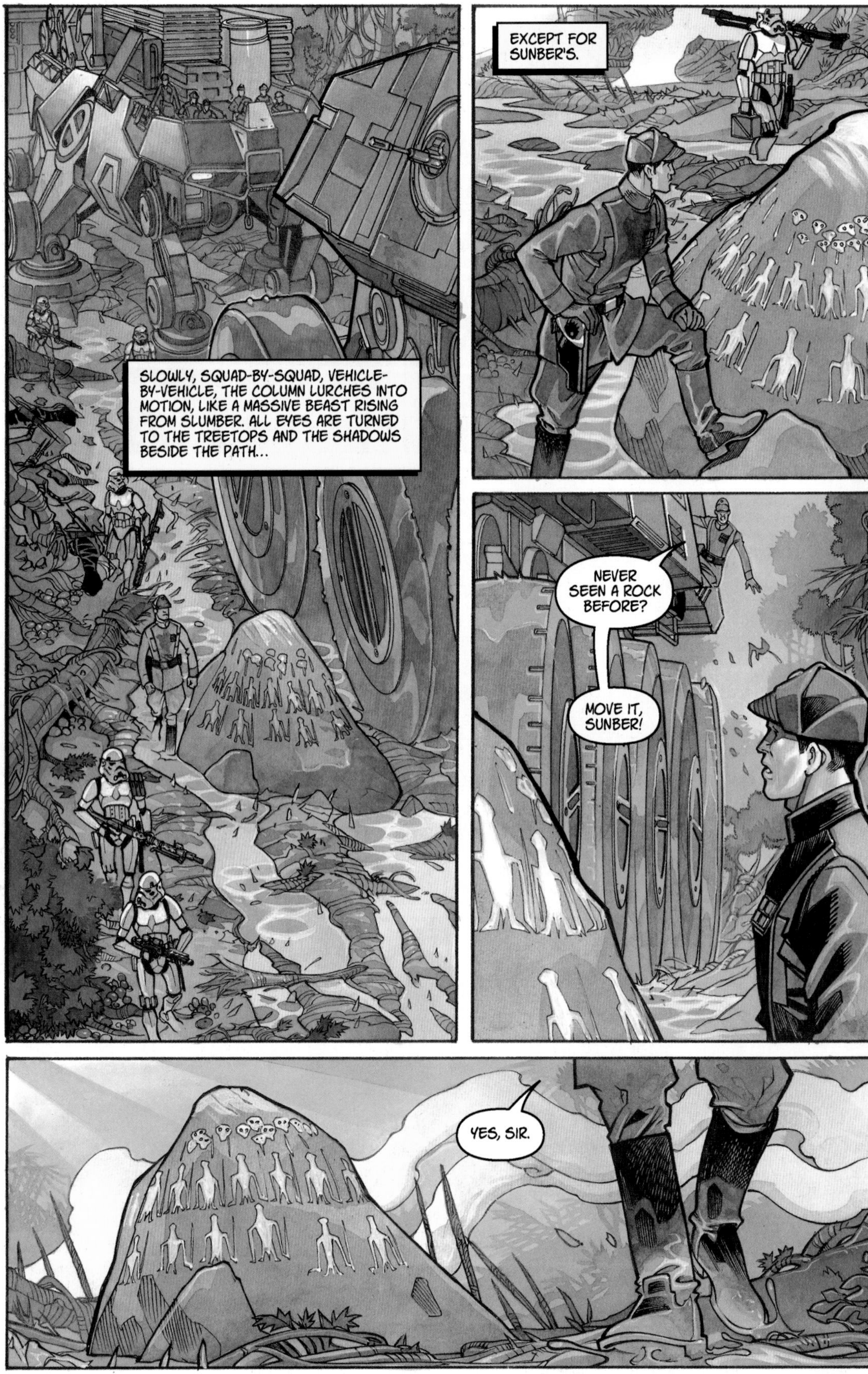
SLOWLY, SQUAD-BY-SQUAD, VEHICLE-BY-VEHICLE, THE COLUMN LURCHES INTO MOTION, LIKE A MASSIVE BEAST RISING FROM SLUMBER. ALL EYES ARE TURNED TO THE TREETOPS AND THE SHADOWS BESIDE THE PATH...
EXCEPT FOR SUNBER'S.
NEVER SEEN A ROCK BEFORE?
MOVE IT, SUNBER!
YES, SIR.

AT MID-DAY, THE SPARSE TRAIL THEY'VE FOLLOWED MEANDERS OUT OF THE JUNGLE AND INTO ONE OF THE VAST ROLLING PLAINS THAT DOT THE SURFACE OF MARIDUN.

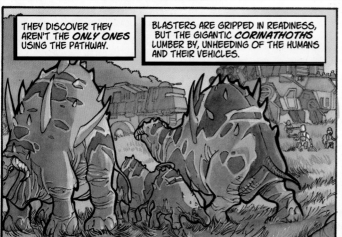

THEY DISCOVER THEY AREN'T THE *ONLY ONES* USING THE PATHWAY.

BLASTERS ARE GRIPPED IN READINESS, BUT THE GIGANTIC *CORINATHOTHS* LUMBER BY, UNHEEDING OF THE HUMANS AND THEIR VEHICLES.

BLIND TO THE *REAL* DANGER, THE COLUMN MARCHES ON.

THE SUN IS A TORCH. THE WAVES OF HUMIDITY RISING UP FROM THE GRASSY PLAIN ARE ALMOST A PHYSICAL OBSTRUCTION.

HIS STORMTROOPERS' COOLING SYSTEMS WHINE IN PROTEST, AND FOR THE FIRST TIME IN HIS SHORT CAREER, SUNBER ENVIES THEM THEIR CUMBERSOME ARMOR.

IT IS ALMOST SUNDOWN WHEN THEY COME WITHIN SIGHT OF THEIR DESTINATION ... A MINING OUTPOST AT THE BASE OF A ROCKY PLATEAU.

THOUGH THE SETTLEMENTS ON MARIDUN ARE SMALL, THEY STILL REQUIRE IMPERIAL OVERSIGHT. THE INFANTRY GOES WHERE IT IS ORDERED.

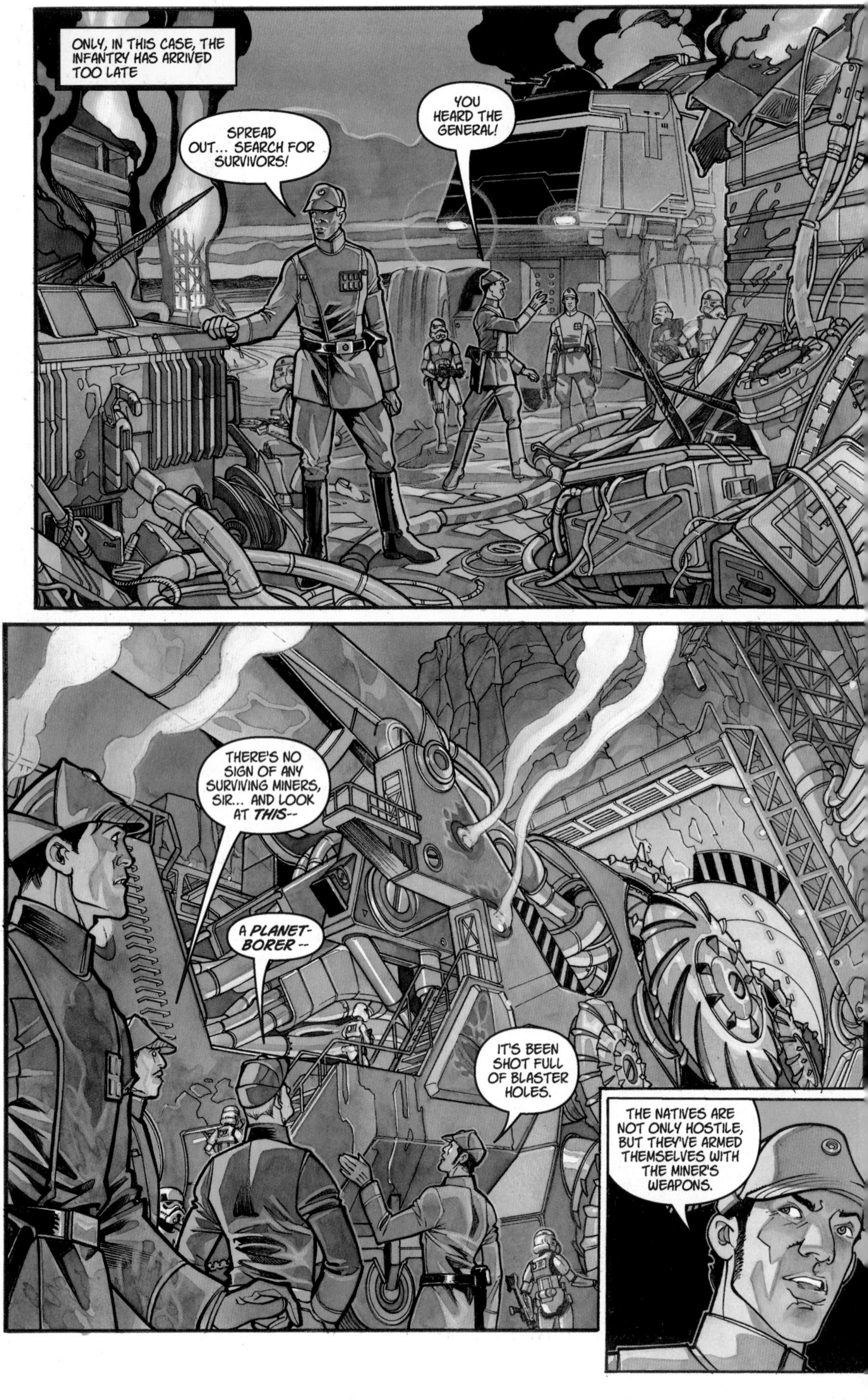

ONLY, IN THIS CASE, THE INFANTRY HAS ARRIVED TOO LATE
SPREAD OUT... SEARCH FOR SURVIVORS!
YOU HEARD THE GENERAL!
THERE'S NO SIGN OF ANY SURVIVING MINERS, SIR... AND LOOK AT *THIS*--
A *PLANET-BORER* --
IT'S BEEN SHOT FULL OF BLASTER HOLES.
THE NATIVES ARE NOT ONLY HOSTILE, BUT THEY'VE ARMED THEMSELVES WITH THE MINER'S WEAPONS.

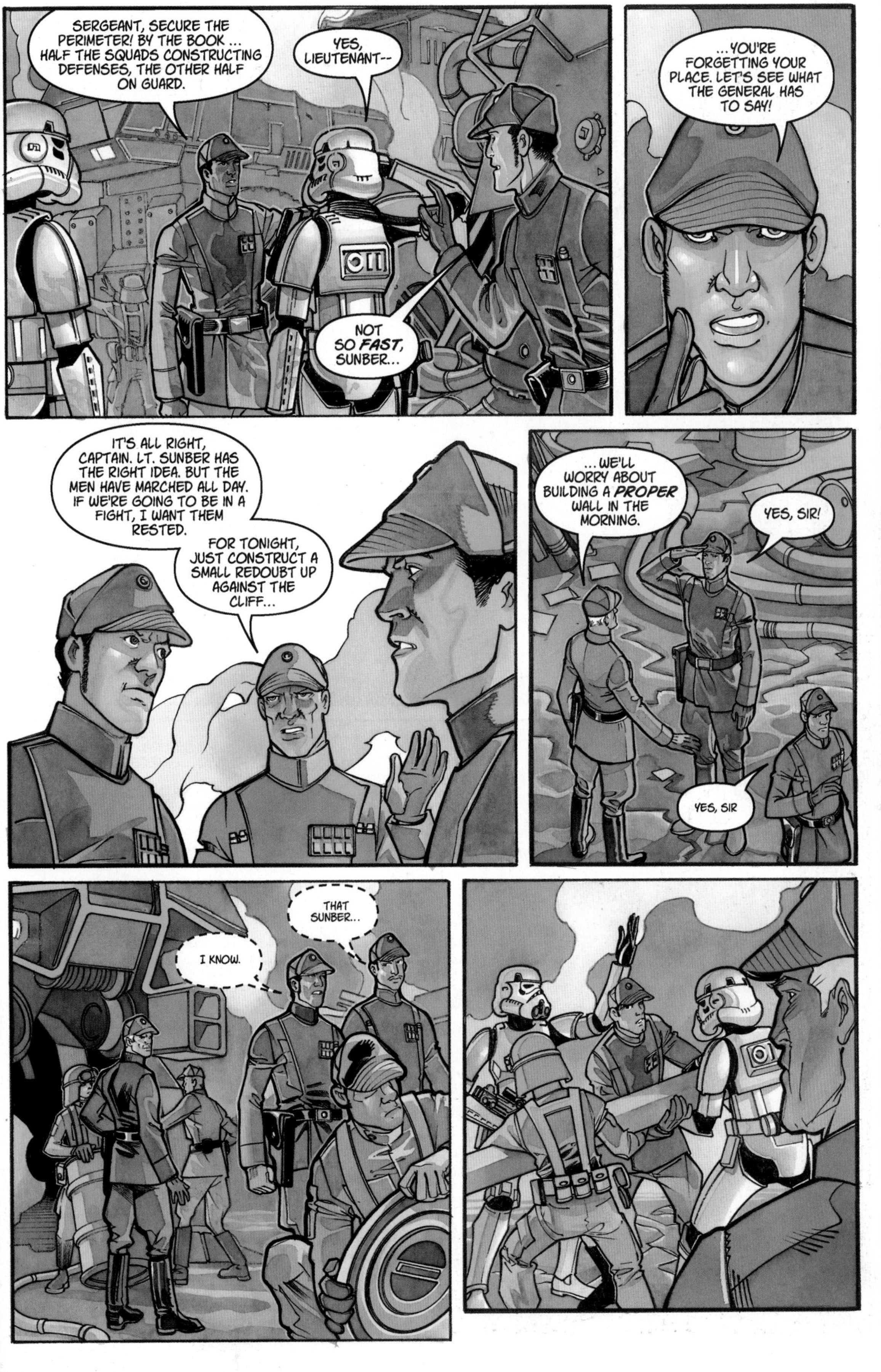

SERGEANT, SECURE THE PERIMETER! BY THE BOOK ... HALF THE SQUADS CONSTRUCTING DEFENSES, THE OTHER HALF ON GUARD.
YES, LIEUTENANT--
NOT SO FAST, SUNBER...
...YOU'RE FORGETTING YOUR PLACE. LET'S SEE WHAT THE GENERAL HAS TO SAY!
IT'S ALL RIGHT, CAPTAIN. LT. SUNBER HAS THE RIGHT IDEA. BUT THE MEN HAVE MARCHED ALL DAY. IF WE'RE GOING TO BE IN A FIGHT, I WANT THEM RESTED.
FOR TONIGHT, JUST CONSTRUCT A SMALL REDOUBT UP AGAINST THE CLIFF...
...WE'LL WORRY ABOUT BUILDING A PROPER WALL IN THE MORNING.
YES, SIR!
YES, SIR
THAT SUNBER...
I KNOW.

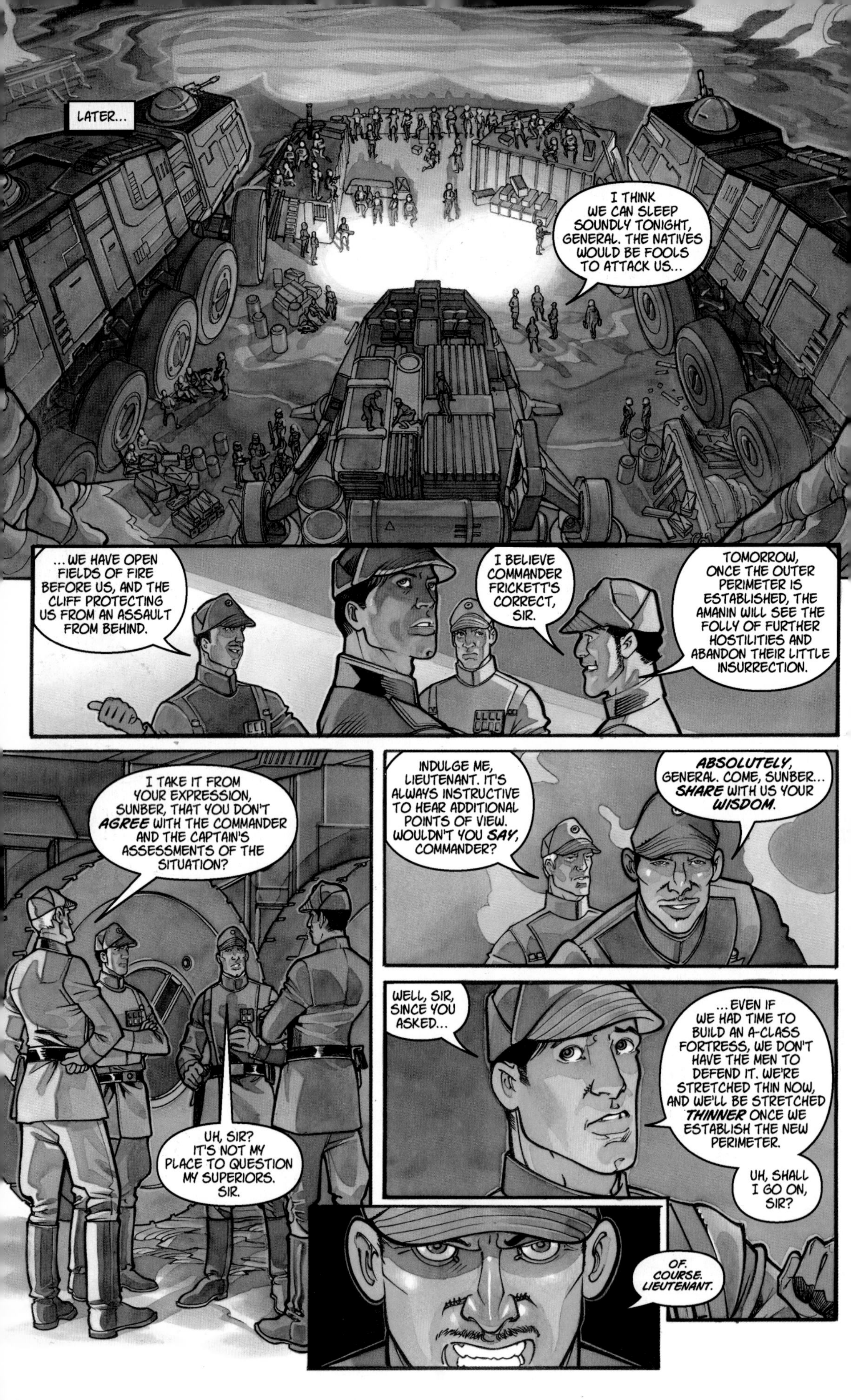
LATER...
I THINK WE CAN SLEEP SOUNDLY TONIGHT, GENERAL. THE NATIVES WOULD BE FOOLS TO ATTACK US...
...WE HAVE OPEN FIELDS OF FIRE BEFORE US, AND THE CLIFF PROTECTING US FROM AN ASSAULT FROM BEHIND.
I BELIEVE COMMANDER FRICKETT'S CORRECT, SIR.
TOMORROW, ONCE THE OUTER PERIMETER IS ESTABLISHED, THE AMANIN WILL SEE THE FOLLY OF FURTHER HOSTILITIES AND ABANDON THEIR LITTLE INSURRECTION.
I TAKE IT FROM YOUR EXPRESSION, SUNBER, THAT YOU DON'T AGREE WITH THE COMMANDER AND THE CAPTAIN'S ASSESSMENTS OF THE SITUATION?
UH, SIR? IT'S NOT MY PLACE TO QUESTION MY SUPERIORS. SIR.
INDULGE ME, LIEUTENANT. IT'S ALWAYS INSTRUCTIVE TO HEAR ADDITIONAL POINTS OF VIEW. WOULDN'T YOU SAY, COMMANDER?
ABSOLUTELY, GENERAL. COME, SUNBER... SHARE WITH US YOUR WISDOM.
WELL, SIR, SINCE YOU ASKED...
...EVEN IF WE HAD TIME TO BUILD AN A-CLASS FORTRESS, WE DON'T HAVE THE MEN TO DEFEND IT. WE'RE STRETCHED THIN NOW, AND WE'LL BE STRETCHED THINNER ONCE WE ESTABLISH THE NEW PERIMETER.
UH, SHALL I GO ON, SIR?
OF. COURSE. LIEUTENANT.

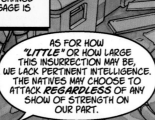

SUNBER *KNOWS* THAT HE IS PLAYING WITH FIRE, AND THAT HE WILL LIKELY SUFFER TOMORROW FOR WHAT HE SAYS TONIGHT. BUT THE GENERAL *HAS* ASKED HIS OPINION, AND THE CHANCE TO SHOW UP FRICKETT AND GAGE IS TOO GOOD TO IGNORE.

AS FOR HOW *"LITTLE"* OR HOW LARGE THIS INSURRECTION MAY BE, WE LACK PERTINENT INTELLIGENCE. THE NATIVES MAY CHOOSE TO ATTACK *REGARDLESS* OF ANY SHOW OF STRENGTH ON OUR PART.

THE AMANIN, THOUGH THEY MAY BE SAVAGES, ARE FAR FROM IGNORANT. WE HAVE NO WAY OF KNOWING HOW *MANY* THEY ARE, OR HOW MANY *BLASTERS* THEY MAY HAVE IN THEIR POSSESSION.

AND WE MAY FIND, SIRS, THAT THE CLIFF AT OUR BACKS IS A *MIXED* BLESSING. WHILE IT PROTECTS OUR BACKS, IT ALSO *BLOCKS* ANY OPPORTUNITY FOR A *RETREAT*...

SHOULD ONE BE NECESSARY.

THANK YOU, LIEUTENANT.

I THINK IT'S TIME YOU CHECKED ON THE SENTRIES.

YES, SIR.

GENERAL, THE IDEA OF AN IMPERIAL INFANTRY COMPANY HAVING TO *RETREAT* FROM A BUNCH OF ALIEN SAVAGES IS RIDICULOUS!

I HOPE THAT YOU'RE RIGHT...

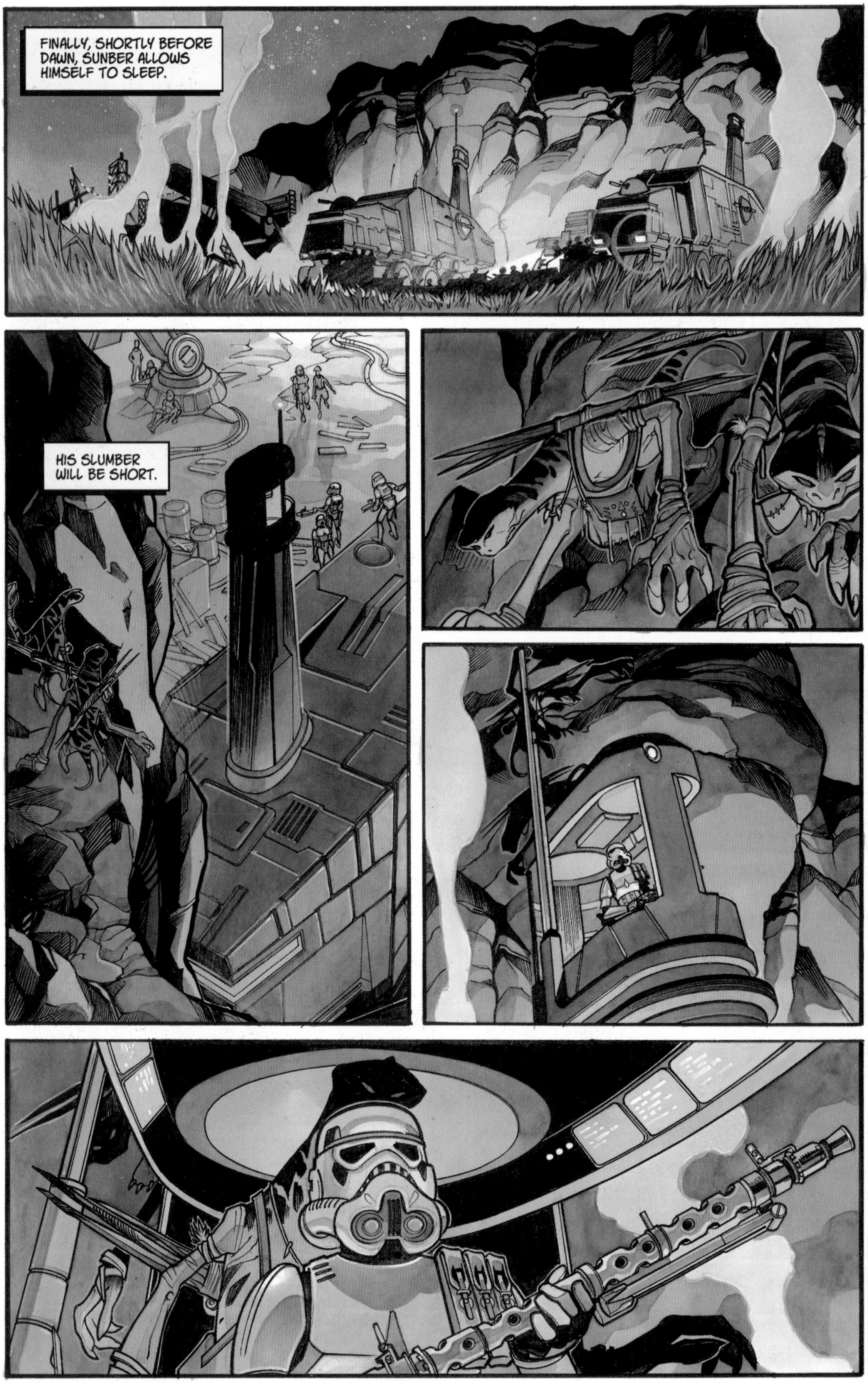
FINALLY, SHORTLY BEFORE DAWN, SUNBER ALLOWS HIMSELF TO SLEEP.
HIS SLUMBER WILL BE SHORT.

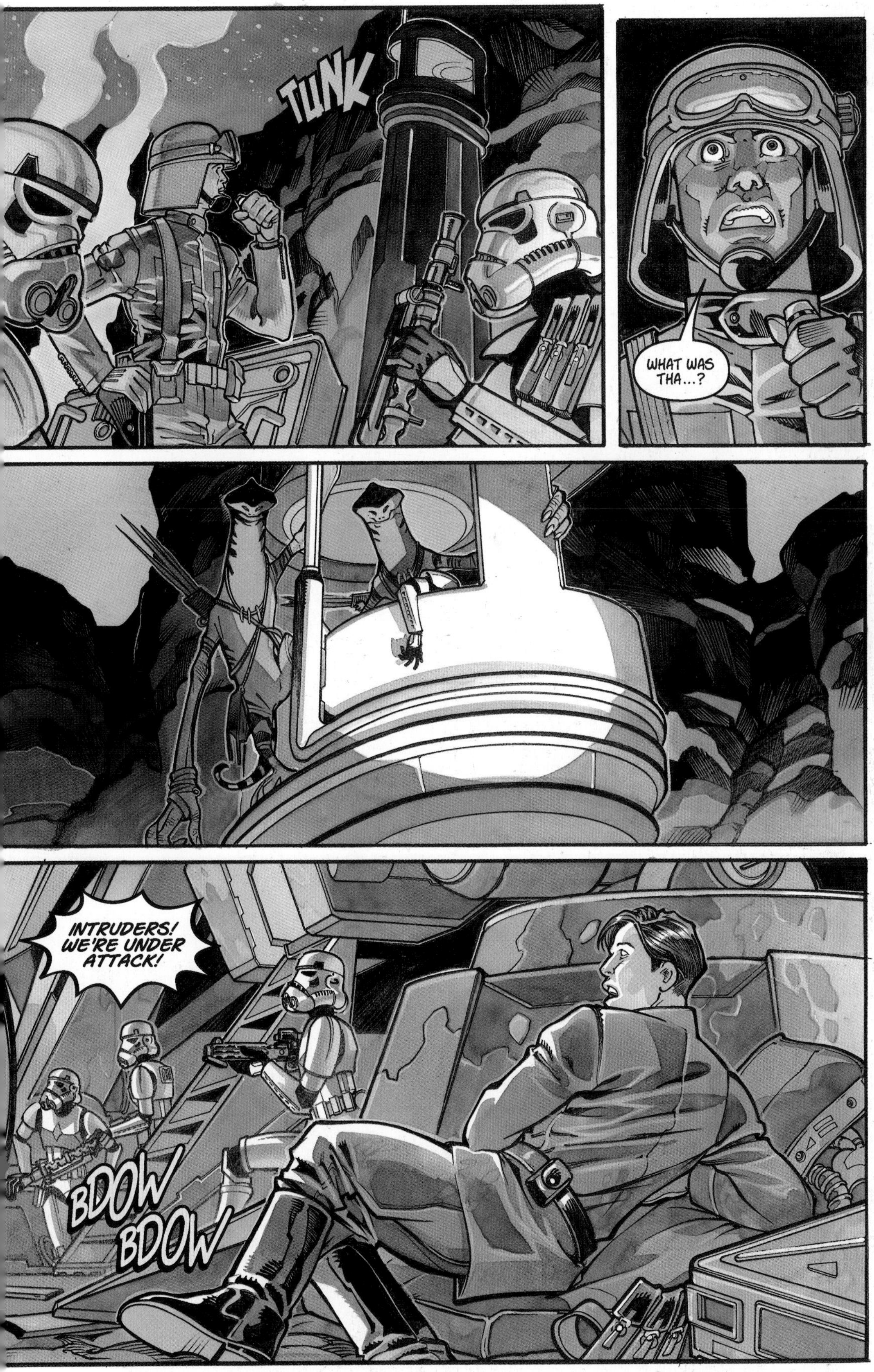
TUNK
WHAT WAS THA...?
INTRUDERS! WE'RE UNDER ATTACK!
BDOW BDOW

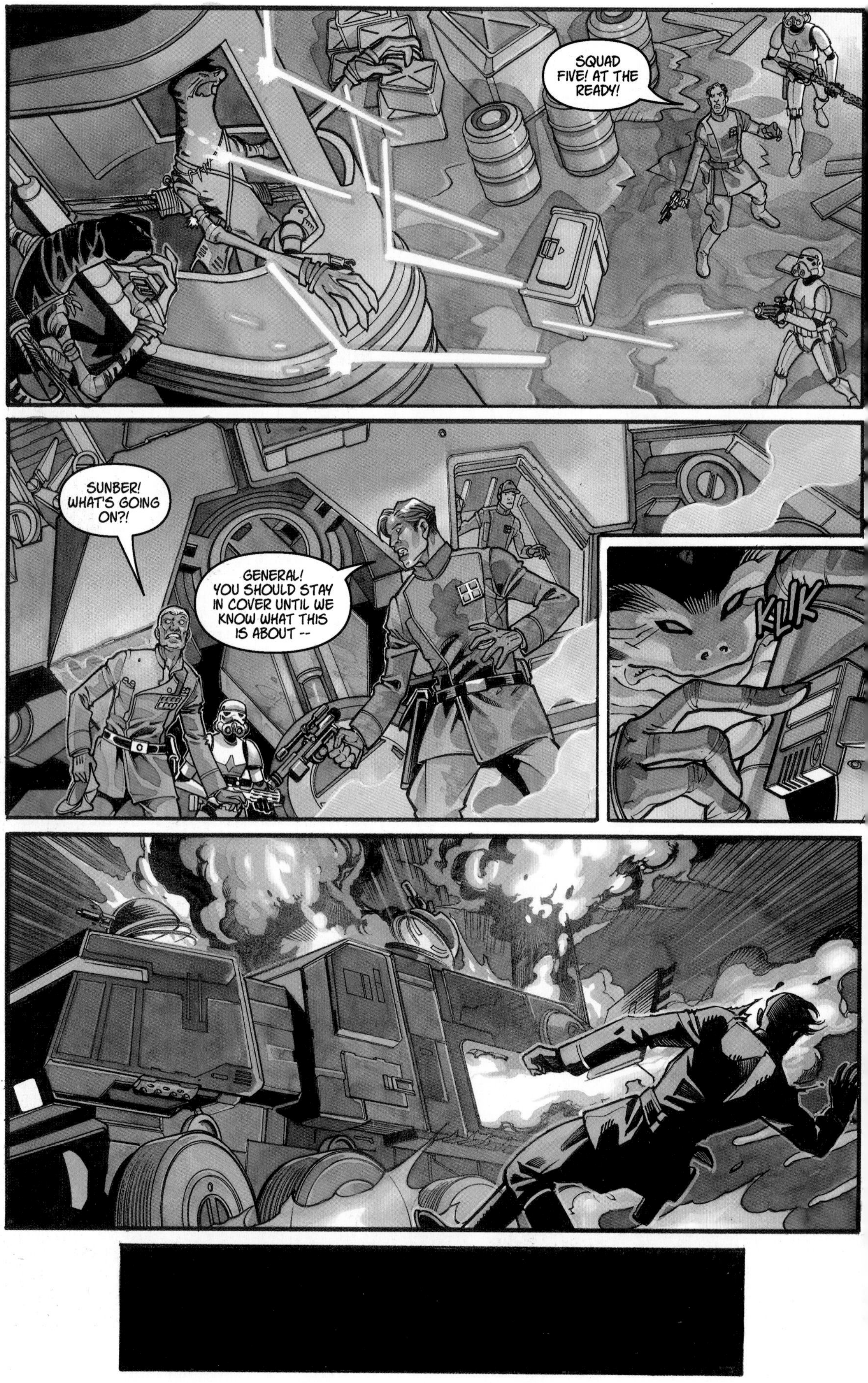
SQUAD FIVE! AT THE READY!
SUNBER! WHAT'S GOING ON?!
GENERAL! YOU SHOULD STAY IN COVER UNTIL WE KNOW WHAT THIS IS ABOUT --
KLIK

[redacted]

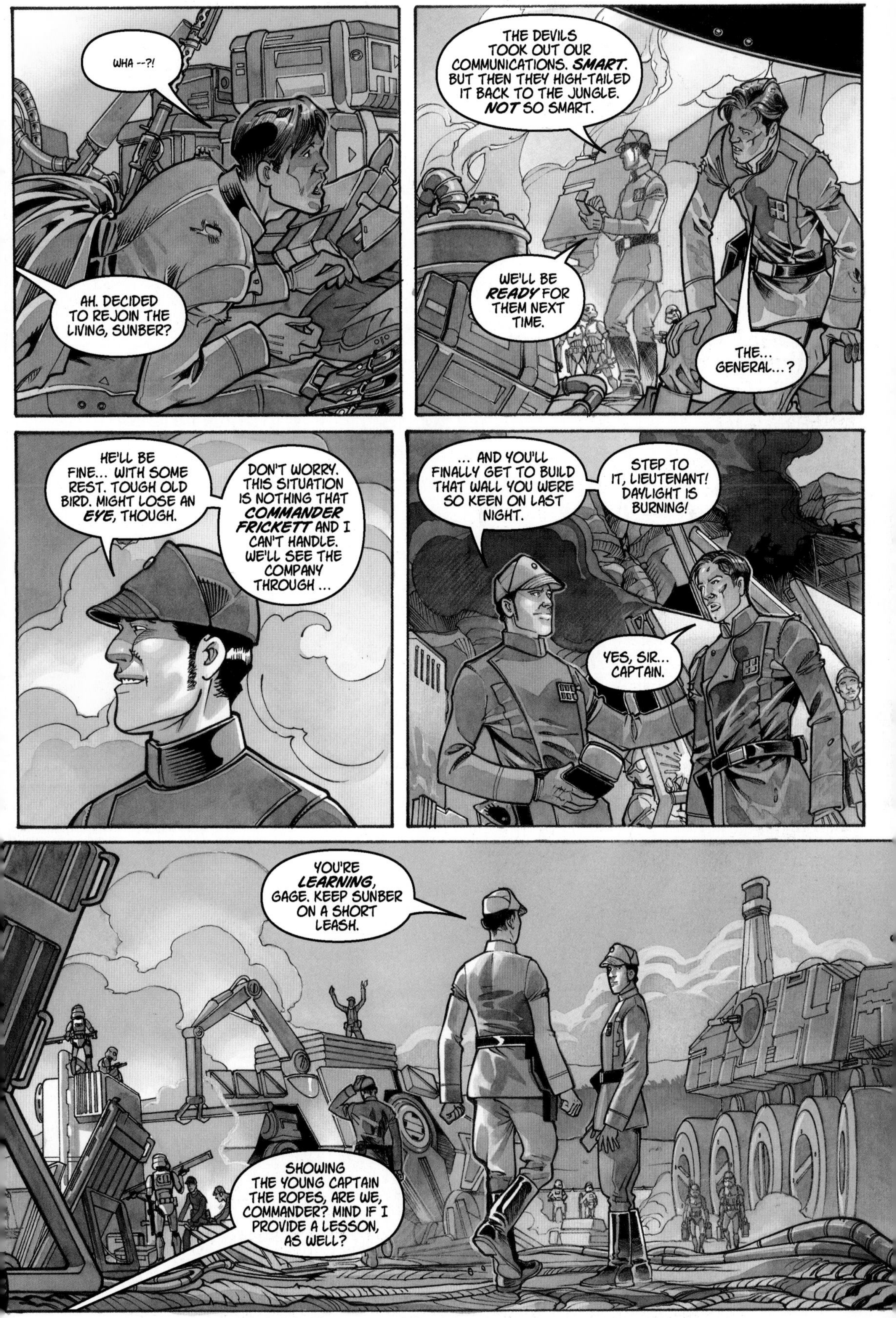
WHA --?!
AH. DECIDED TO REJOIN THE LIVING, SUNBER?
THE DEVILS TOOK OUT OUR COMMUNICATIONS. SMART. BUT THEN THEY HIGH-TAILED IT BACK TO THE JUNGLE. NOT SO SMART.
WE'LL BE READY FOR THEM NEXT TIME.
THE... GENERAL...?
HE'LL BE FINE... WITH SOME REST. TOUGH OLD BIRD. MIGHT LOSE AN EYE, THOUGH.
DON'T WORRY. THIS SITUATION IS NOTHING THAT COMMANDER FRICKETT AND I CAN'T HANDLE. WE'LL SEE THE COMPANY THROUGH ...
... AND YOU'LL FINALLY GET TO BUILD THAT WALL YOU WERE SO KEEN ON LAST NIGHT.
STEP TO IT, LIEUTENANT! DAYLIGHT IS BURNING!
YES, SIR... CAPTAIN.
YOU'RE LEARNING, GAGE. KEEP SUNBER ON A SHORT LEASH.
SHOWING THE YOUNG CAPTAIN THE ROPES, ARE WE, COMMANDER? MIND IF I PROVIDE A LESSON, AS WELL?

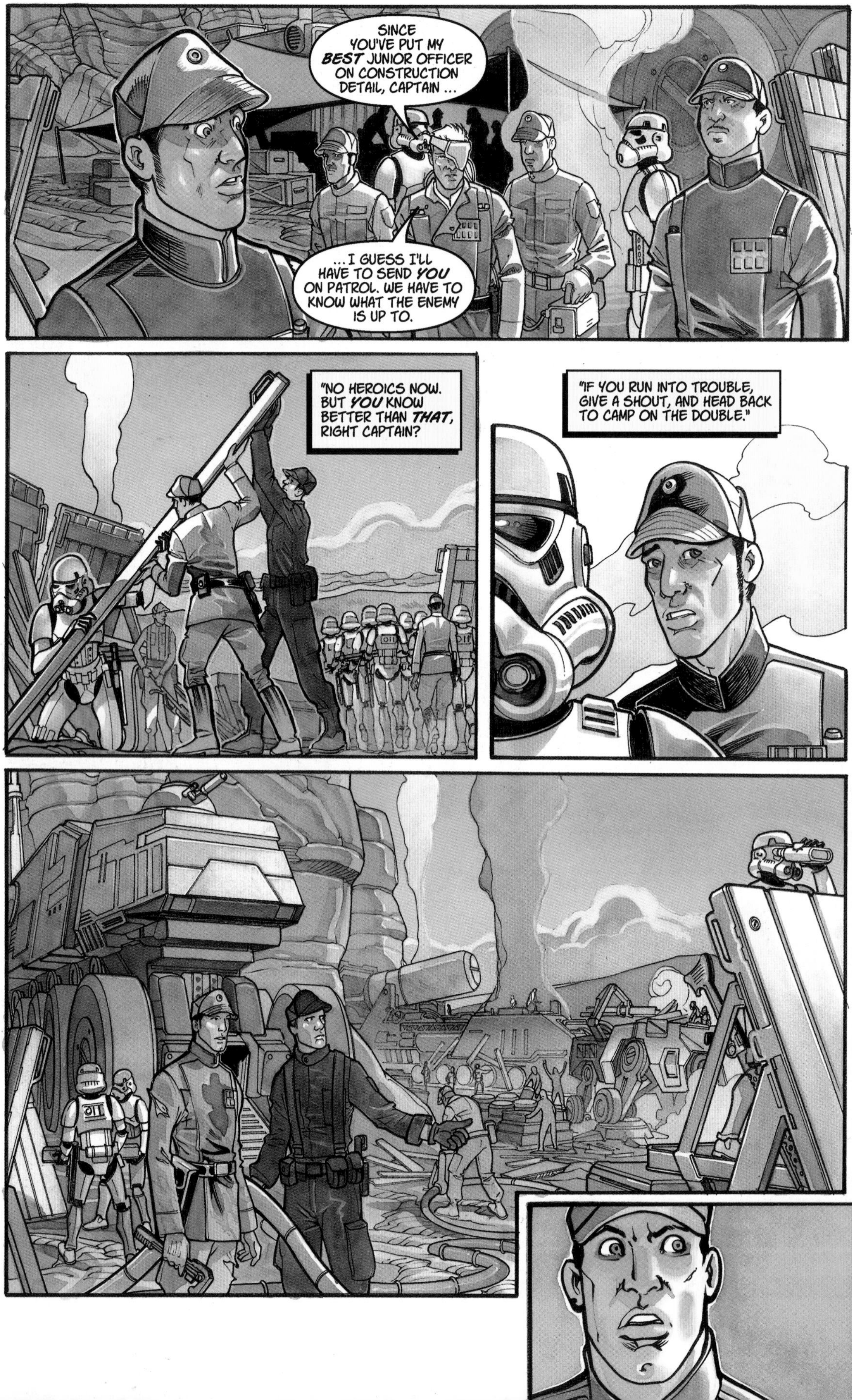
SINCE YOU'VE PUT MY BEST JUNIOR OFFICER ON CONSTRUCTION DETAIL, CAPTAIN ...
... I GUESS I'LL HAVE TO SEND YOU ON PATROL. WE HAVE TO KNOW WHAT THE ENEMY IS UP TO.
"NO HEROICS NOW. BUT YOU KNOW BETTER THAN THAT, RIGHT CAPTAIN?
"IF YOU RUN INTO TROUBLE, GIVE A SHOUT, AND HEAD BACK TO CAMP ON THE DOUBLE."

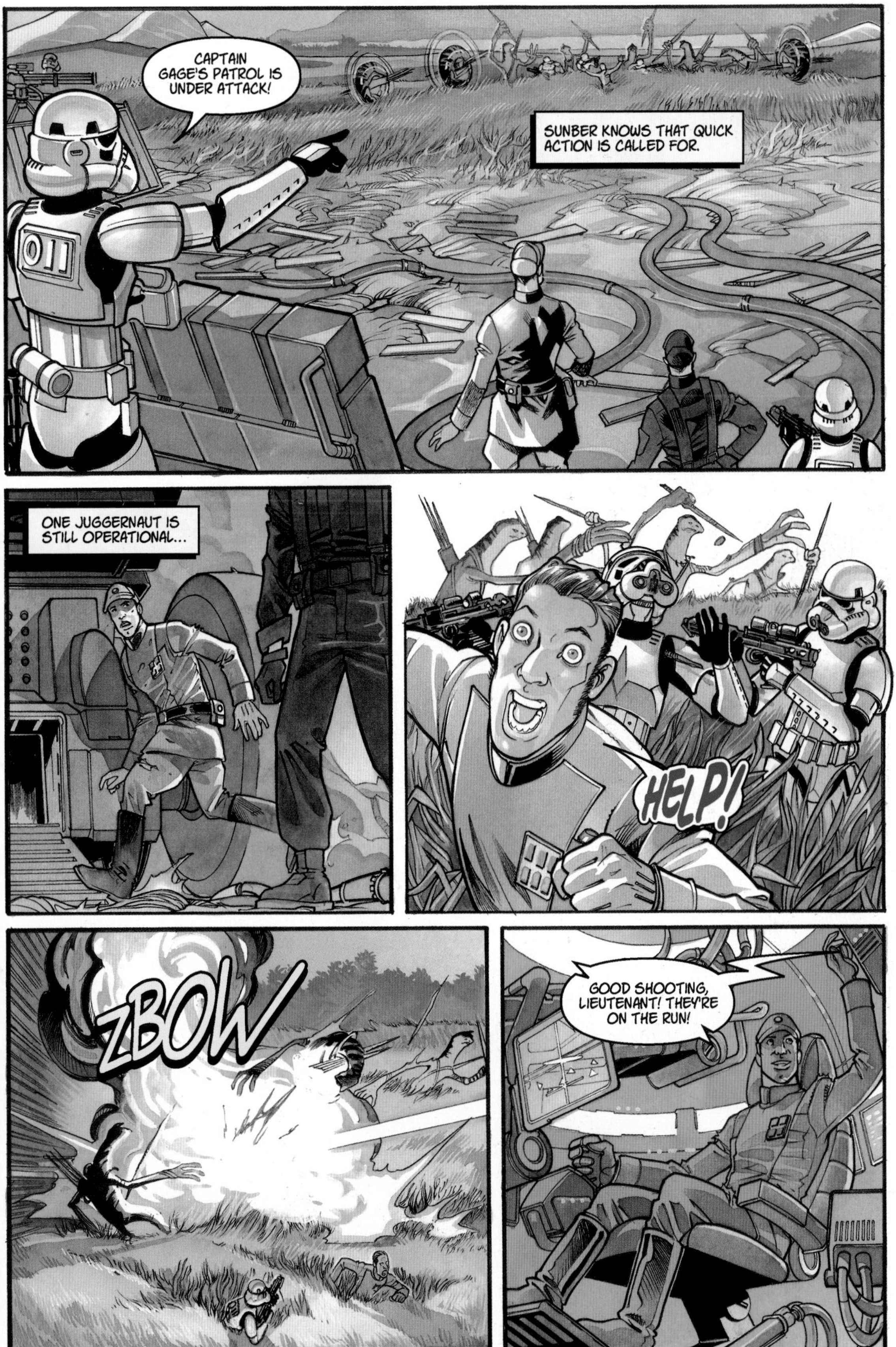
CAPTAIN GAGE'S PATROL IS UNDER ATTACK!
SUNBER KNOWS THAT QUICK ACTION IS CALLED FOR.
ONE JUGGERNAUT IS STILL OPERATIONAL...
HELP!
ZBOW
GOOD SHOOTING, LIEUTENANT! THEY'RE ON THE RUN!

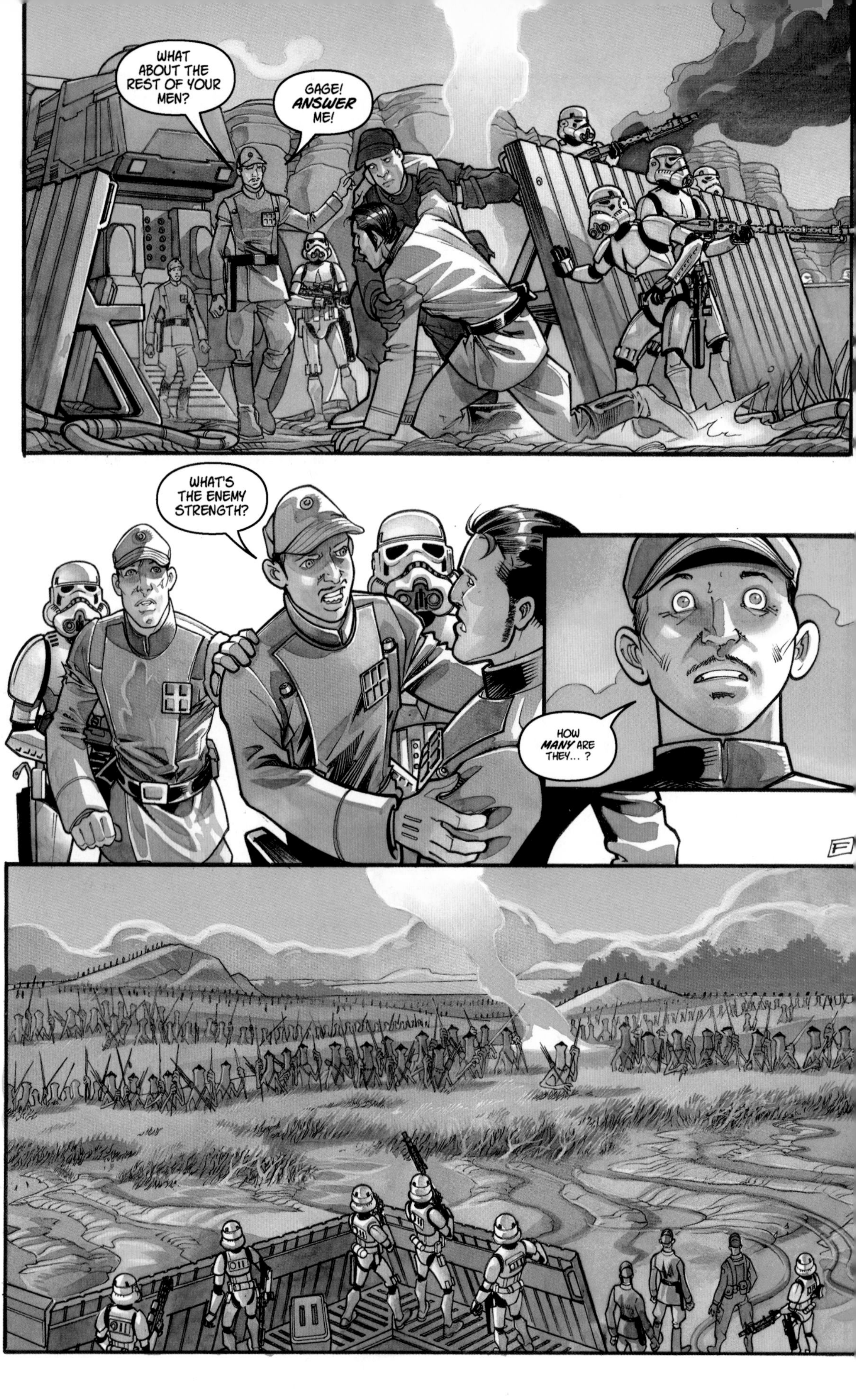
WHAT ABOUT THE REST OF YOUR MEN?
GAGE! ANSWER ME!
WHAT'S THE ENEMY STRENGTH?
HOW MANY ARE THEY... ?

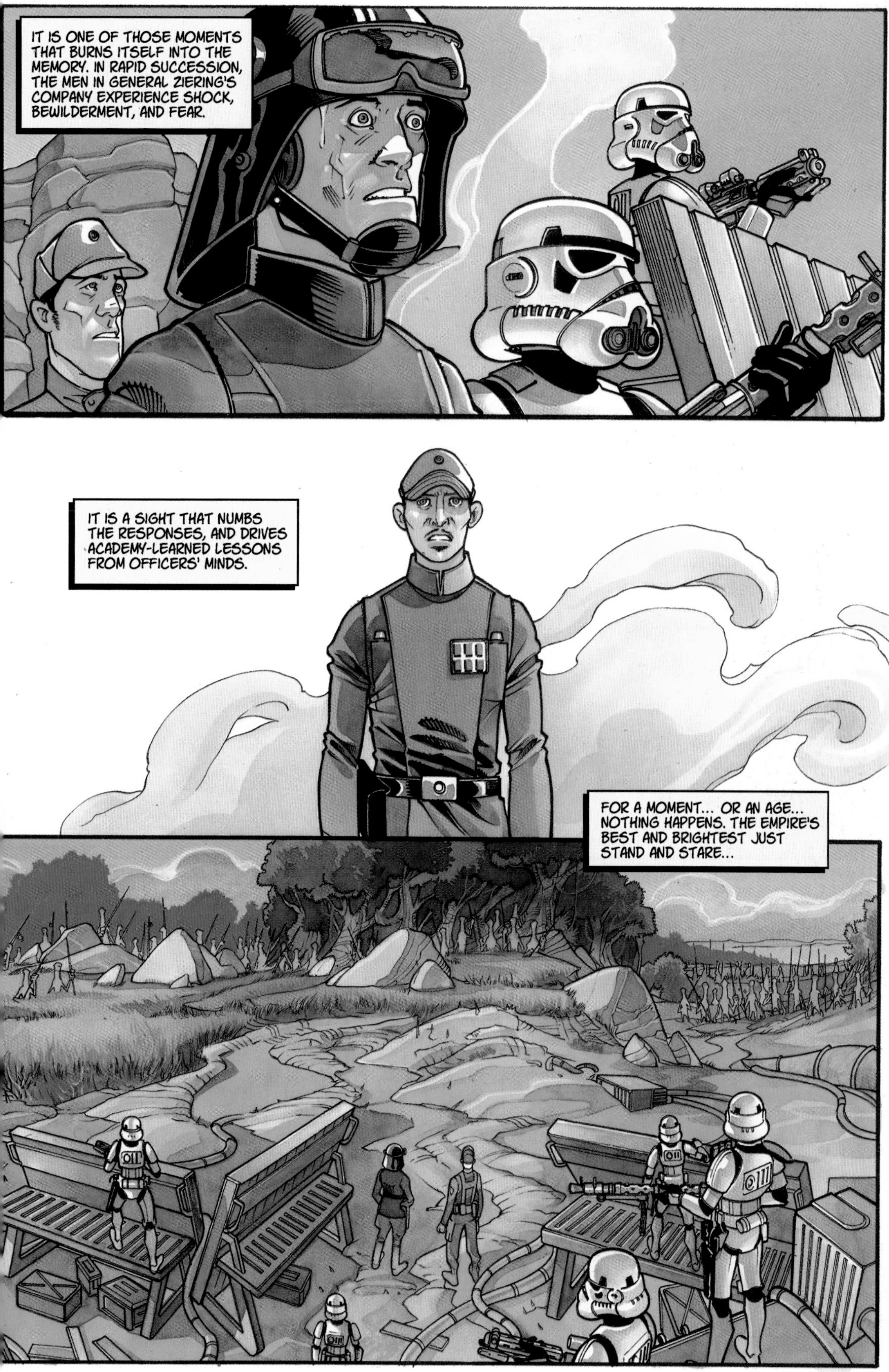
IT IS ONE OF THOSE MOMENTS THAT BURNS ITSELF INTO THE MEMORY. IN RAPID SUCCESSION, THE MEN IN GENERAL ZIERING'S COMPANY EXPERIENCE SHOCK, BEWILDERMENT, AND FEAR.
IT IS A SIGHT THAT NUMBS THE RESPONSES, AND DRIVES ACADEMY-LEARNED LESSONS FROM OFFICERS' MINDS.
FOR A MOMENT... OR AN AGE... NOTHING HAPPENS. THE EMPIRE'S BEST AND BRIGHTEST JUST STAND AND STARE...

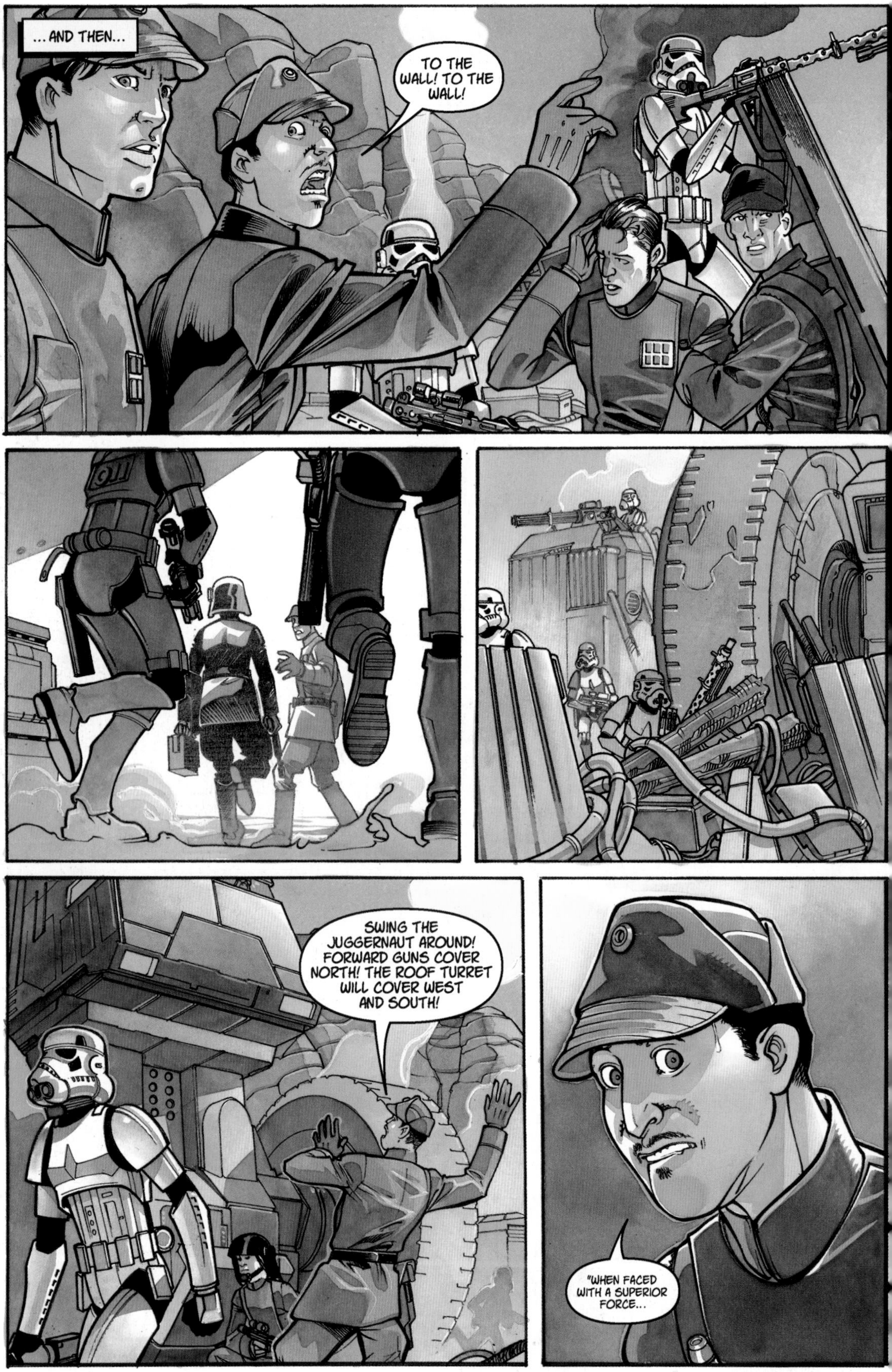
...AND THEN...
TO THE WALL! TO THE WALL!
SWING THE JUGGERNAUT AROUND! FORWARD GUNS COVER NORTH! THE ROOF TURRET WILL COVER WEST AND SOUTH!
"WHEN FACED WITH A SUPERIOR FORCE...

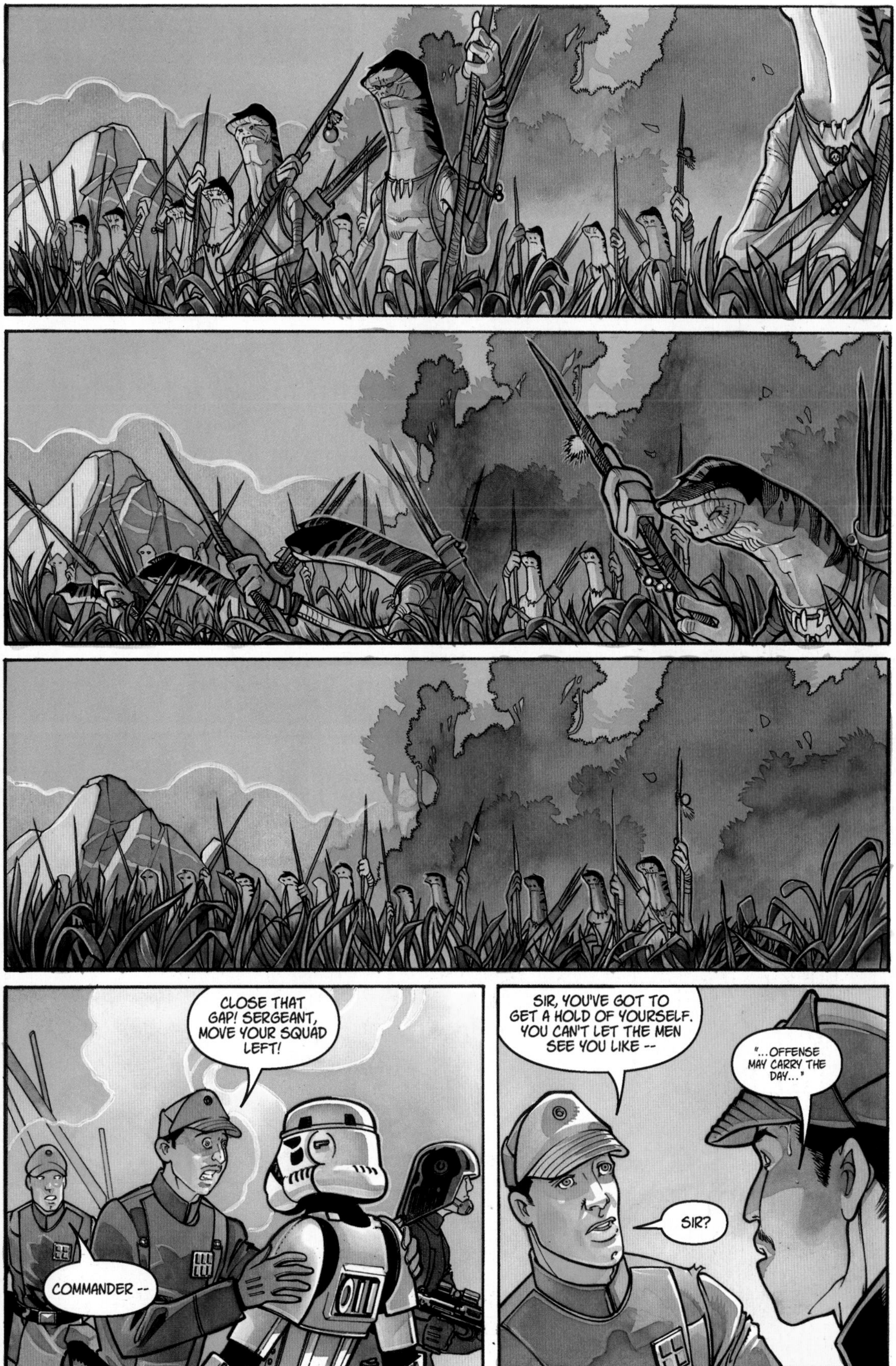
CLOSE THAT GAP! SERGEANT, MOVE YOUR SQUAD LEFT!
COMMANDER --
SIR, YOU'VE GOT TO GET A HOLD OF YOURSELF. YOU CAN'T LET THE MEN SEE YOU LIKE --
"...OFFENSE MAY CARRY THE DAY..."
SIR?

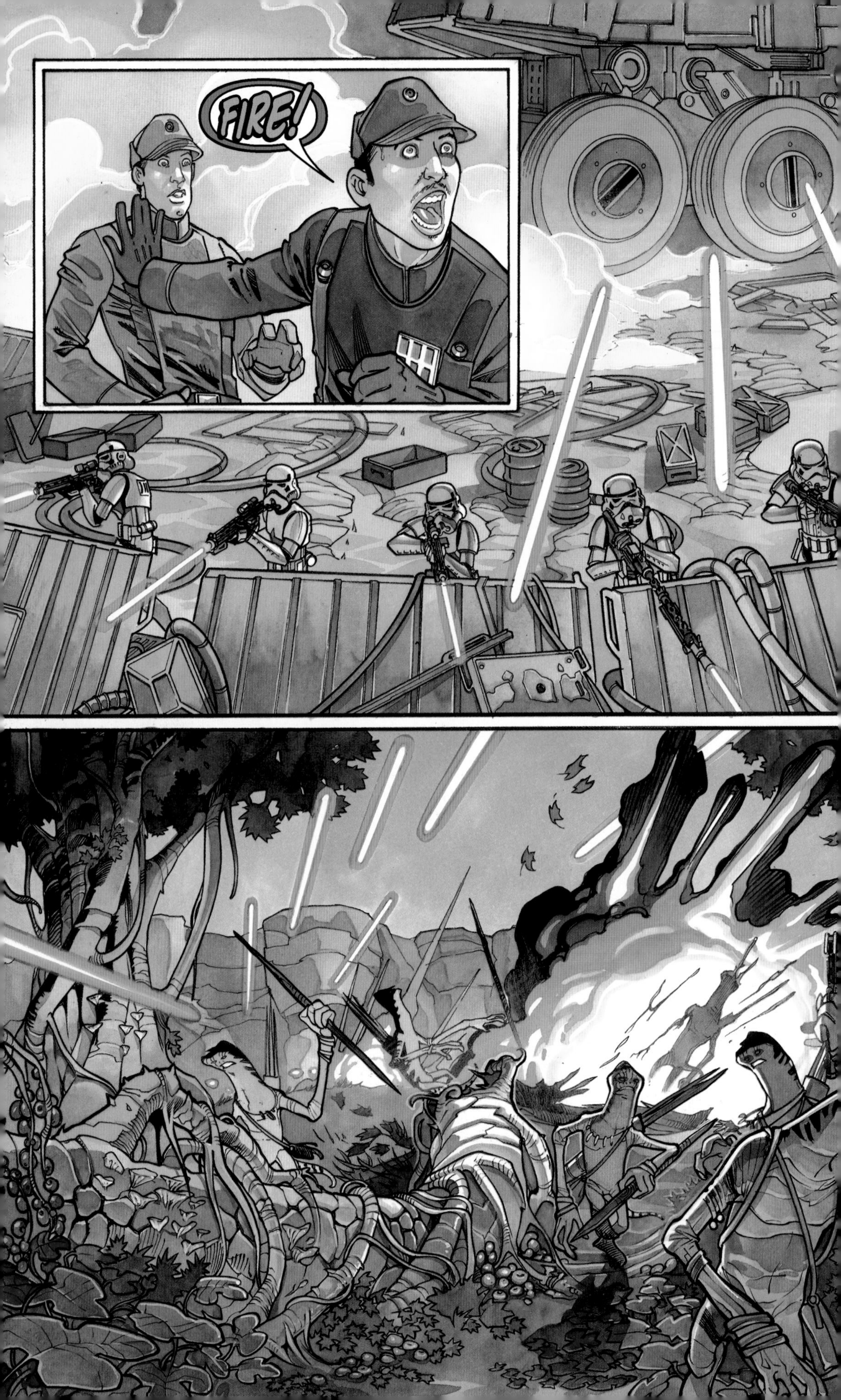
FIRE!

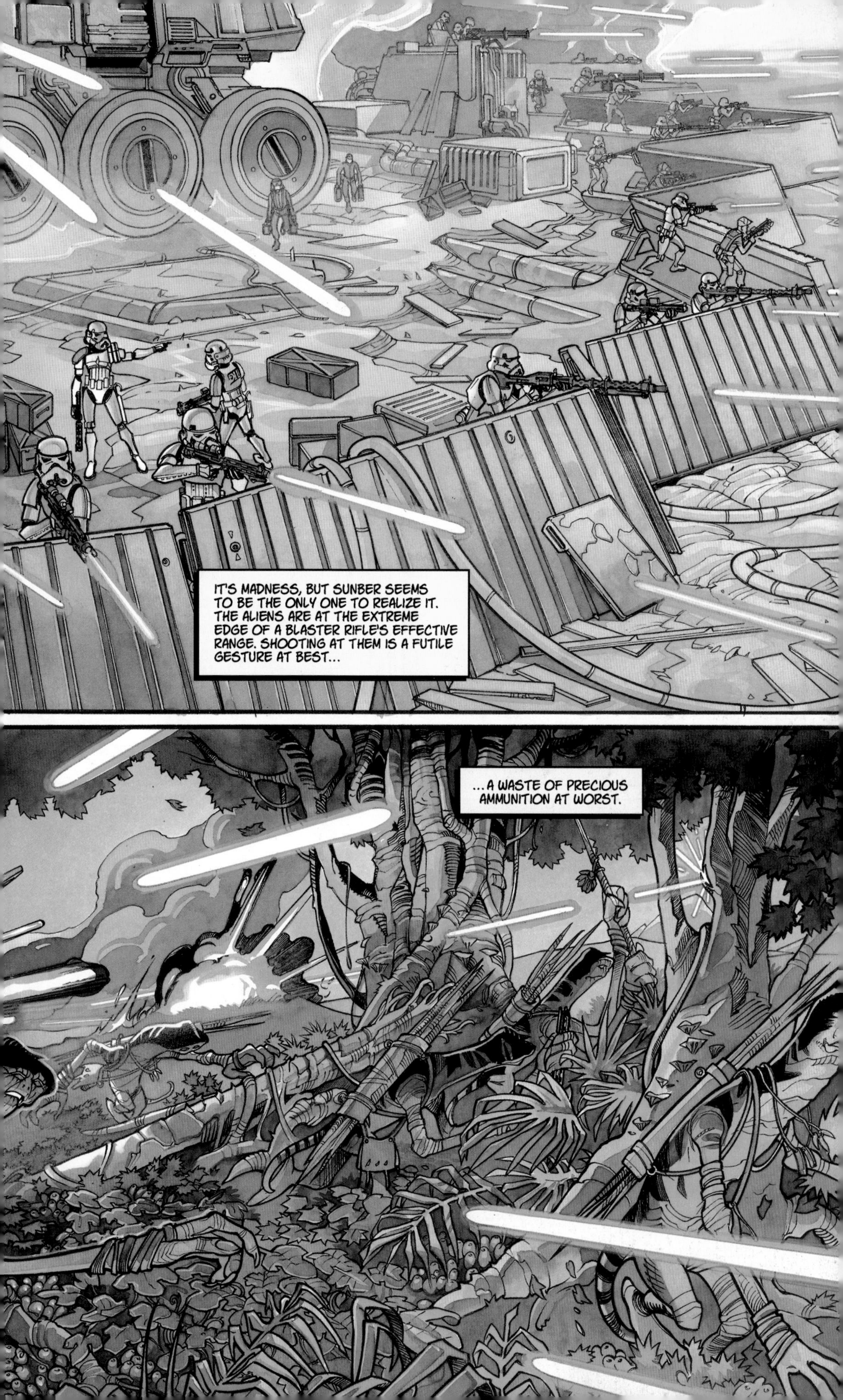
IT'S MADNESS, BUT SUNBER SEEMS TO BE THE ONLY ONE TO REALIZE IT. THE ALIENS ARE AT THE EXTREME EDGE OF A BLASTER RIFLE'S EFFECTIVE RANGE. SHOOTING AT THEM IS A FUTILE GESTURE AT BEST...
...A WASTE OF PRECIOUS AMMUNITION AT WORST.

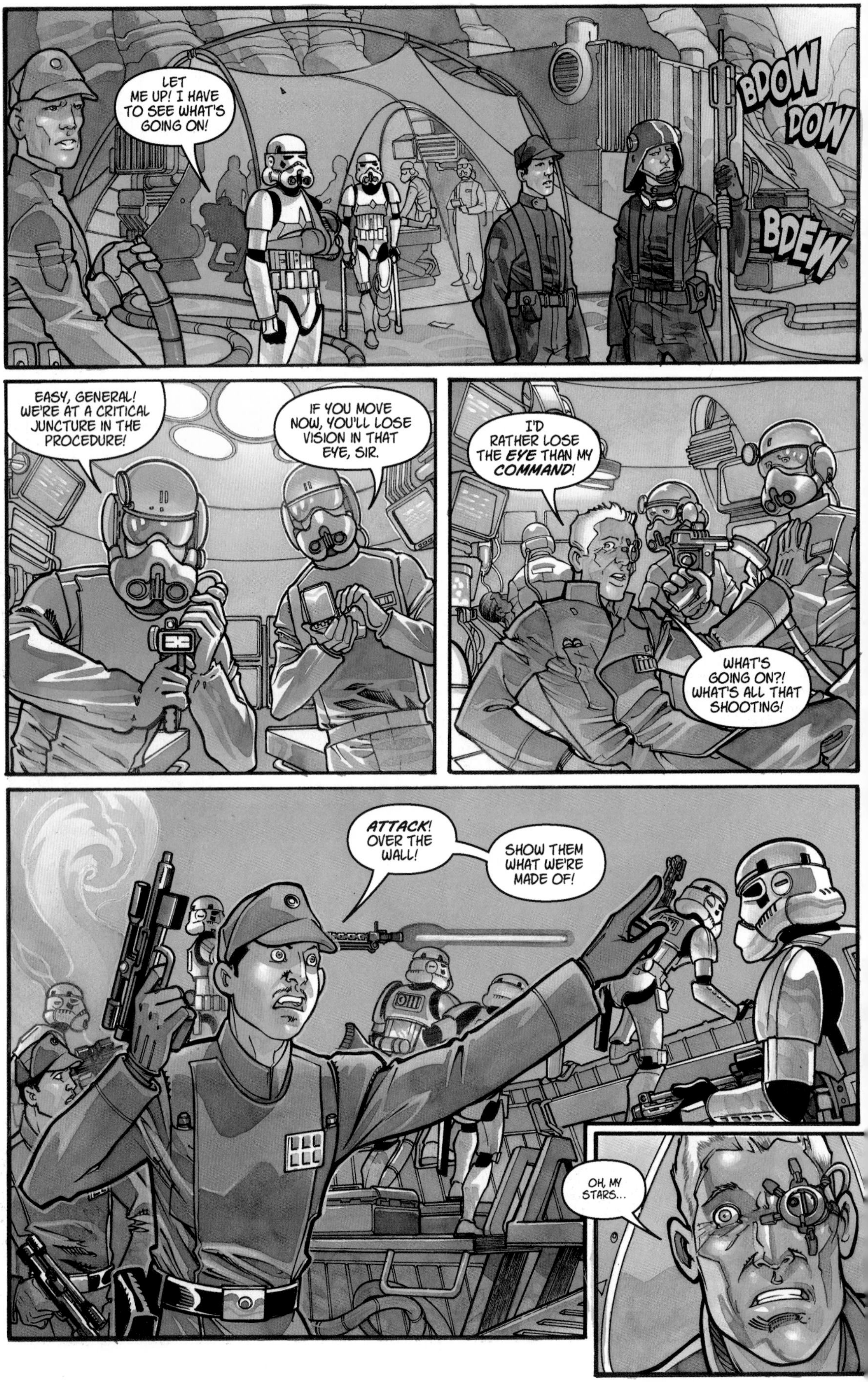
LET ME UP! I HAVE TO SEE WHAT'S GOING ON!
BDOW
DOW
BDEW
EASY, GENERAL! WE'RE AT A CRITICAL JUNCTURE IN THE PROCEDURE!
IF YOU MOVE NOW, YOU'LL LOSE VISION IN THAT EYE, SIR.
I'D RATHER LOSE THE EYE THAN MY COMMAND!
WHAT'S GOING ON?! WHAT'S ALL THAT SHOOTING!
ATTACK! OVER THE WALL!
SHOW THEM WHAT WE'RE MADE OF!
OH, MY STARS...

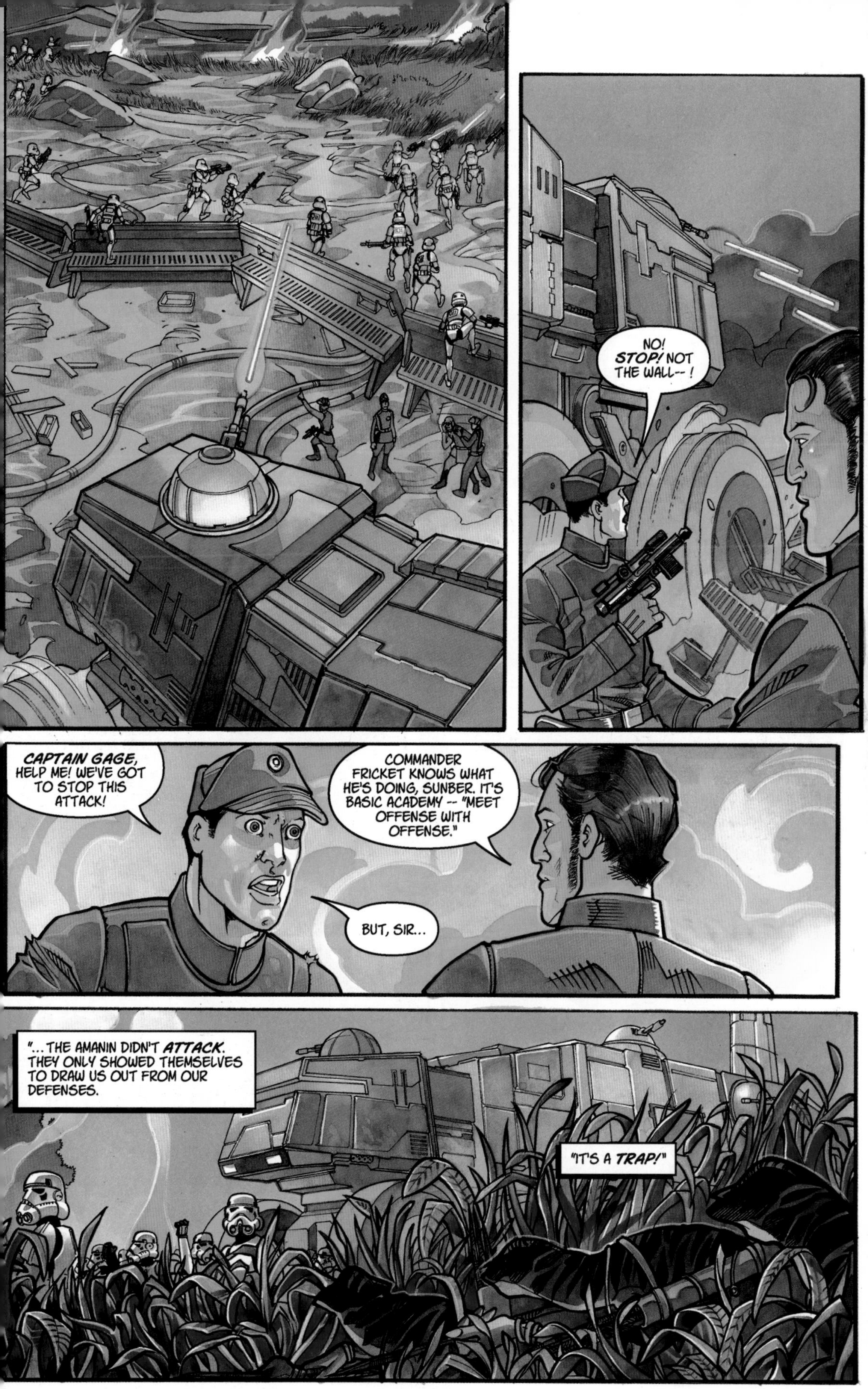
NO! STOP! NOT THE WALL-- !
CAPTAIN GAGE, HELP ME! WE'VE GOT TO STOP THIS ATTACK!
COMMANDER FRICKET KNOWS WHAT HE'S DOING, SUNBER. IT'S BASIC ACADEMY -- "MEET OFFENSE WITH OFFENSE."
BUT, SIR...
"... THE AMANIN DIDN'T ATTACK. THEY ONLY SHOWED THEMSELVES TO DRAW US OUT FROM OUR DEFENSES.
"IT'S A TRAP!"

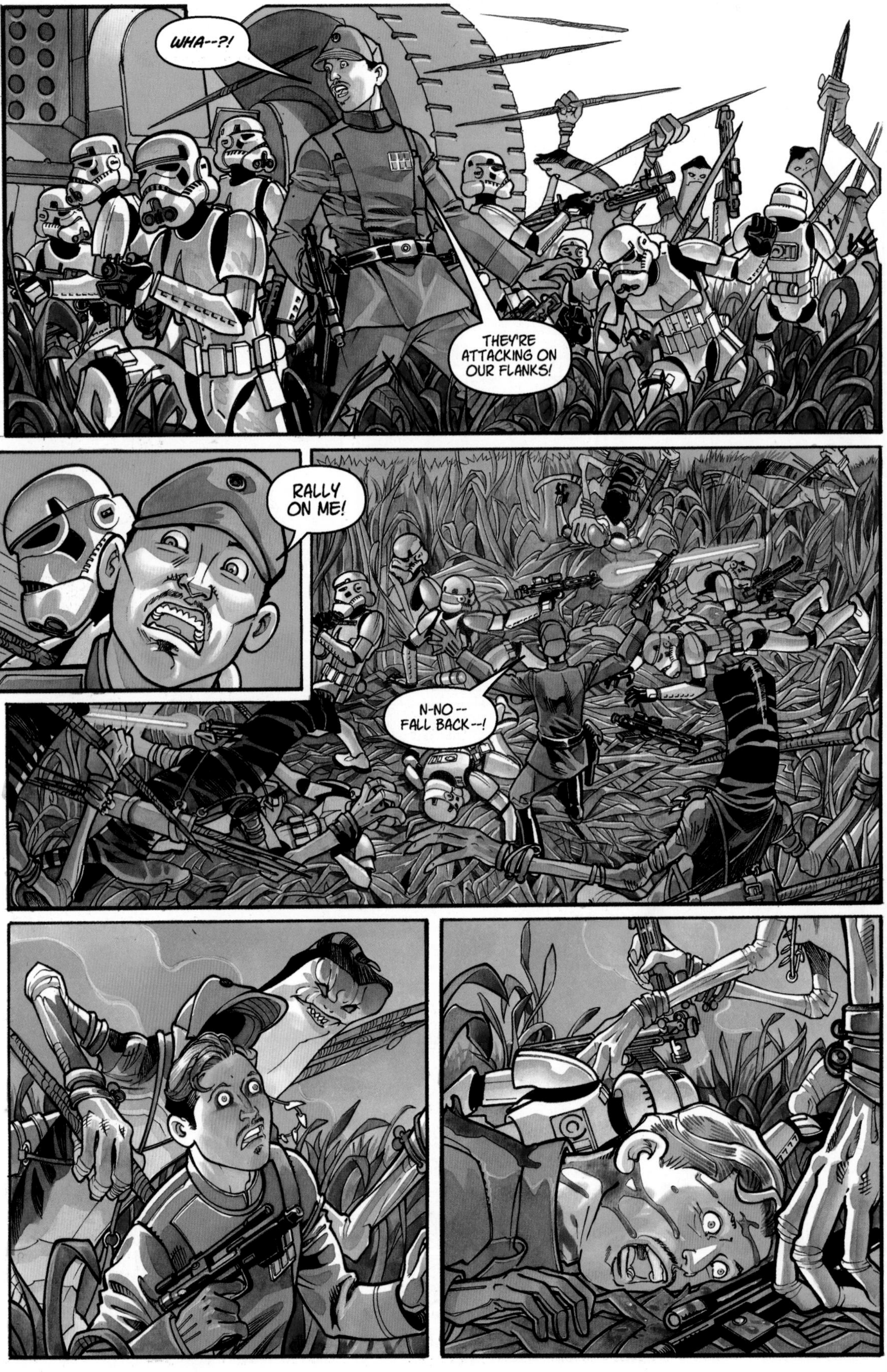
WHA--?!
THEY'RE ATTACKING ON OUR FLANKS!
RALLY ON ME!
N-NO -- FALL BACK--!

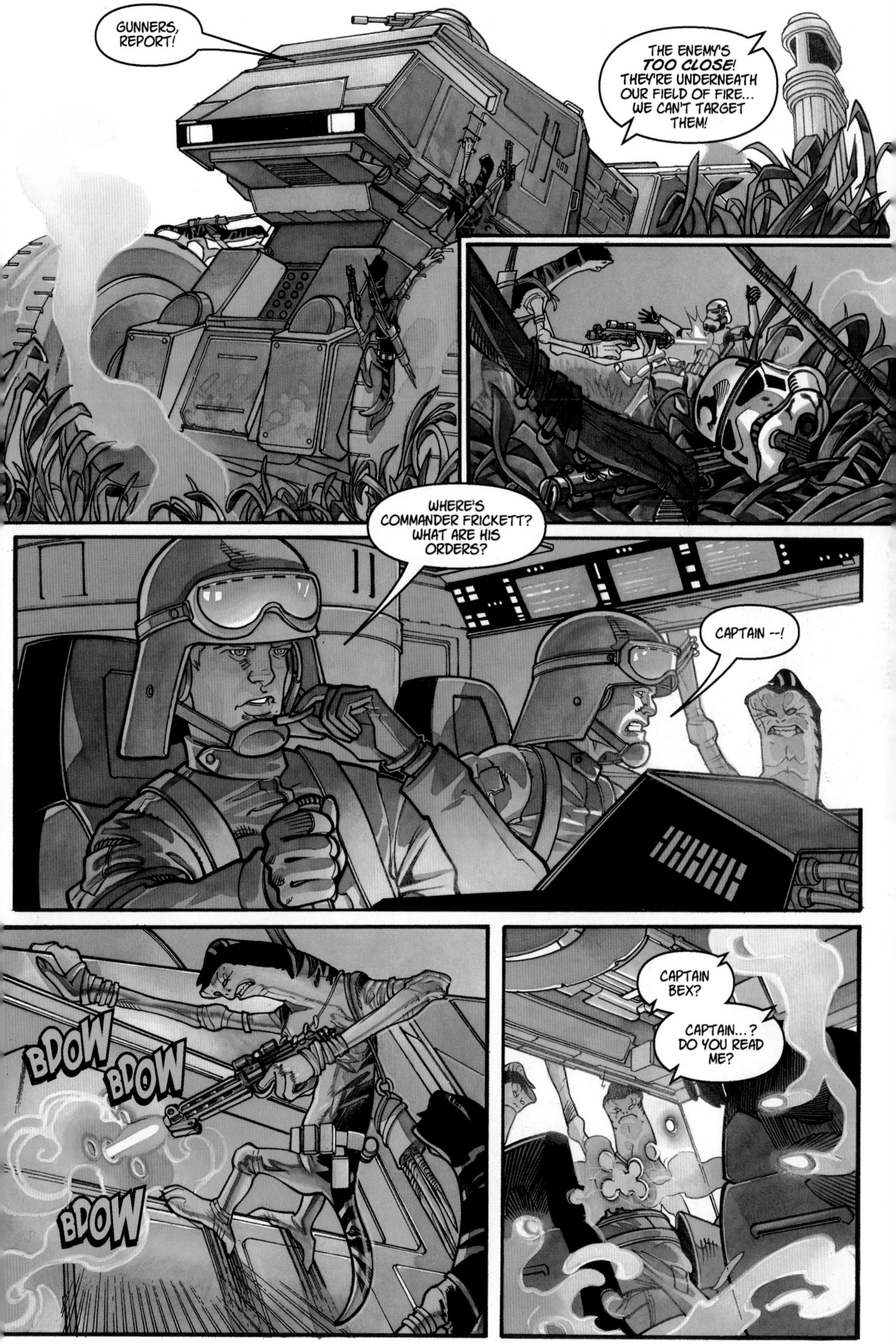
GUNNERS, REPORT!
THE ENEMY'S TOO CLOSE! THEY'RE UNDERNEATH OUR FIELD OF FIRE... WE CAN'T TARGET THEM!
WHERE'S COMMANDER FRICKETT? WHAT ARE HIS ORDERS?
CAPTAIN --!
BDOW
BDOW
BDOW
CAPTAIN BEX?
CAPTAIN...? DO YOU READ ME?

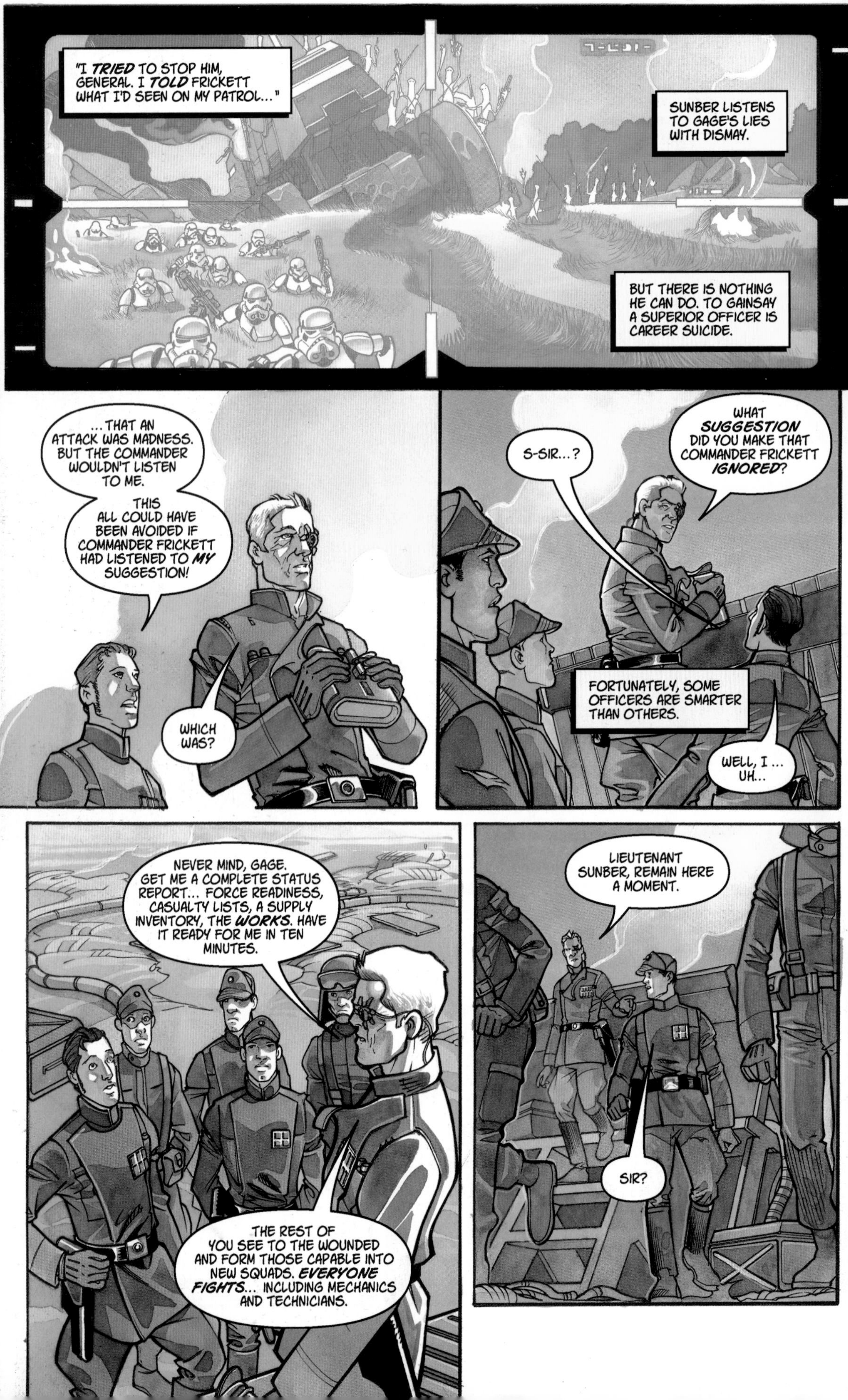
"I TRIED TO STOP HIM, GENERAL. I TOLD FRICKETT WHAT I'D SEEN ON MY PATROL..."
SUNBER LISTENS TO GAGE'S LIES WITH DISMAY.
BUT THERE IS NOTHING HE CAN DO. TO GAINSAY A SUPERIOR OFFICER IS CAREER SUICIDE.
...THAT AN ATTACK WAS MADNESS. BUT THE COMMANDER WOULDN'T LISTEN TO ME.
THIS ALL COULD HAVE BEEN AVOIDED IF COMMANDER FRICKETT HAD LISTENED TO MY SUGGESTION!
WHICH WAS?
S-SIR...?
WHAT SUGGESTION DID YOU MAKE THAT COMMANDER FRICKETT IGNORED?
FORTUNATELY, SOME OFFICERS ARE SMARTER THAN OTHERS.
WELL, I ... UH...
NEVER MIND, GAGE. GET ME A COMPLETE STATUS REPORT... FORCE READINESS, CASUALTY LISTS, A SUPPLY INVENTORY, THE WORKS. HAVE IT READY FOR ME IN TEN MINUTES.
THE REST OF YOU SEE TO THE WOUNDED AND FORM THOSE CAPABLE INTO NEW SQUADS. EVERYONE FIGHTS... INCLUDING MECHANICS AND TECHNICIANS.
LIEUTENANT SUNBER, REMAIN HERE A MOMENT.
SIR?

THIS IS *NOT* THE PLACE WHERE I WANTED TO *END* MY CAREER. MY PLAN WAS TO RETIRE, GET A QUIET LITTLE PLACE OUTSIDE THE CORPORATE HUB, SPEND TIME WITH MY WIFE AND GRANDCHILDREN, AND DIE IN MY SLEEP... MANY YEARS FROM NOW.

BUT THAT ISN'T GOING TO HAPPEN.

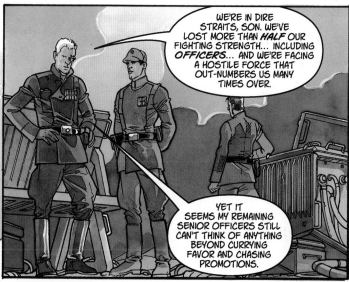

WE'RE IN DIRE STRAITS, SON. WE'VE LOST MORE THAN *HALF* OUR FIGHTING STRENGTH... INCLUDING *OFFICERS*... AND WE'RE FACING A HOSTILE FORCE THAT OUT-NUMBERS US MANY TIMES OVER.

YET IT SEEMS MY REMAINING SENIOR OFFICERS STILL CAN'T THINK OF ANYTHING BEYOND CURRYING FAVOR AND CHASING PROMOTIONS.

WHAT WOULD YOU DO, LIEUTENANT?

ME, SIR?

WELL, SIR, AT THE ACADEMY THEY TAUGHT US THAT WHEN FACED WITH AN OVERWHELMING FORCE, ONE SHOULD LOOK FOR AN OPPORTUNITY TO RETREAT AND REJOIN THE MAIN IMPERIAL LINES. IF THAT'S NOT POSSIBLE...

...YOU DIG IN AND HOLD YOUR CURRENT POSITION... UNTIL REINFORCEMENTS ARRIVE...

NOT MUCH CHANCE OF THAT, *NOW*, IS THERE?

THAT'S THE *ACADEMY'S* ANSWER. THE ARMCHAIR GENERALS WHO CAME UP WITH THAT PLAN AREN'T HERE. WE *ARE*. WHAT WOULD *YOU* DO, SUNBER... GIVEN OUR CURRENT SITUATION?

SIR, THE AMANIN ARE GOING TO OVERRUN OUR POSITION AND KILL US ALL, NO MATTER WHAT WE DO.

I WOULD HAVE US TAKE AS MANY OF THEM WITH US AS POSSIBLE. MAKE THEM THINK TWICE ABOUT EVER DEFYING IMPERIAL AUTHORITY AGAIN.

I SAY WE USE THE AMANIN'S *OWN* TACTIC AGAINST THEM... DRAW THEM IN, AND SUBJECT THEM TO OVERLAPPING FIELDS OF FIRE.

WE SET UP OUR WALLS AND TRENCHES LIKE THIS... THREE *"LETH"* SYMBOLS, EACH *"NESTED"* INTO THE NEXT, ALL POINTING TOWARD A FINAL REDOUBT.

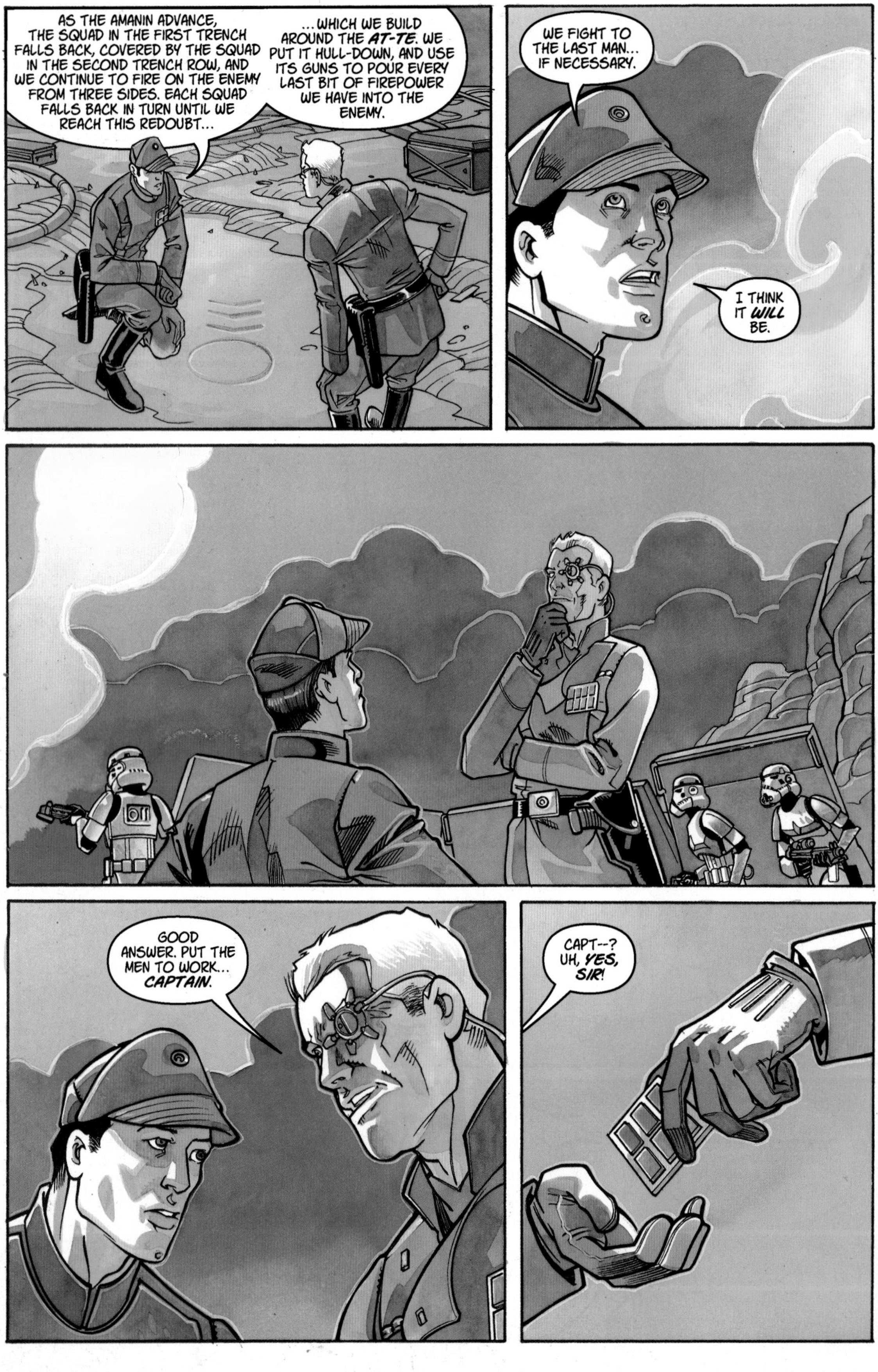
AS THE AMANIN ADVANCE, THE SQUAD IN THE FIRST TRENCH FALLS BACK, COVERED BY THE SQUAD IN THE SECOND TRENCH ROW, AND WE CONTINUE TO FIRE ON THE ENEMY FROM THREE SIDES. EACH SQUAD FALLS BACK IN TURN UNTIL WE REACH THIS REDOUBT...
...WHICH WE BUILD AROUND THE AT-TE. WE PUT IT HULL-DOWN, AND USE ITS GUNS TO POUR EVERY LAST BIT OF FIREPOWER WE HAVE INTO THE ENEMY.
WE FIGHT TO THE LAST MAN... IF NECESSARY.
I THINK IT WILL BE.
GOOD ANSWER. PUT THE MEN TO WORK... CAPTAIN.
CAPT--? UH, YES, SIR!

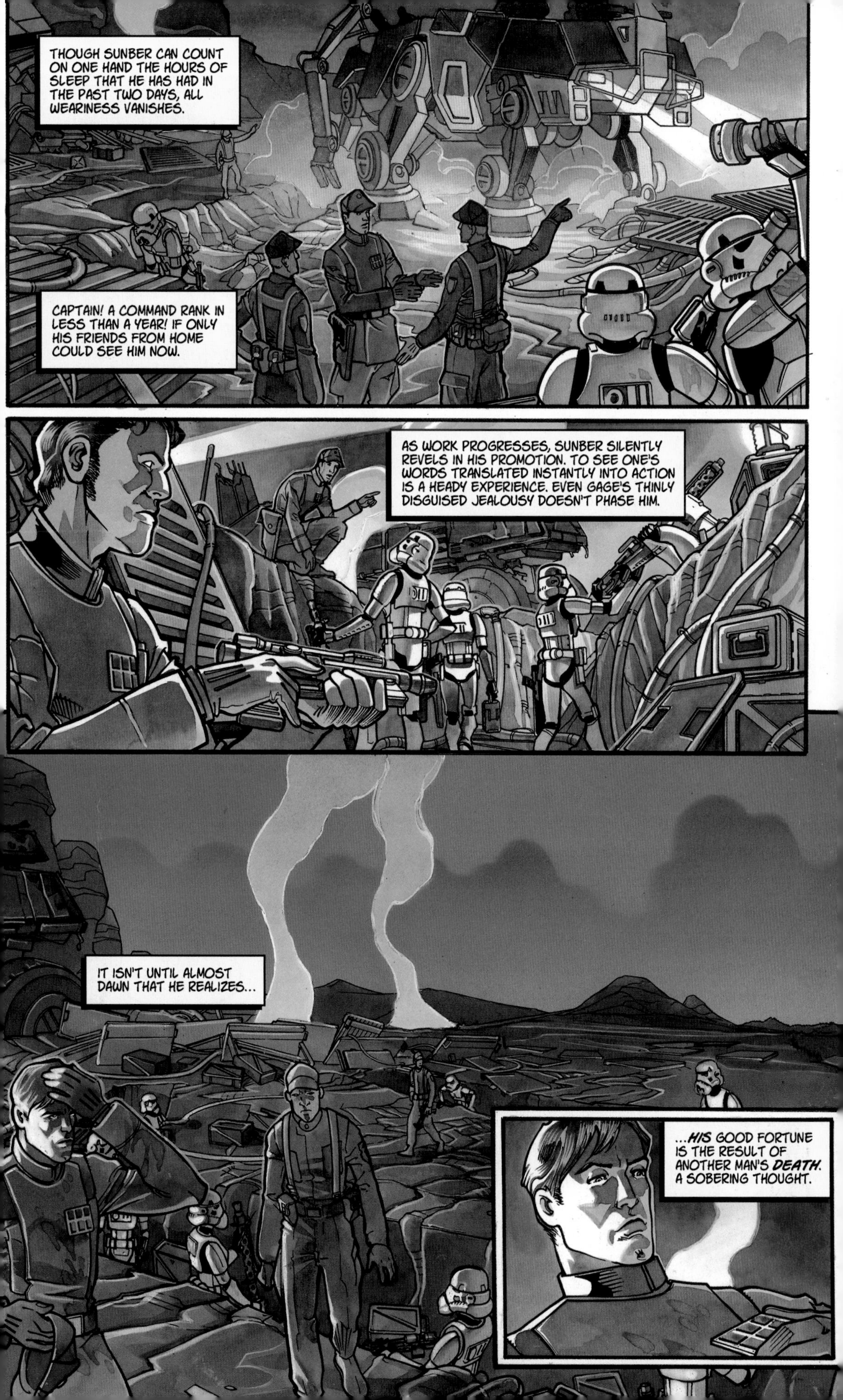
THOUGH SUNBER CAN COUNT ON ONE HAND THE HOURS OF SLEEP THAT HE HAS HAD IN THE PAST TWO DAYS, ALL WEARINESS VANISHES.
CAPTAIN! A COMMAND RANK IN LESS THAN A YEAR! IF ONLY HIS FRIENDS FROM HOME COULD SEE HIM NOW.
AS WORK PROGRESSES, SUNBER SILENTLY REVELS IN HIS PROMOTION. TO SEE ONE'S WORDS TRANSLATED INSTANTLY INTO ACTION IS A HEADY EXPERIENCE. EVEN GAGE'S THINLY DISGUISED JEALOUSY DOESN'T PHASE HIM.
IT ISN'T UNTIL ALMOST DAWN THAT HE REALIZES...
...*HIS* GOOD FORTUNE IS THE RESULT OF ANOTHER MAN'S *DEATH*. A SOBERING THOUGHT.

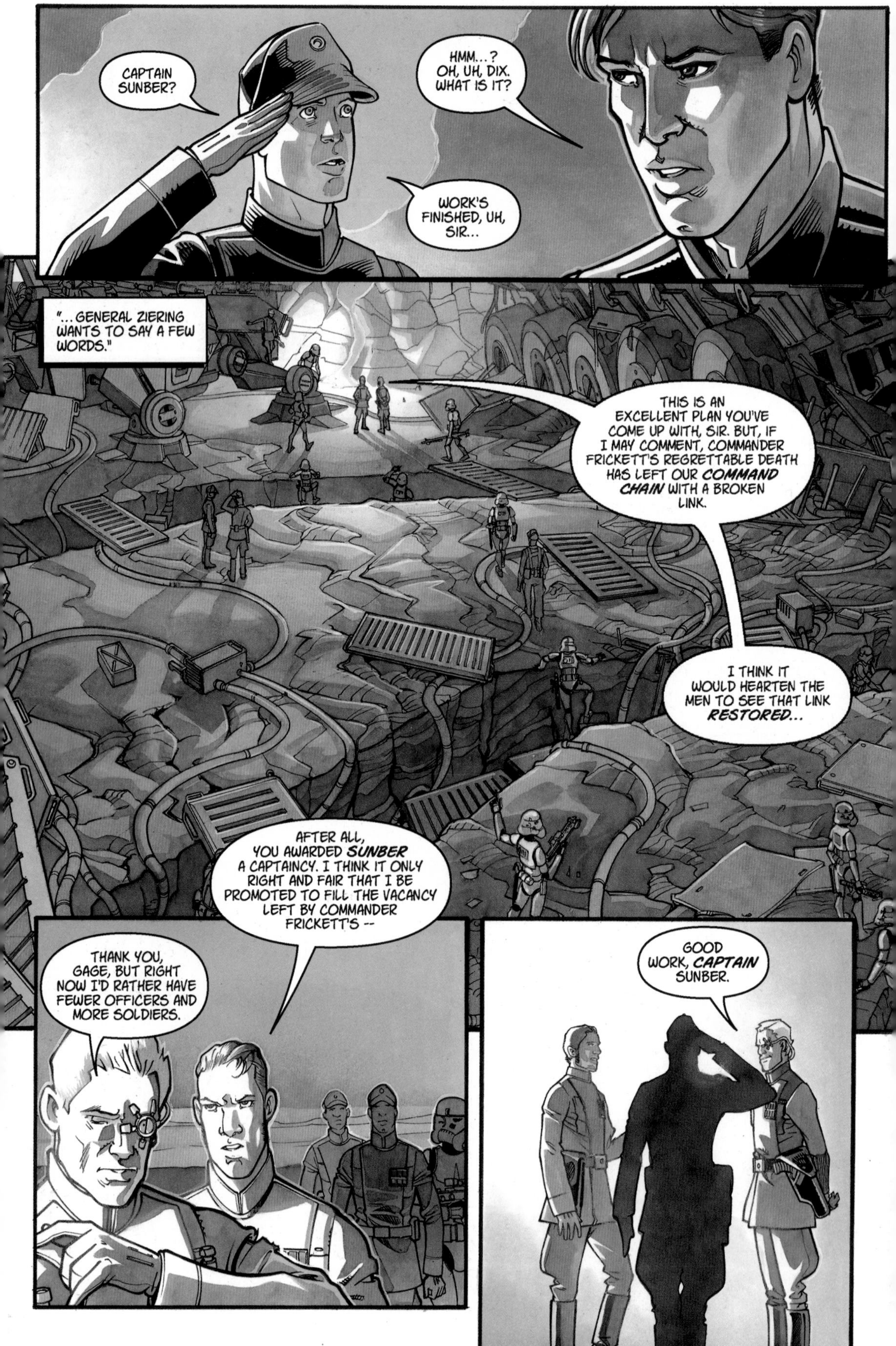
CAPTAIN SUNBER?
HMM...? OH, UH, DIX. WHAT IS IT?
WORK'S FINISHED, UH, SIR...
"...GENERAL ZIERING WANTS TO SAY A FEW WORDS."
THIS IS AN EXCELLENT PLAN YOU'VE COME UP WITH, SIR. BUT, IF I MAY COMMENT, COMMANDER FRICKETT'S REGRETTABLE DEATH HAS LEFT OUR COMMAND CHAIN WITH A BROKEN LINK.
I THINK IT WOULD HEARTEN THE MEN TO SEE THAT LINK RESTORED...
AFTER ALL, YOU AWARDED SUNBER A CAPTAINCY. I THINK IT ONLY RIGHT AND FAIR THAT I BE PROMOTED TO FILL THE VACANCY LEFT BY COMMANDER FRICKETT'S --
THANK YOU, GAGE, BUT RIGHT NOW I'D RATHER HAVE FEWER OFFICERS AND MORE SOLDIERS.
GOOD WORK, CAPTAIN SUNBER.

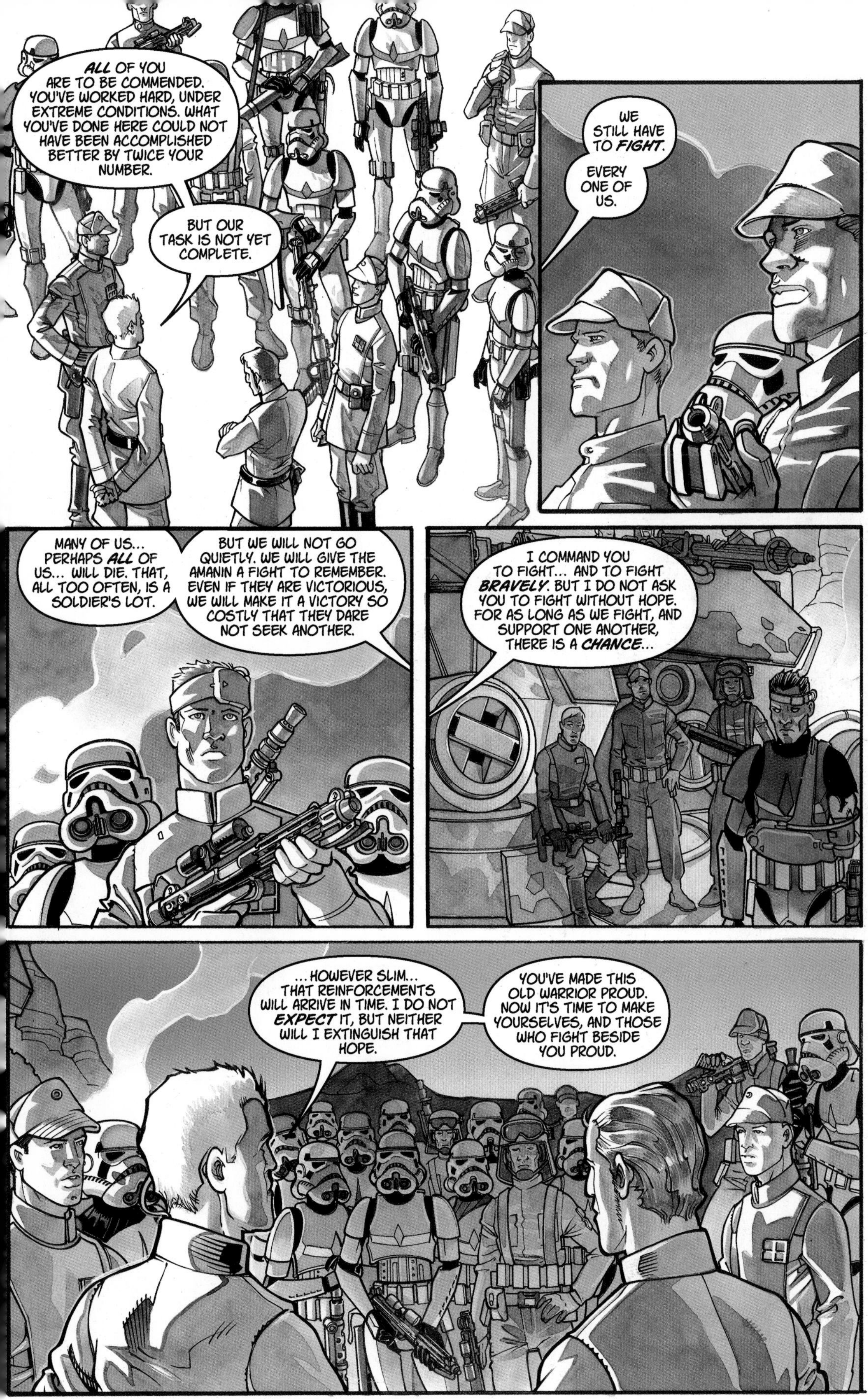
ALL OF YOU ARE TO BE COMMENDED. YOU'VE WORKED HARD, UNDER EXTREME CONDITIONS. WHAT YOU'VE DONE HERE COULD NOT HAVE BEEN ACCOMPLISHED BETTER BY TWICE YOUR NUMBER.
BUT OUR TASK IS NOT YET COMPLETE.
WE STILL HAVE TO FIGHT.
EVERY ONE OF US.
MANY OF US... PERHAPS ALL OF US... WILL DIE. THAT, ALL TOO OFTEN, IS A SOLDIER'S LOT.
BUT WE WILL NOT GO QUIETLY. WE WILL GIVE THE AMANIN A FIGHT TO REMEMBER. EVEN IF THEY ARE VICTORIOUS, WE WILL MAKE IT A VICTORY SO COSTLY THAT THEY DARE NOT SEEK ANOTHER.
I COMMAND YOU TO FIGHT... AND TO FIGHT BRAVELY. BUT I DO NOT ASK YOU TO FIGHT WITHOUT HOPE. FOR AS LONG AS WE FIGHT, AND SUPPORT ONE ANOTHER, THERE IS A CHANCE...
...HOWEVER SLIM... THAT REINFORCEMENTS WILL ARRIVE IN TIME. I DO NOT EXPECT IT, BUT NEITHER WILL I EXTINGUISH THAT HOPE.
YOU'VE MADE THIS OLD WARRIOR PROUD. NOW IT'S TIME TO MAKE YOURSELVES, AND THOSE WHO FIGHT BESIDE YOU PROUD.

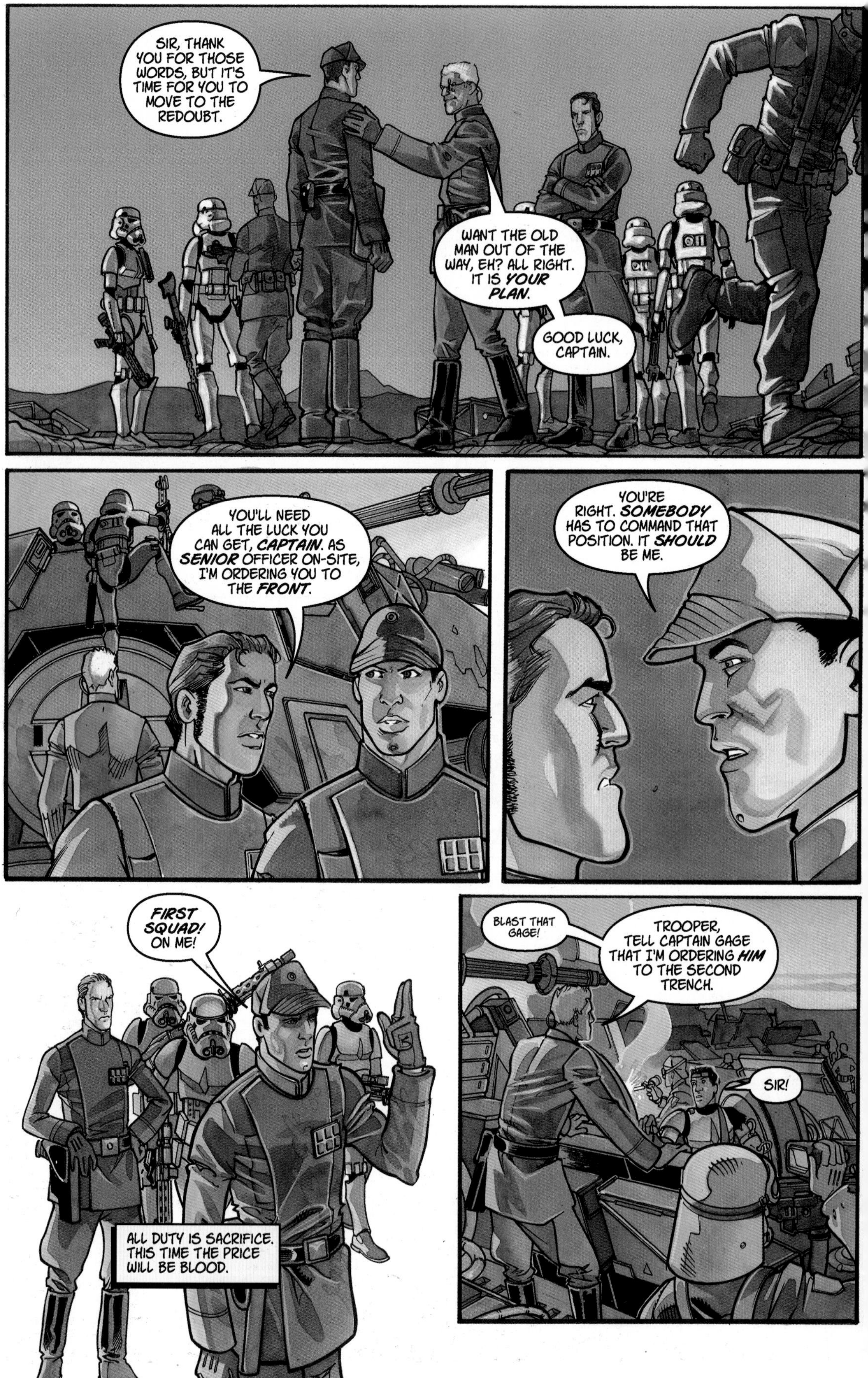
SIR, THANK YOU FOR THOSE WORDS, BUT IT'S TIME FOR YOU TO MOVE TO THE REDOUBT.
WANT THE OLD MAN OUT OF THE WAY, EH? ALL RIGHT. IT IS *YOUR PLAN*.
GOOD LUCK, CAPTAIN.
YOU'LL NEED ALL THE LUCK YOU CAN GET, *CAPTAIN*. AS *SENIOR* OFFICER ON-SITE, I'M ORDERING YOU TO THE *FRONT*.
YOU'RE RIGHT. *SOMEBODY* HAS TO COMMAND THAT POSITION. IT *SHOULD* BE ME.
FIRST SQUAD! ON ME!
ALL DUTY IS SACRIFICE. THIS TIME THE PRICE WILL BE BLOOD.
BLAST THAT GAGE!
TROOPER, TELL CAPTAIN GAGE THAT I'M ORDERING *HIM* TO THE SECOND TRENCH.
SIR!

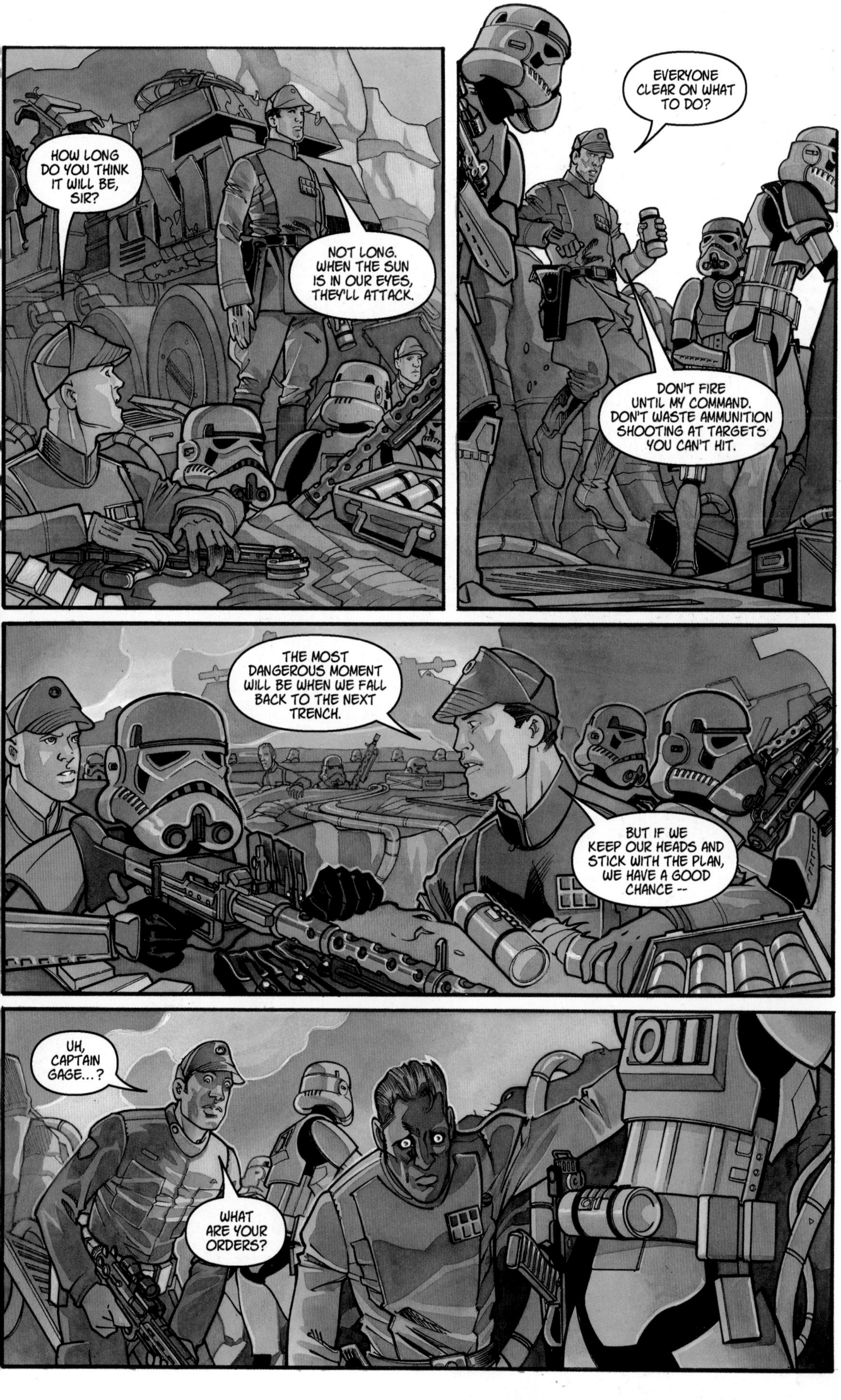
HOW LONG DO YOU THINK IT WILL BE, SIR?
NOT LONG. WHEN THE SUN IS IN OUR EYES, THEY'LL ATTACK.
EVERYONE CLEAR ON WHAT TO DO?
DON'T FIRE UNTIL MY COMMAND. DON'T WASTE AMMUNITION SHOOTING AT TARGETS YOU CAN'T HIT.
THE MOST DANGEROUS MOMENT WILL BE WHEN WE FALL BACK TO THE NEXT TRENCH.
BUT IF WE KEEP OUR HEADS AND STICK WITH THE PLAN, WE HAVE A GOOD CHANCE --
UH, CAPTAIN GAGE...?
WHAT ARE YOUR ORDERS?

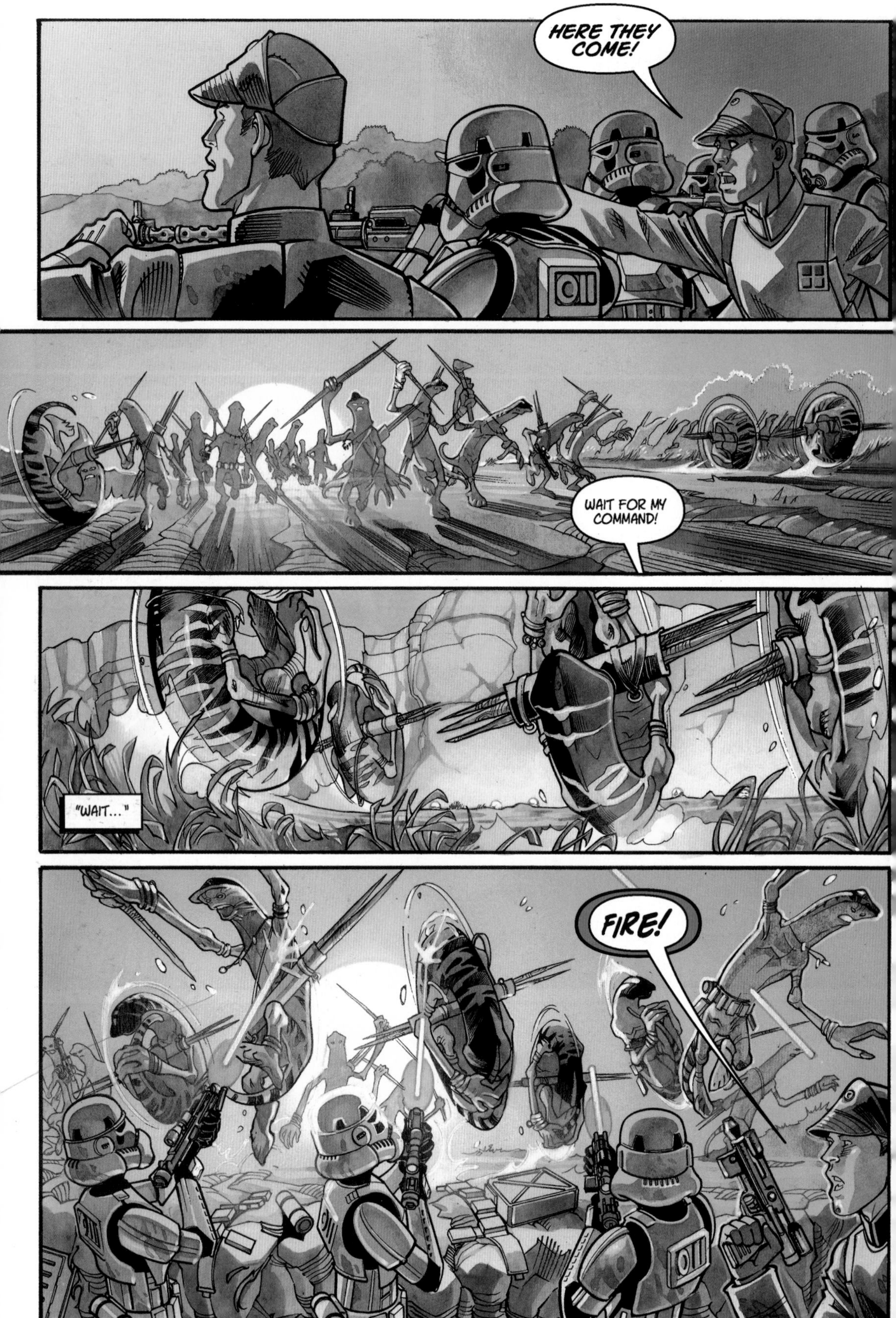
HERE THEY COME!
WAIT FOR MY COMMAND!
"WAIT..."
FIRE!

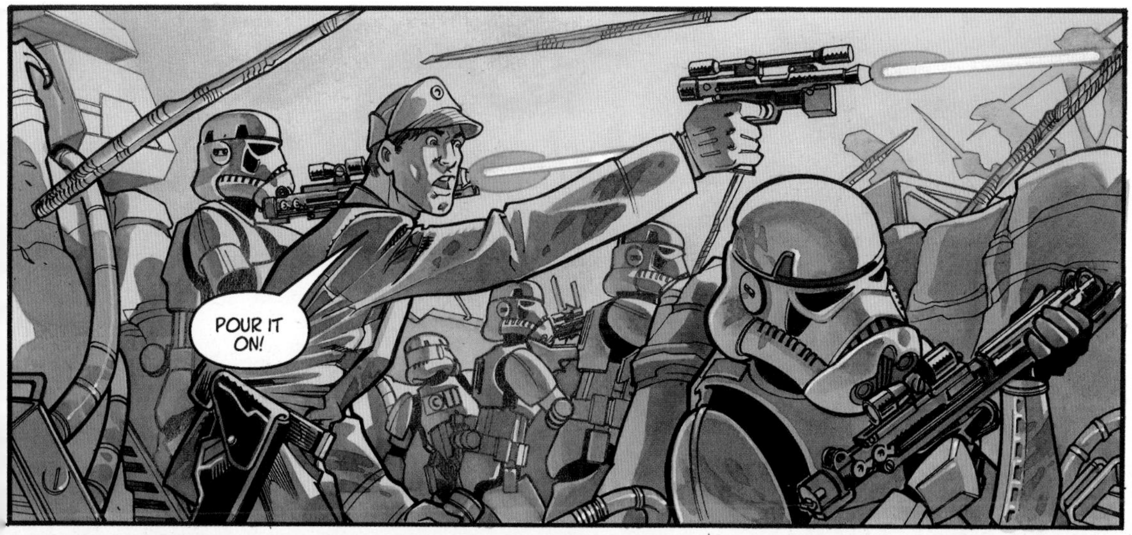
POUR IT ON!

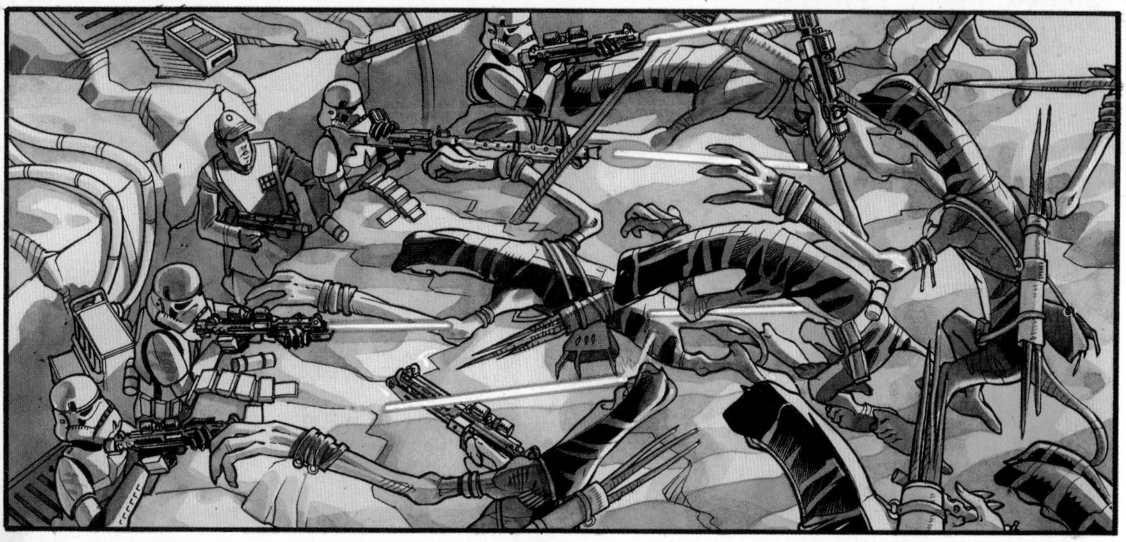

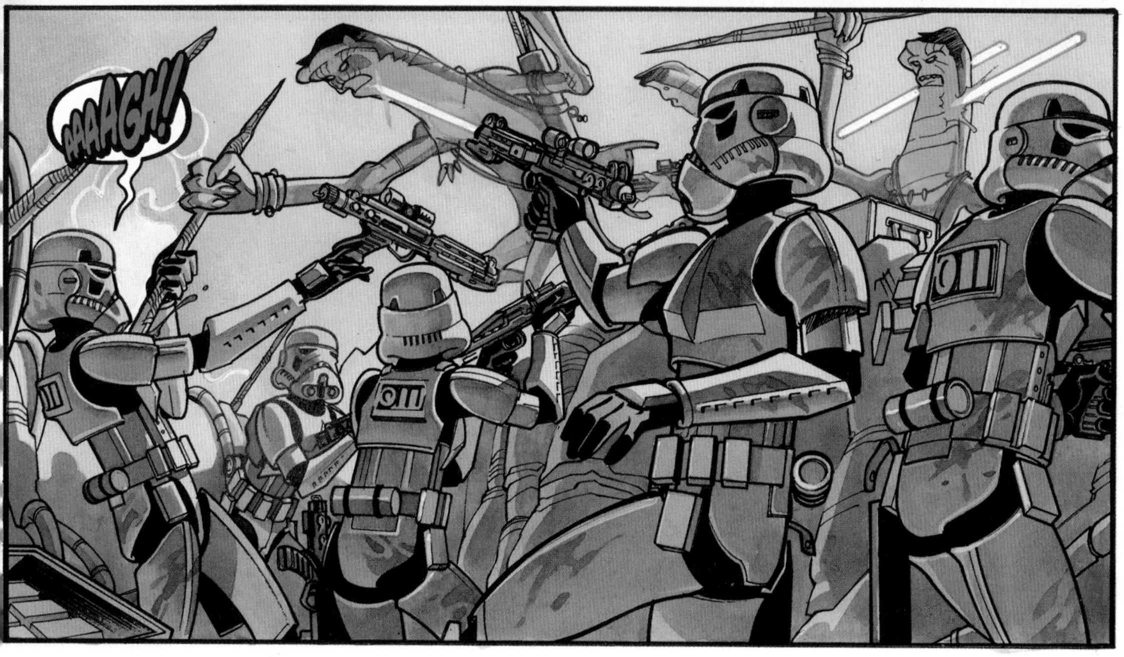
AAAAGH!!

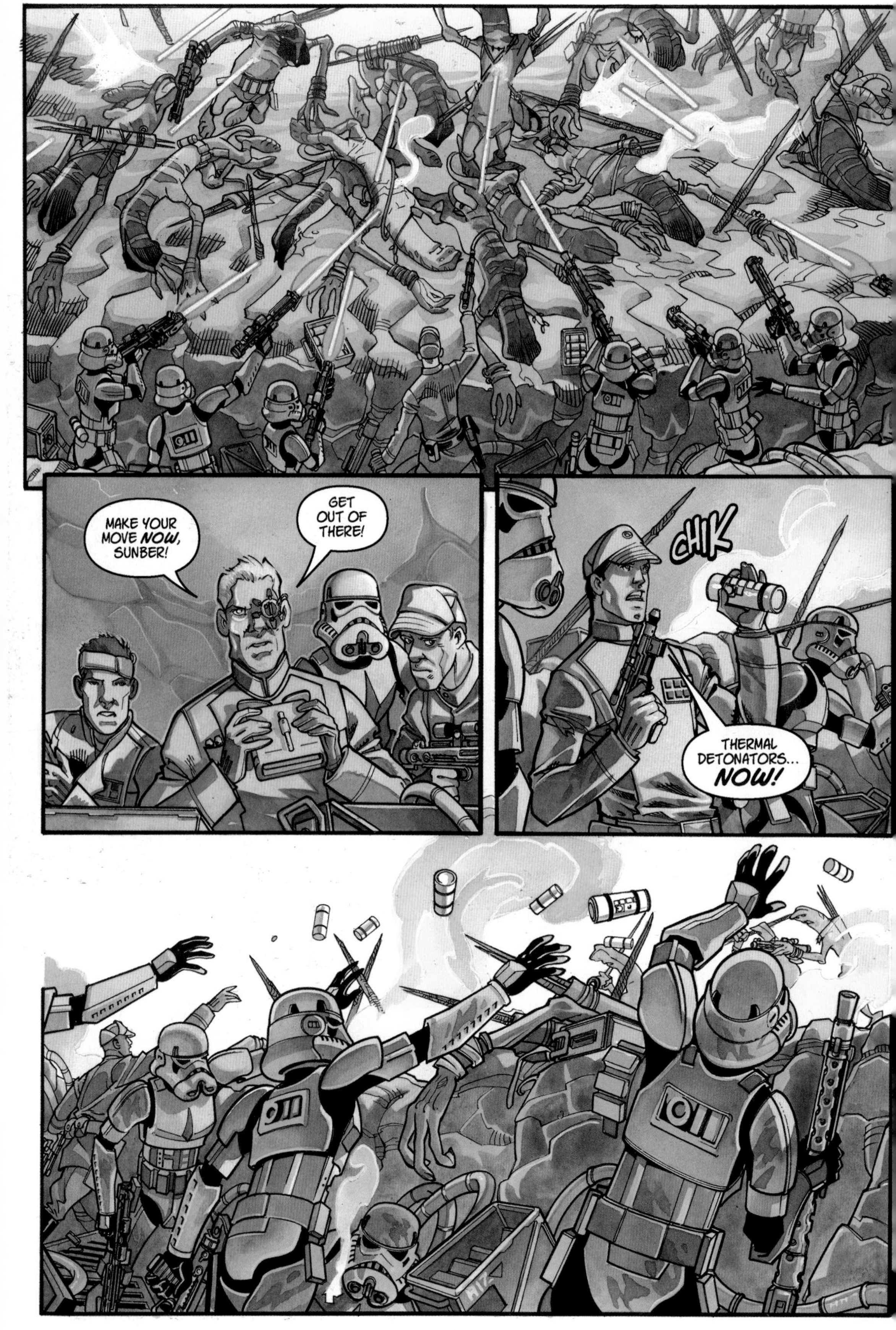
MAKE YOUR MOVE NOW, SUNBER!
GET OUT OF THERE!
CHIK
THERMAL DETONATORS... NOW!

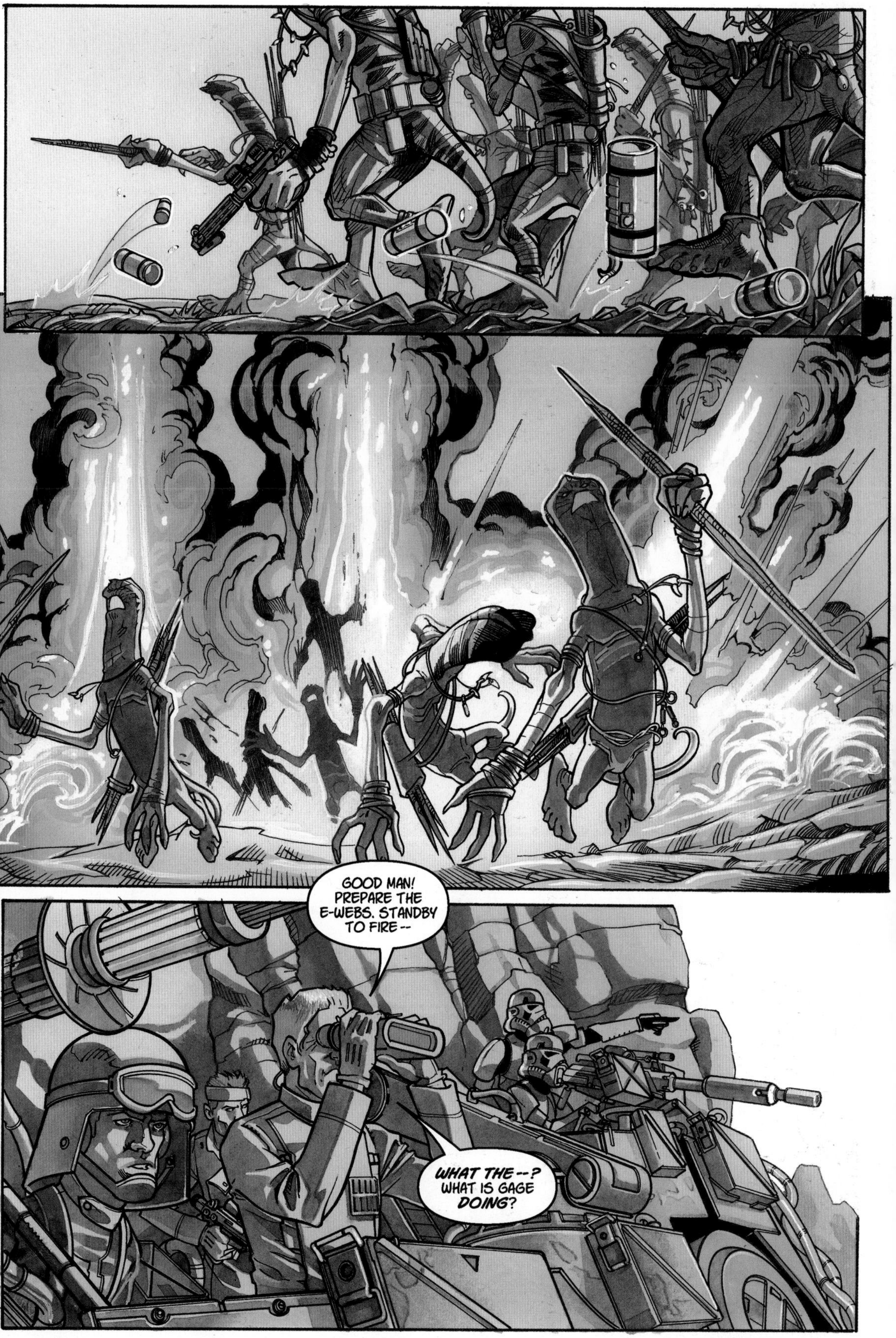
GOOD MAN! PREPARE THE E-WEBS. STANDBY TO FIRE--
WHAT THE--? WHAT IS GAGE DOING?

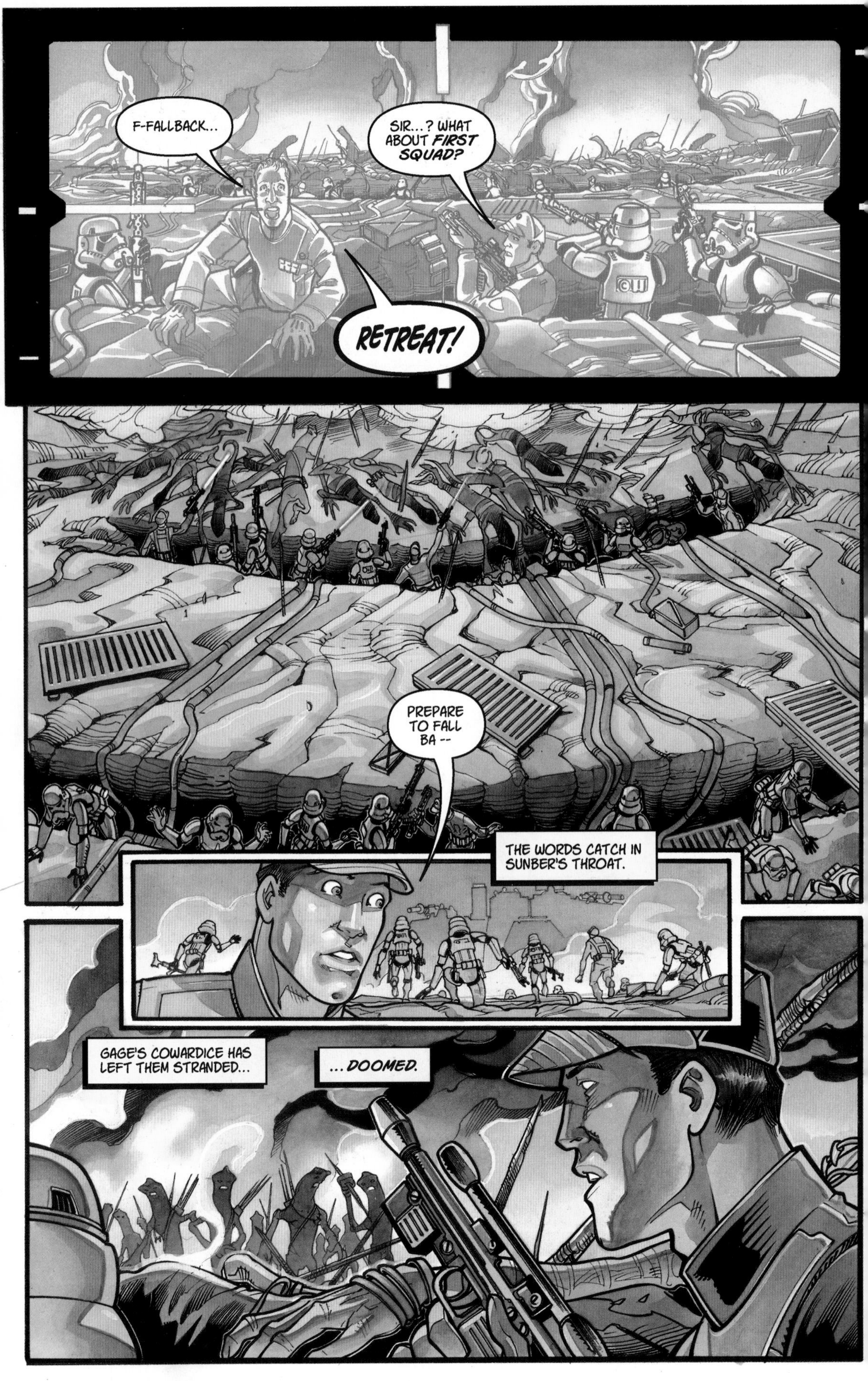
F-FALLBACK...
SIR...? WHAT ABOUT FIRST SQUAD?
RETREAT!
PREPARE TO FALL BA --
THE WORDS CATCH IN SUNBER'S THROAT.
GAGE'S COWARDICE HAS LEFT THEM STRANDED...
...DOOMED.

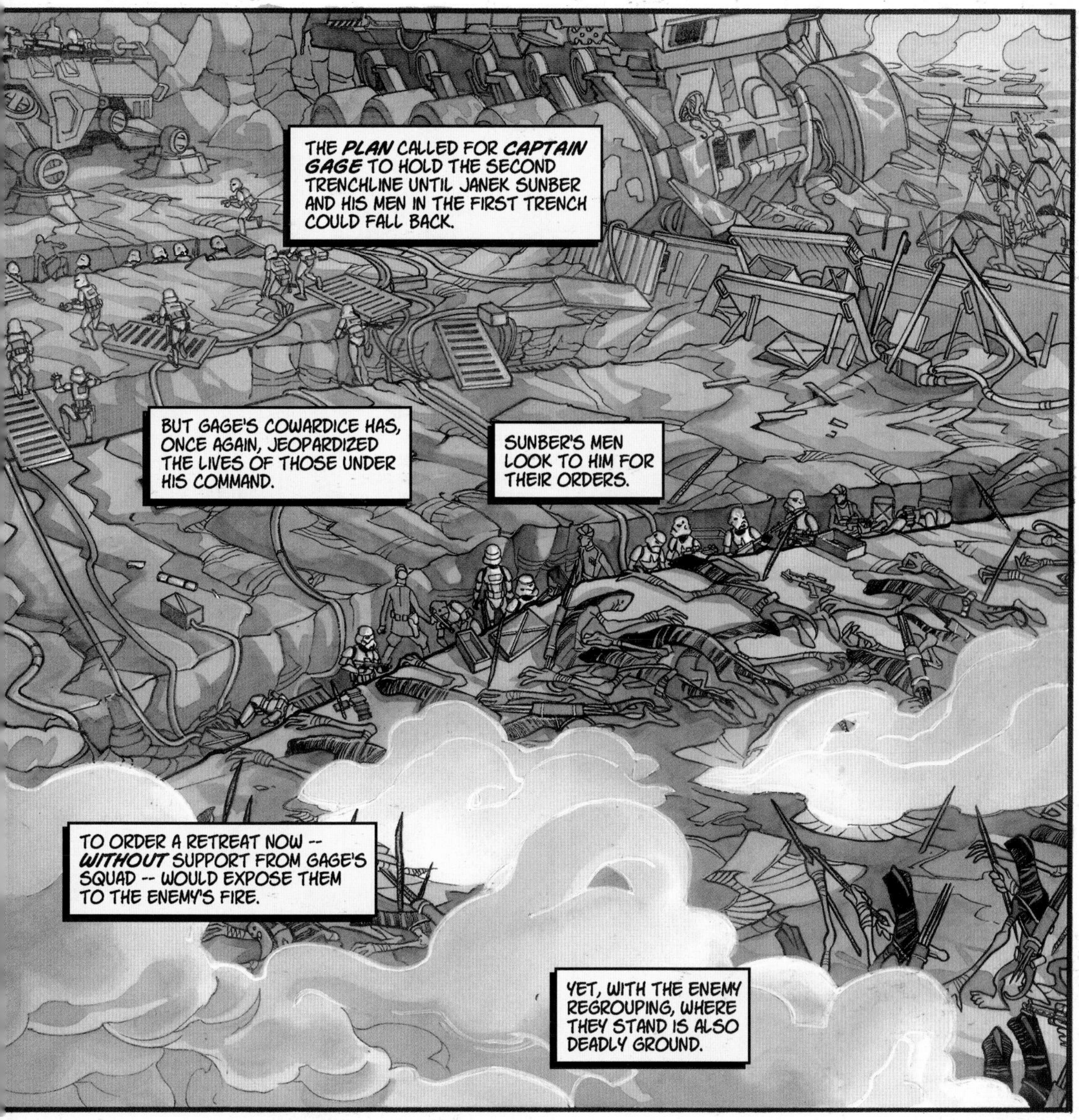

THE *PLAN* CALLED FOR *CAPTAIN GAGE* TO HOLD THE SECOND TRENCHLINE UNTIL JANEK SUNBER AND HIS MEN IN THE FIRST TRENCH COULD FALL BACK.
BUT GAGE'S COWARDICE HAS, ONCE AGAIN, JEOPARDIZED THE LIVES OF THOSE UNDER HIS COMMAND.
SUNBER'S MEN LOOK TO HIM FOR THEIR ORDERS.
TO ORDER A RETREAT NOW -- *WITHOUT* SUPPORT FROM GAGE'S SQUAD -- WOULD EXPOSE THEM TO THE ENEMY'S FIRE.
YET, WITH THE ENEMY REGROUPING, WHERE THEY STAND IS ALSO DEADLY GROUND.

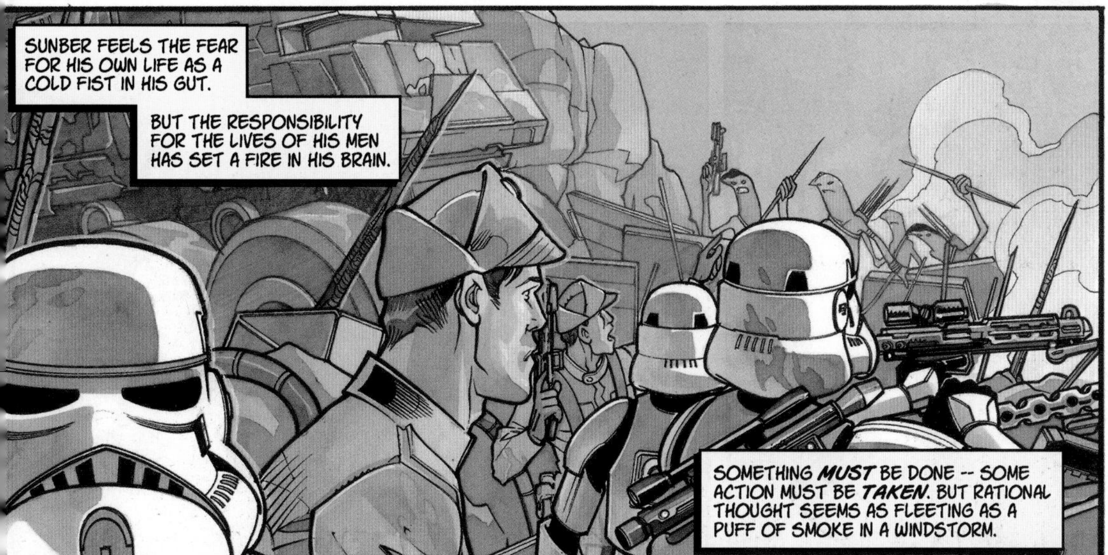

SUNBER FEELS THE FEAR FOR HIS OWN LIFE AS A COLD FIST IN HIS GUT.
BUT THE RESPONSIBILITY FOR THE LIVES OF HIS MEN HAS SET A FIRE IN HIS BRAIN.
SOMETHING *MUST* BE DONE -- SOME ACTION MUST BE *TAKEN*. BUT RATIONAL THOUGHT SEEMS AS FLEETING AS A PUFF OF SMOKE IN A WINDSTORM.

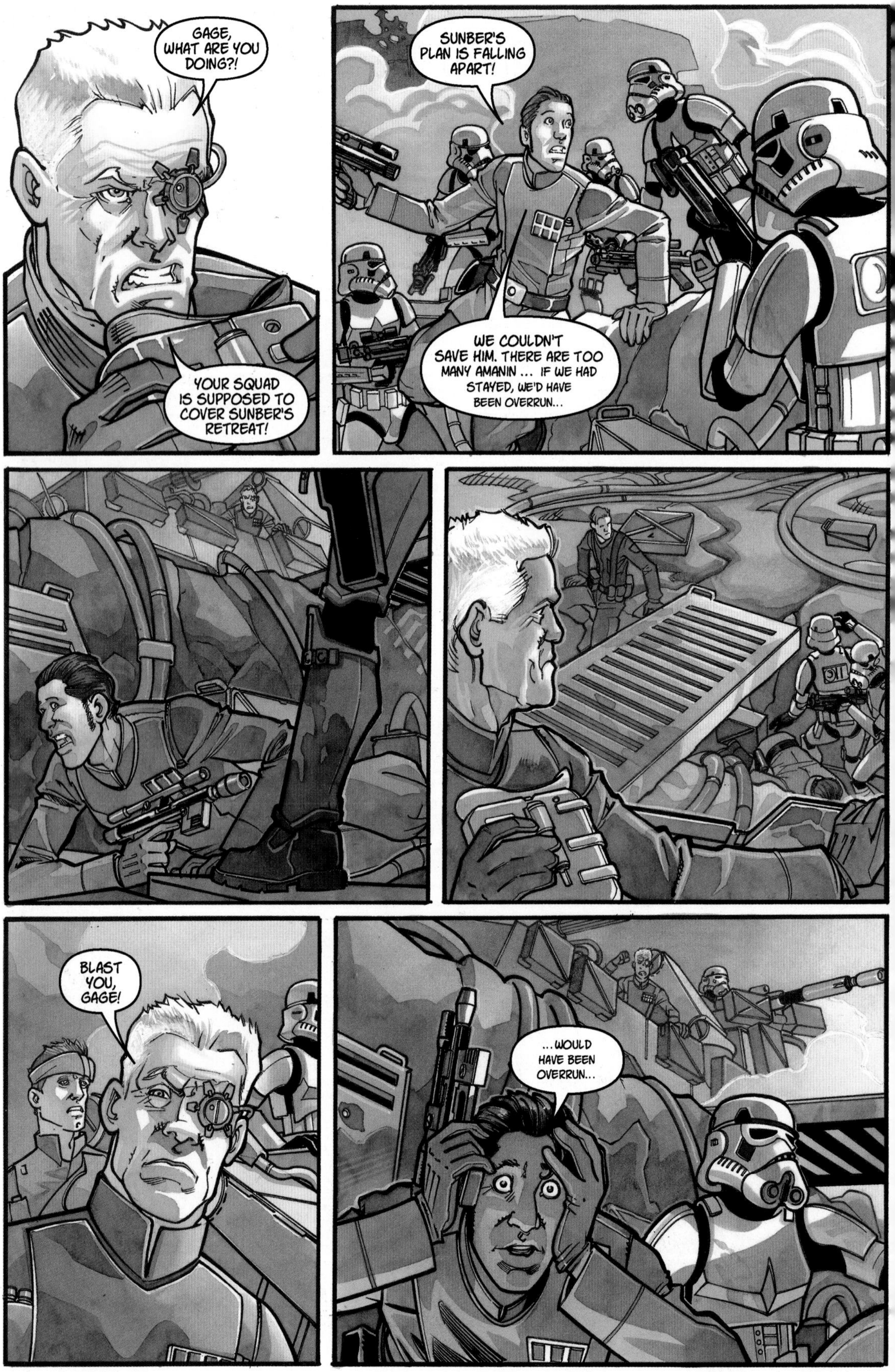
GAGE, WHAT ARE YOU DOING?!
YOUR SQUAD IS SUPPOSED TO COVER SUNBER'S RETREAT!
SUNBER'S PLAN IS FALLING APART!
WE COULDN'T SAVE HIM. THERE ARE TOO MANY AMANIN ... IF WE HAD STAYED, WE'D HAVE BEEN OVERRUN...
BLAST YOU, GAGE!
...WOULD HAVE BEEN OVERRUN...

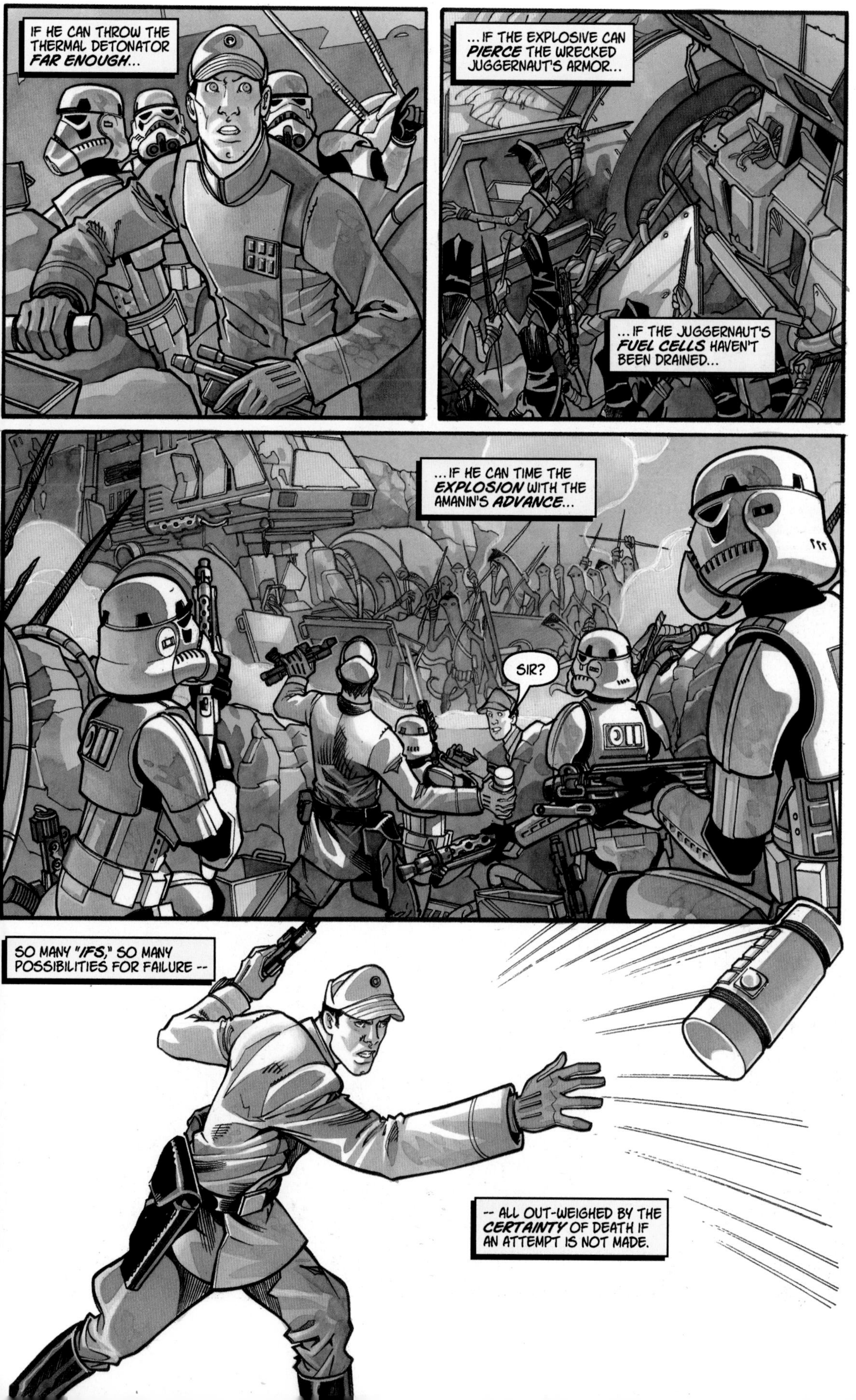
IF HE CAN THROW THE THERMAL DETONATOR FAR ENOUGH...
...IF THE EXPLOSIVE CAN PIERCE THE WRECKED JUGGERNAUT'S ARMOR...
...IF THE JUGGERNAUT'S FUEL CELLS HAVEN'T BEEN DRAINED...
...IF HE CAN TIME THE EXPLOSION WITH THE AMANIN'S ADVANCE...
SIR?
SO MANY "IFS," SO MANY POSSIBILITIES FOR FAILURE --
-- ALL OUT-WEIGHED BY THE CERTAINTY OF DEATH IF AN ATTEMPT IS NOT MADE.

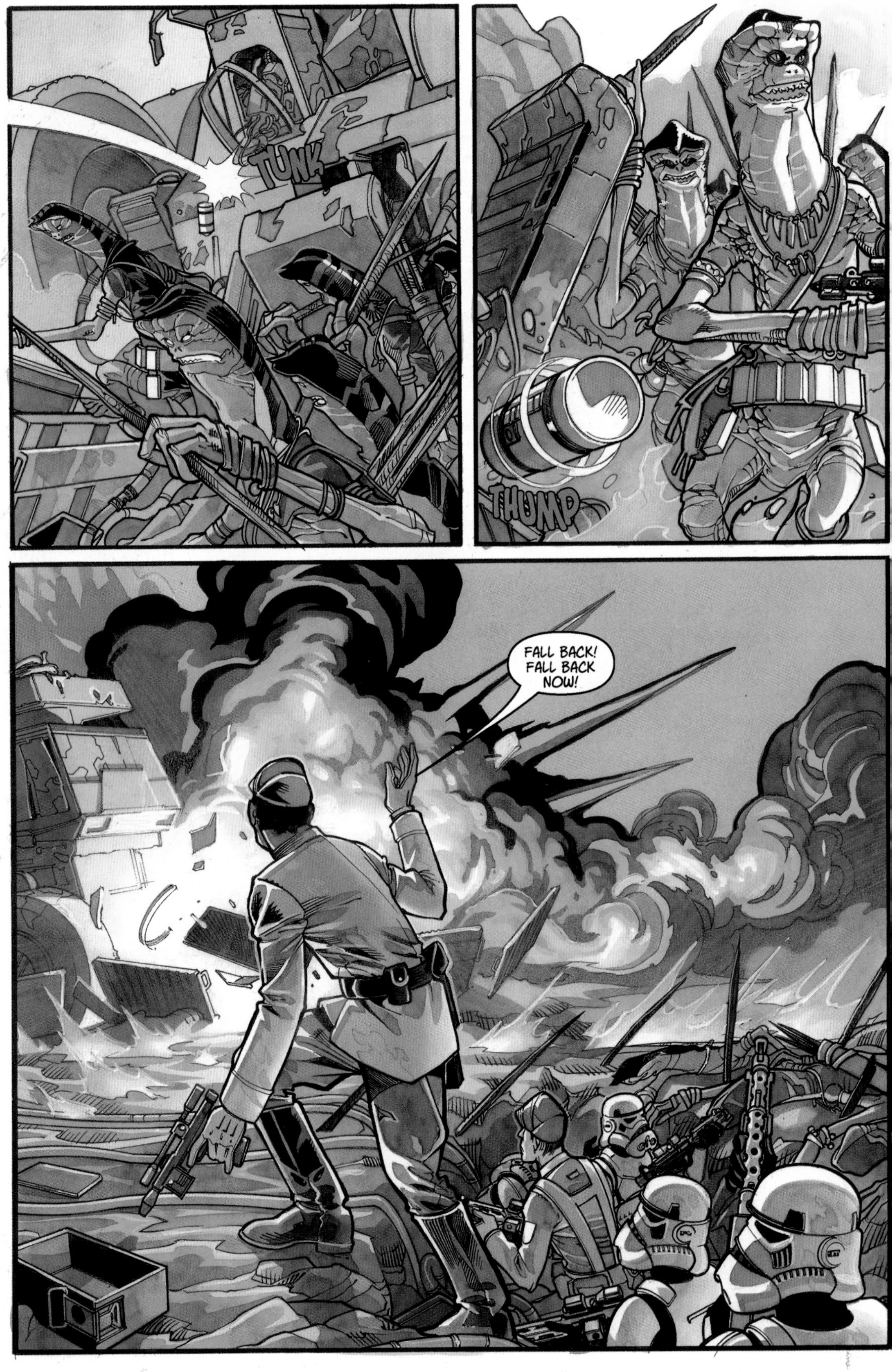
TUNK
THUMP
FALL BACK!
FALL BACK
NOW!

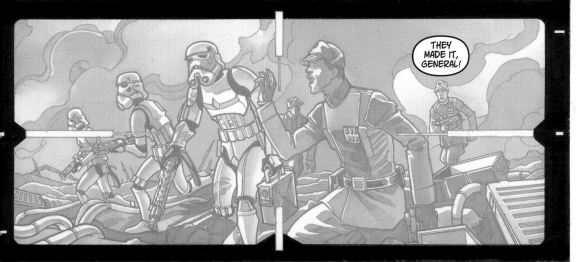

THEY MADE IT, GENERAL!

WE'LL BE ABLE TO COVER THEIR NEXT RETREAT FROM HERE.

LUCKY FOR YOU SUNBER SURVIVED, GAGE. IF HE HADN'T, I'D HAVE SHOT YOU MYSELF.

NOW YOU CAN LIVE LONG ENOUGH TO DIE BY AN AMANIN SPEAR.

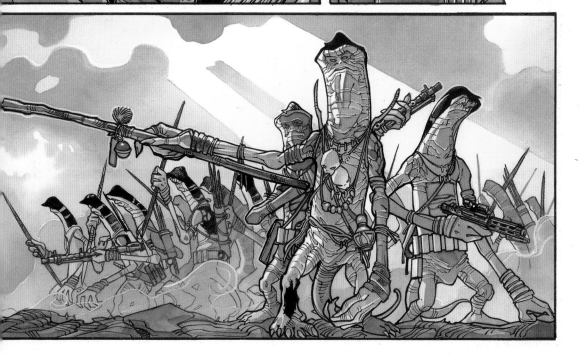

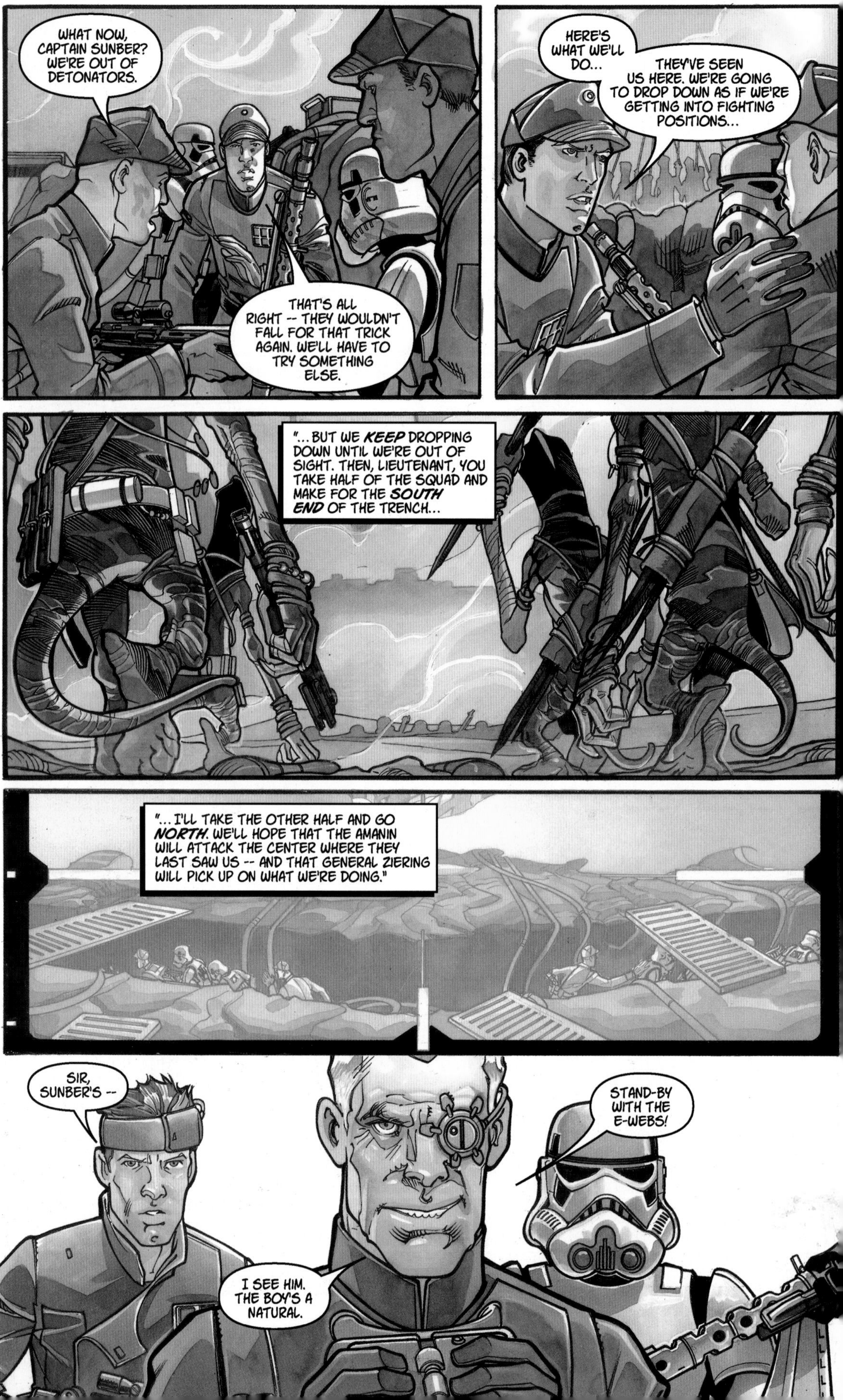
WHAT NOW, CAPTAIN SUNBER? WE'RE OUT OF DETONATORS.
THAT'S ALL RIGHT -- THEY WOULDN'T FALL FOR THAT TRICK AGAIN. WE'LL HAVE TO TRY SOMETHING ELSE.
HERE'S WHAT WE'LL DO...
THEY'VE SEEN US HERE. WE'RE GOING TO DROP DOWN AS IF WE'RE GETTING INTO FIGHTING POSITIONS...
"...BUT WE KEEP DROPPING DOWN UNTIL WE'RE OUT OF SIGHT. THEN, LIEUTENANT, YOU TAKE HALF OF THE SQUAD AND MAKE FOR THE SOUTH END OF THE TRENCH...
"...I'LL TAKE THE OTHER HALF AND GO NORTH. WE'LL HOPE THAT THE AMANIN WILL ATTACK THE CENTER WHERE THEY LAST SAW US -- AND THAT GENERAL ZIERING WILL PICK UP ON WHAT WE'RE DOING."
SIR, SUNBER'S --
STAND-BY WITH THE E-WEBS!
I SEE HIM. THE BOY'S A NATURAL.

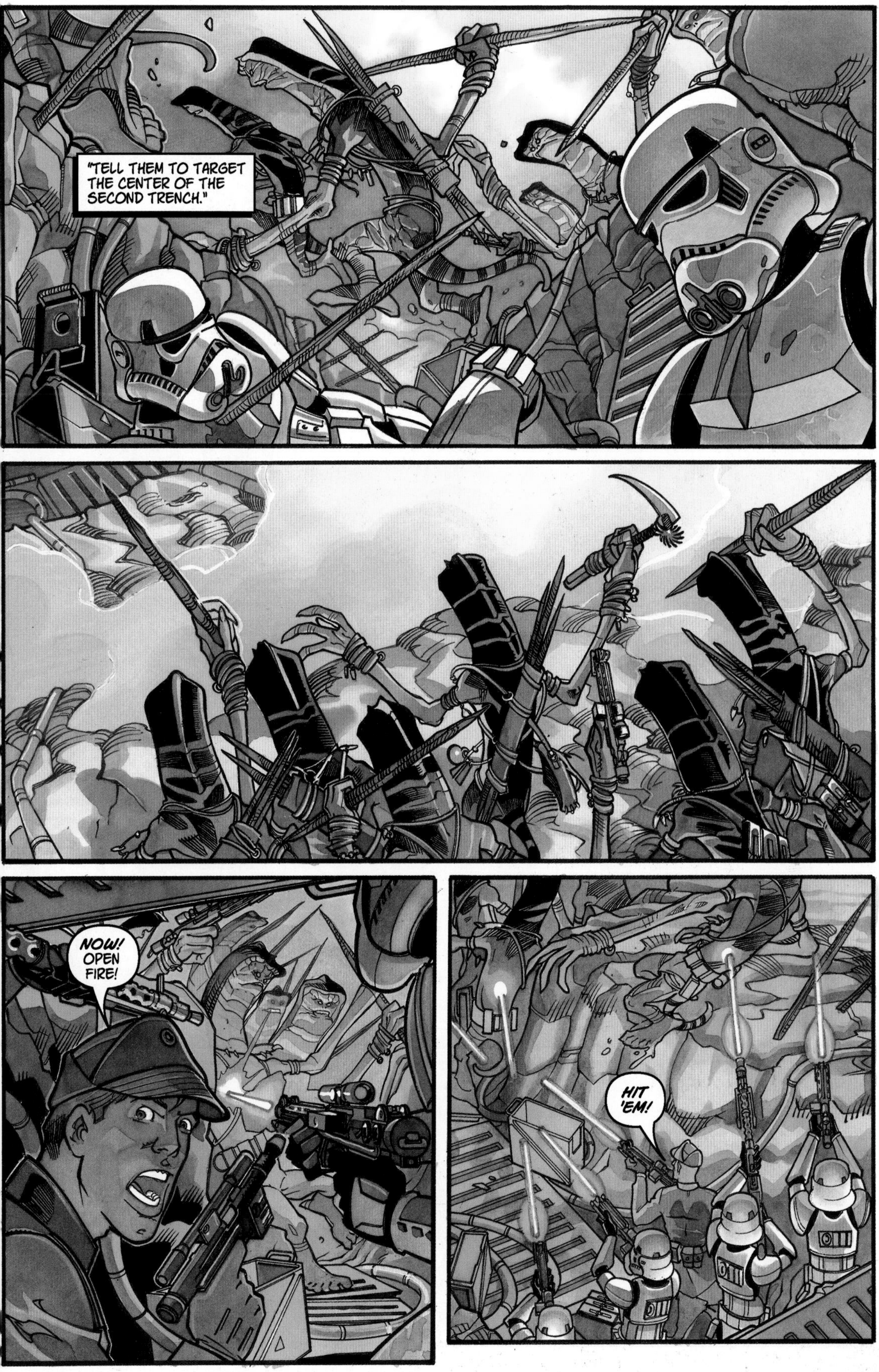
"TELL THEM TO TARGET THE CENTER OF THE SECOND TRENCH."
NOW! OPEN FIRE!
HIT 'EM!

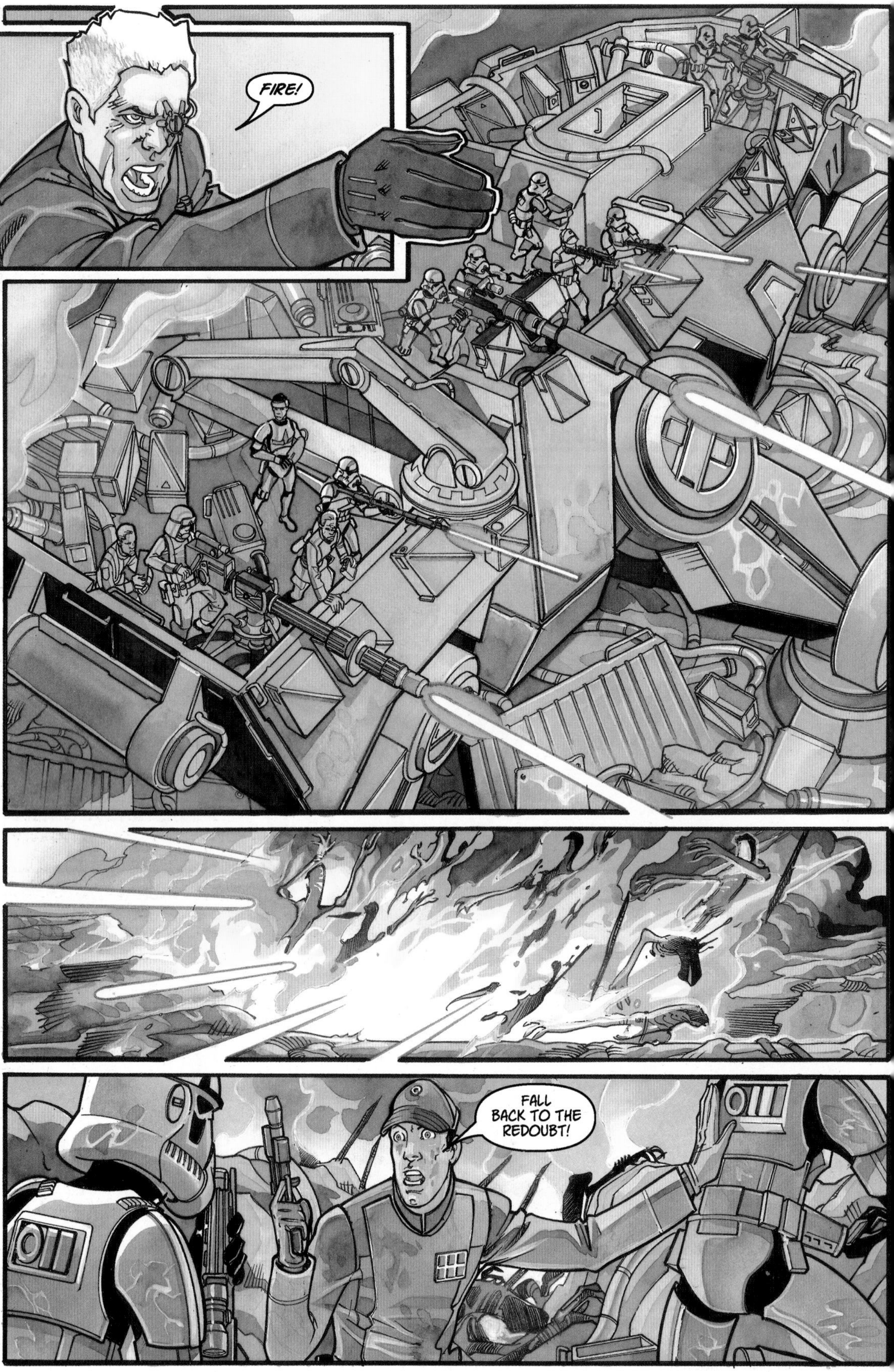
FIRE!
FALL BACK TO THE REDOUBT!

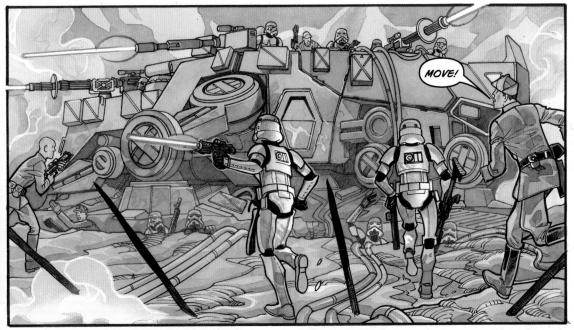

MOVE!

UGH!

IT IS SAID OF MEN IN BATTLE THAT THE FIRST INVOLUNTARY EMOTION EXPERIENCED AT THE SIGHT OF A COMRADE'S DEATH IS *RELIEF* THAT IT WASN'T THEY THEMSELVES WHO FELL TO THE ENEMY'S WEAPONS.

BUT FOR THOSE FOR WHO BEAR THE *WEIGHT* OF COMMAND, EVERY SOLDIER'S DEATH *INCREASES* -- RATHER THAN *LIGHTENS* -- THEIR BURDEN.

SIR, HE'S DEAD!

SUNBER REALIZES THAT HE NEVER KNEW -- NEVER WILL *KNOW* -- THE FALLEN TROOPER'S NAME...

...WHETHER THE MAN WAS A CLONE OR, LIKE HE HIMSELF, A RECRUIT FROM SOME BACKWATER WORLD FOR WHOM THE IMPERIAL ACADEMY OFFERED A PROMISE OF ADVENTURE AND A BETTER LIFE.

WORSE YET, HE REALIZES THAT IT DOESN'T MATTER. THERE ARE OTHERS IN HIS SERVICE WHO YET LIVE -- WHO STILL REQUIRE HIS LEADERSHIP.

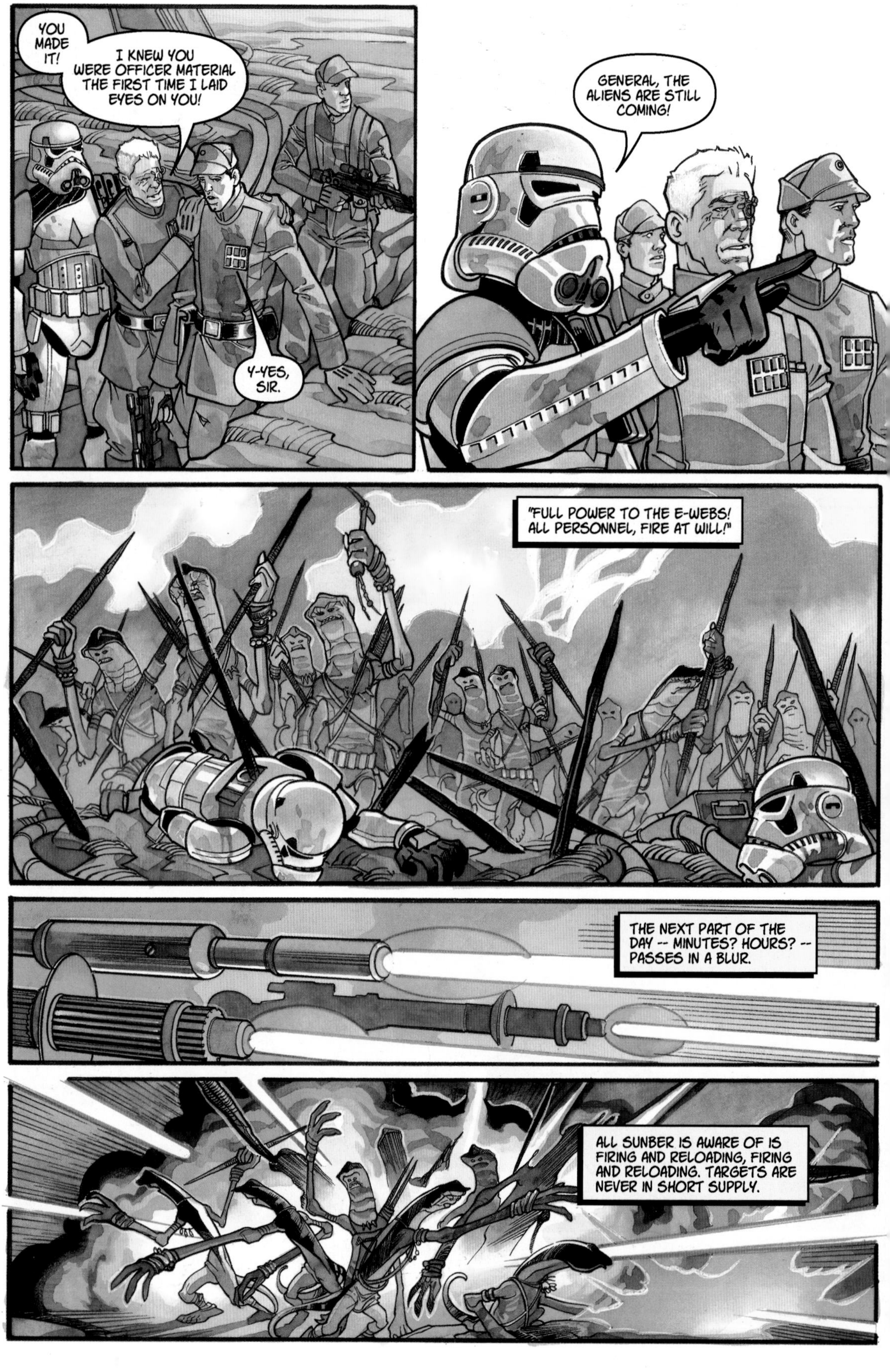
YOU MADE IT!
I KNEW YOU WERE OFFICER MATERIAL THE FIRST TIME I LAID EYES ON YOU!
Y-YES, SIR.
GENERAL, THE ALIENS ARE STILL COMING!
"FULL POWER TO THE E-WEBS! ALL PERSONNEL, FIRE AT WILL!"
THE NEXT PART OF THE DAY -- MINUTES? HOURS? -- PASSES IN A BLUR.
ALL SUNBER IS AWARE OF IS FIRING AND RELOADING, FIRING AND RELOADING. TARGETS ARE NEVER IN SHORT SUPPLY.

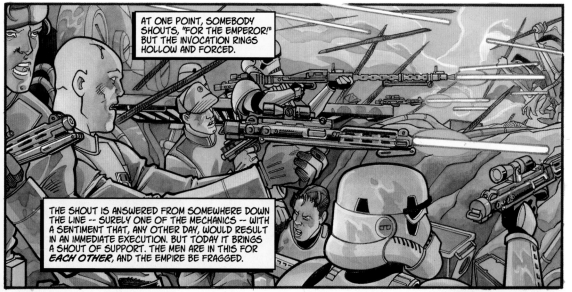

AT ONE POINT, SOMEBODY SHOUTS, "FOR THE EMPEROR!" BUT THE INVOCATION RINGS HOLLOW AND FORCED.

THE SHOUT IS ANSWERED FROM SOMEWHERE DOWN THE LINE -- SURELY ONE OF THE MECHANICS -- WITH A SENTIMENT THAT, ANY OTHER DAY, WOULD RESULT IN AN IMMEDIATE EXECUTION. BUT TODAY IT BRINGS A SHOUT OF SUPPORT. THE MEN ARE IN THIS FOR *EACH OTHER*, AND THE EMPIRE BE FRAGGED.

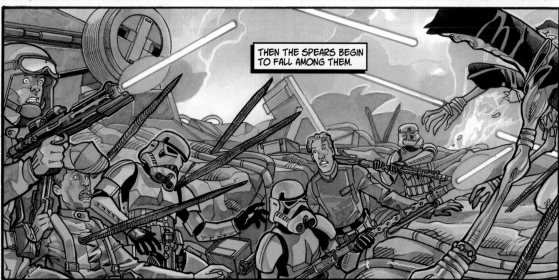

THEN THE SPEARS BEGIN TO FALL AMONG THEM.

BUT THE DEATHS OF THEIR COMRADES, RATHER THAN INSPIRE FEAR OR DESPAIR --

-- FIRES THE DEFENDERS WITH A FURY TO REDOUBLE THEIR EFFORTS.

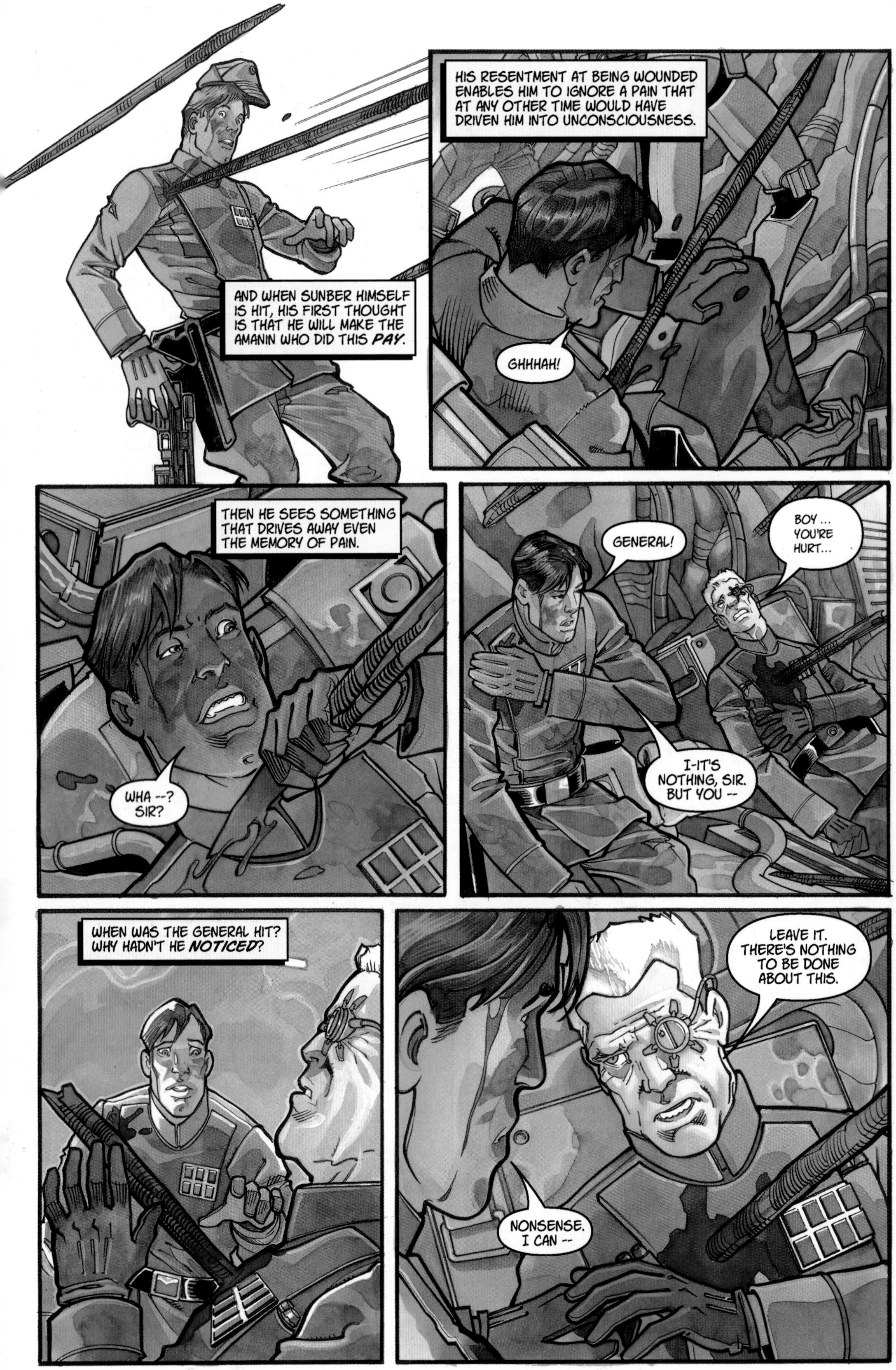
AND WHEN SUNBER HIMSELF IS HIT, HIS FIRST THOUGHT IS THAT HE WILL MAKE THE AMANIN WHO DID THIS *PAY*.
HIS RESENTMENT AT BEING WOUNDED ENABLES HIM TO IGNORE A PAIN THAT AT ANY OTHER TIME WOULD HAVE DRIVEN HIM INTO UNCONSCIOUSNESS.
GHHHAH!
THEN HE SEES SOMETHING THAT DRIVES AWAY EVEN THE MEMORY OF PAIN.
WHA --? SIR?
GENERAL!
BOY ... YOU'RE HURT...
I-IT'S NOTHING, SIR. BUT YOU --
WHEN WAS THE GENERAL HIT? WHY HADN'T HE *NOTICED*?
LEAVE IT. THERE'S NOTHING TO BE DONE ABOUT THIS.
NONSENSE. I CAN --

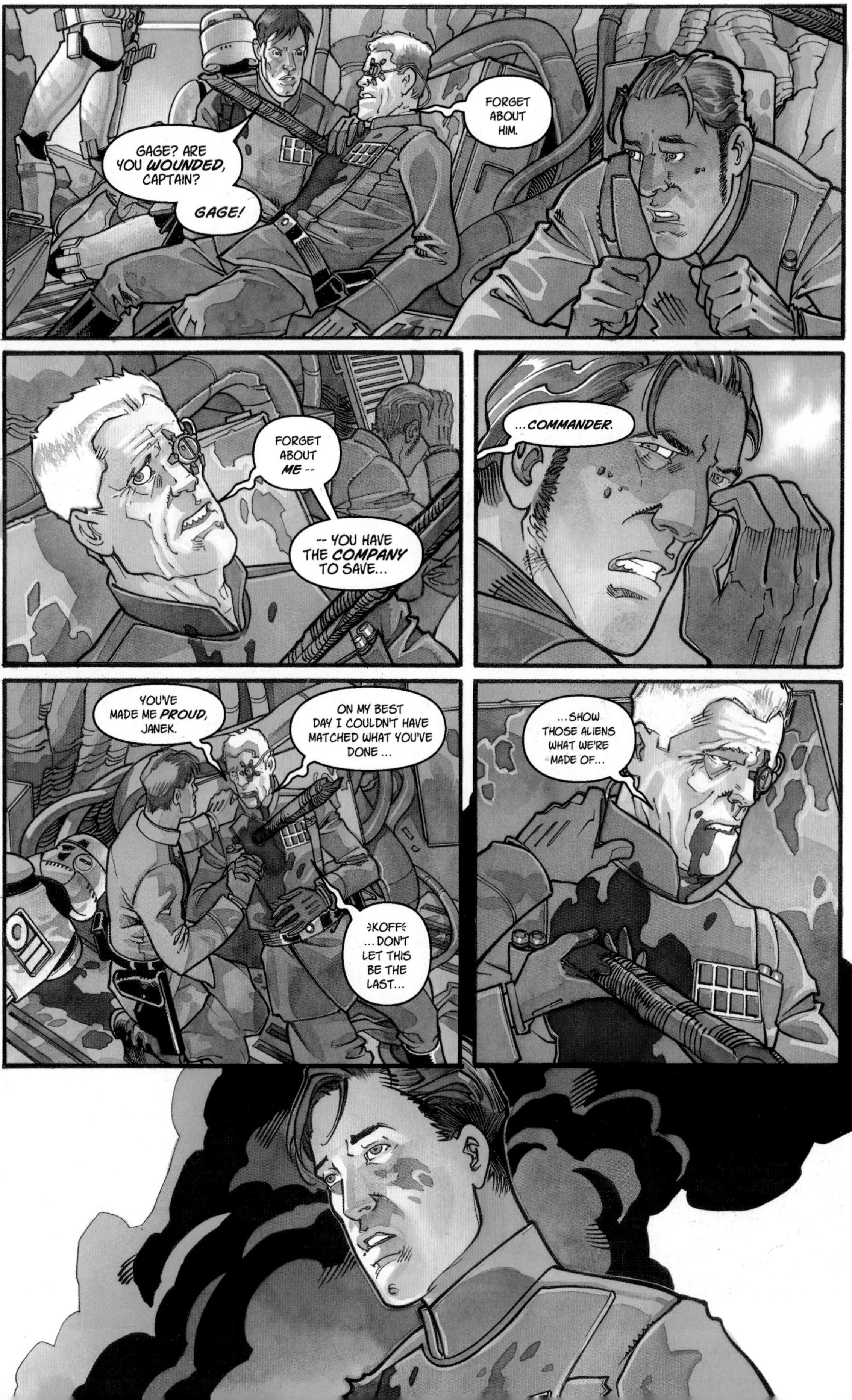
GAGE? ARE YOU WOUNDED, CAPTAIN?
GAGE!
FORGET ABOUT HIM.
FORGET ABOUT ME --
-- YOU HAVE THE COMPANY TO SAVE...
...COMMANDER.
YOU'VE MADE ME PROUD, JANEK.
ON MY BEST DAY I COULDN'T HAVE MATCHED WHAT YOU'VE DONE...
KOFF ...DON'T LET THIS BE THE LAST...
...SHOW THOSE ALIENS WHAT WE'RE MADE OF...

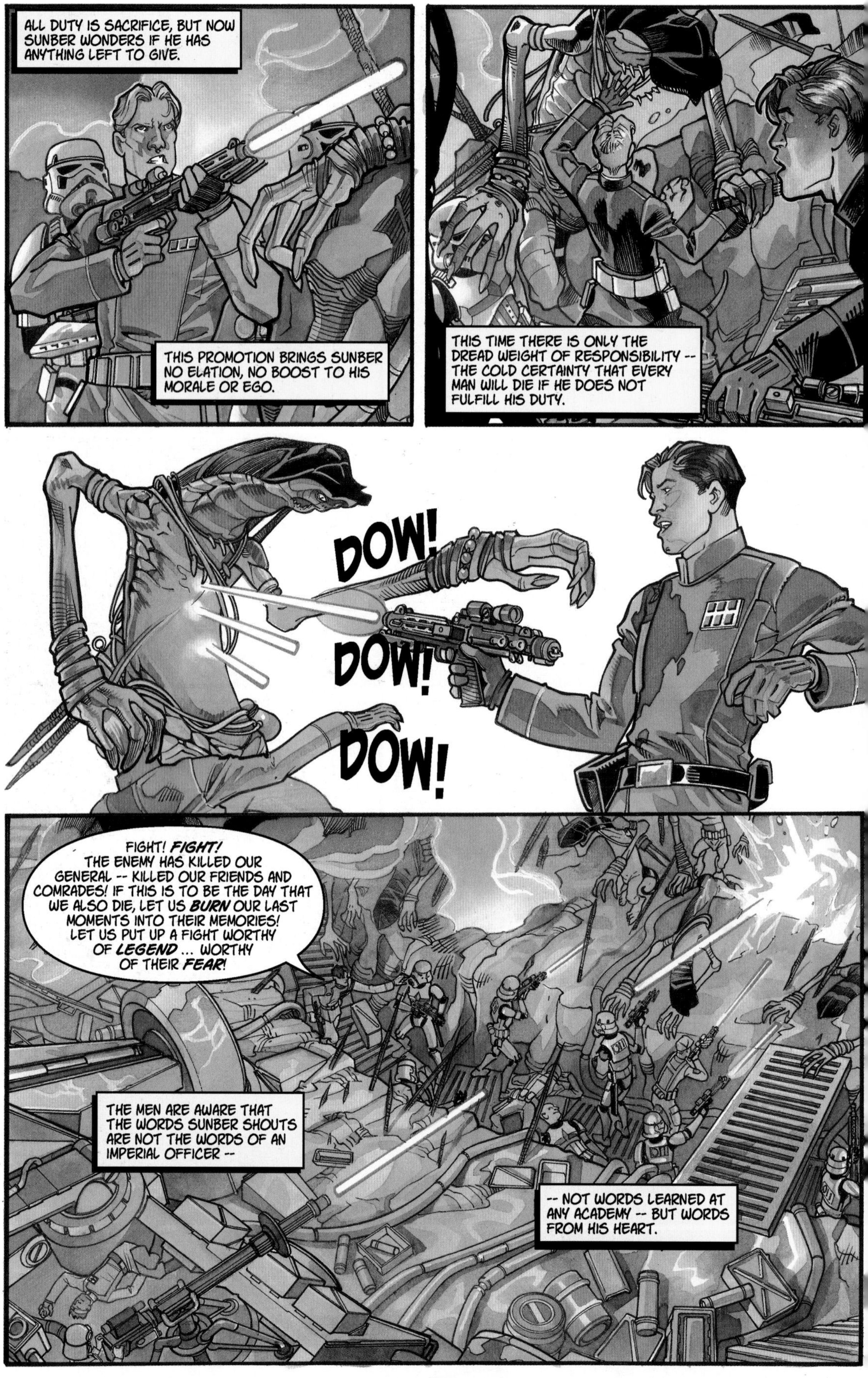
ALL DUTY IS SACRIFICE, BUT NOW SUNBER WONDERS IF HE HAS ANYTHING LEFT TO GIVE.
THIS PROMOTION BRINGS SUNBER NO ELATION, NO BOOST TO HIS MORALE OR EGO.
THIS TIME THERE IS ONLY THE DREAD WEIGHT OF RESPONSIBILITY -- THE COLD CERTAINTY THAT EVERY MAN WILL DIE IF HE DOES NOT FULFILL HIS DUTY.
DOW!
DOW!
DOW!
FIGHT! FIGHT! THE ENEMY HAS KILLED OUR GENERAL -- KILLED OUR FRIENDS AND COMRADES! IF THIS IS TO BE THE DAY THAT WE ALSO DIE, LET US BURN OUR LAST MOMENTS INTO THEIR MEMORIES! LET US PUT UP A FIGHT WORTHY OF LEGEND ... WORTHY OF THEIR FEAR!
THE MEN ARE AWARE THAT THE WORDS SUNBER SHOUTS ARE NOT THE WORDS OF AN IMPERIAL OFFICER --
-- NOT WORDS LEARNED AT ANY ACADEMY -- BUT WORDS FROM HIS HEART.

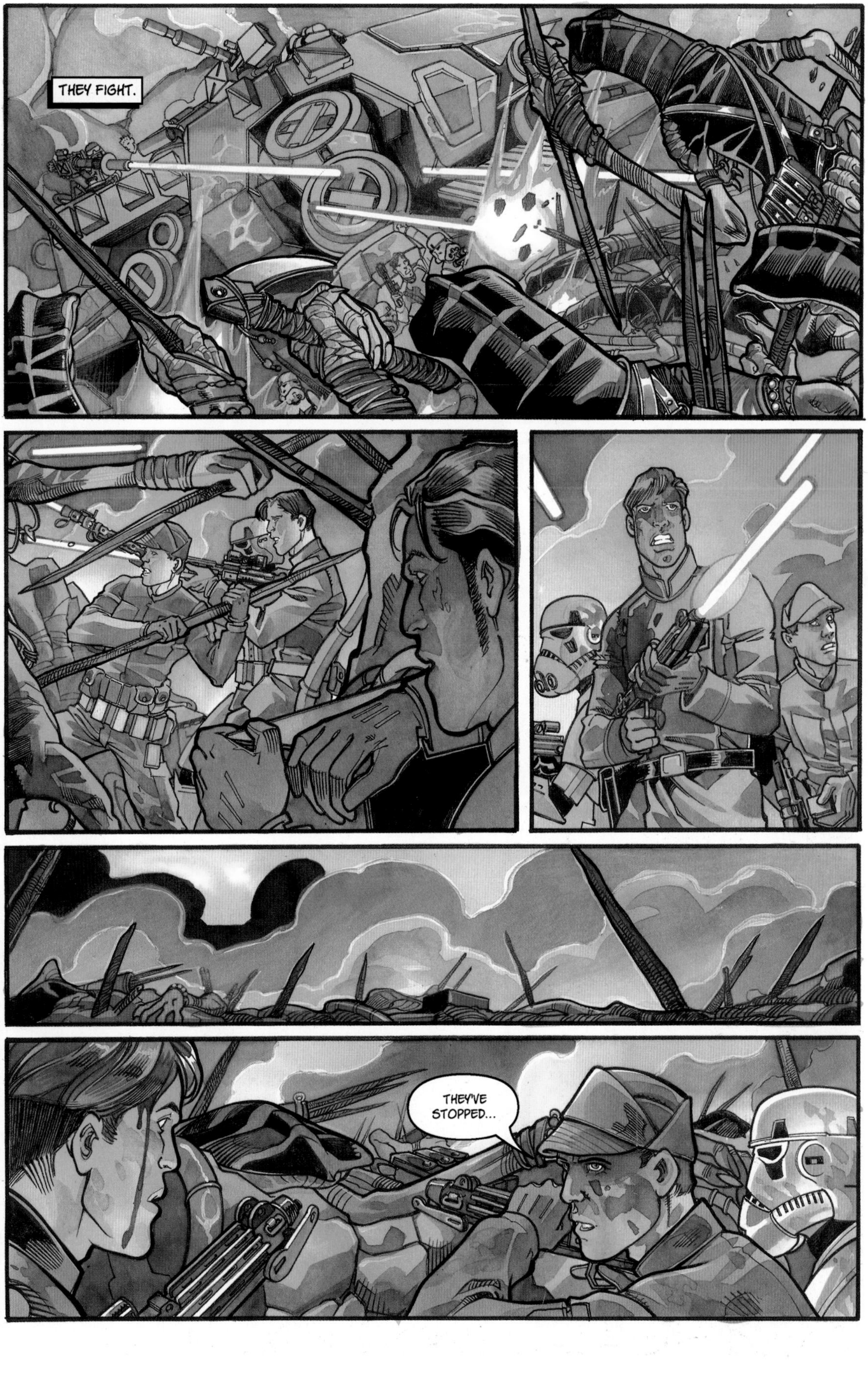
THEY FIGHT.
THEY'VE STOPPED...

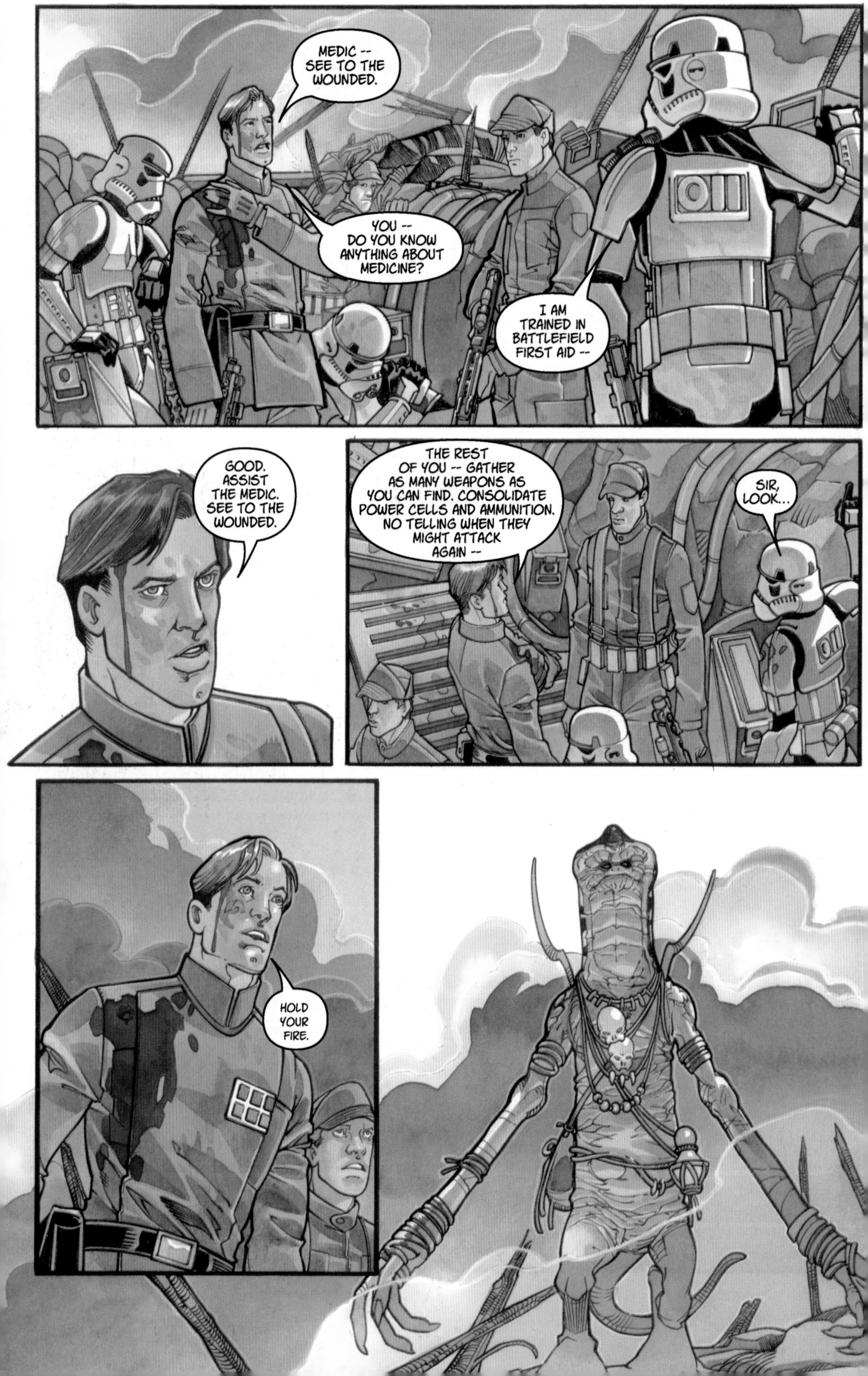
MEDIC -- SEE TO THE WOUNDED.
YOU -- DO YOU KNOW ANYTHING ABOUT MEDICINE?
I AM TRAINED IN BATTLEFIELD FIRST AID --
GOOD. ASSIST THE MEDIC. SEE TO THE WOUNDED.
THE REST OF YOU -- GATHER AS MANY WEAPONS AS YOU CAN FIND. CONSOLIDATE POWER CELLS AND AMMUNITION. NO TELLING WHEN THEY MIGHT ATTACK AGAIN --
SIR, LOOK...
HOLD YOUR FIRE.

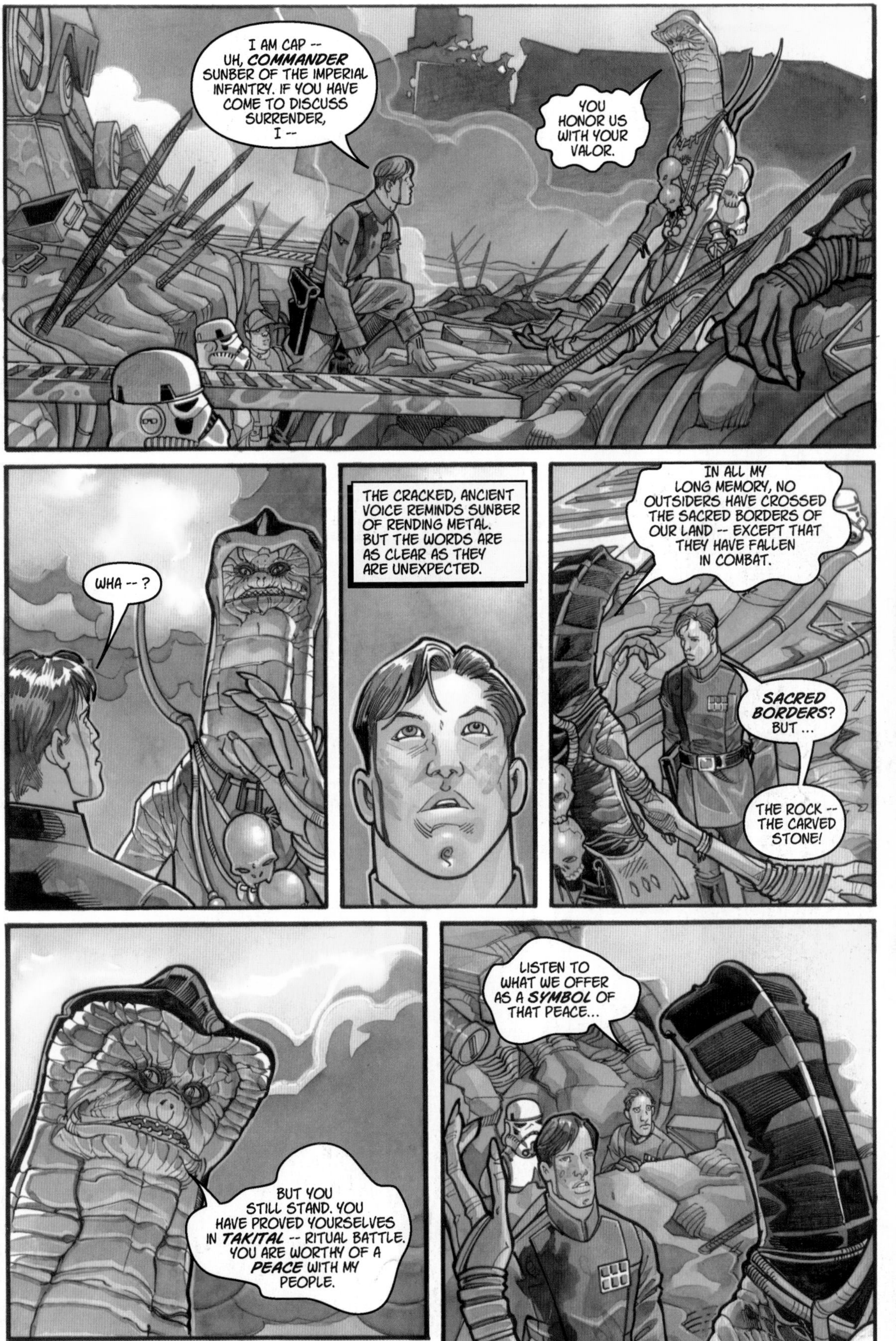
I AM CAP -- UH, COMMANDER SUNBER OF THE IMPERIAL INFANTRY. IF YOU HAVE COME TO DISCUSS SURRENDER, I --
YOU HONOR US WITH YOUR VALOR.
WHA -- ?
THE CRACKED, ANCIENT VOICE REMINDS SUNBER OF RENDING METAL. BUT THE WORDS ARE AS CLEAR AS THEY ARE UNEXPECTED.
IN ALL MY LONG MEMORY, NO OUTSIDERS HAVE CROSSED THE SACRED BORDERS OF OUR LAND -- EXCEPT THAT THEY HAVE FALLEN IN COMBAT.
SACRED BORDERS? BUT ...
THE ROCK -- THE CARVED STONE!
BUT YOU STILL STAND. YOU HAVE PROVED YOURSELVES IN TAKITAL -- RITUAL BATTLE. YOU ARE WORTHY OF A PEACE WITH MY PEOPLE.
LISTEN TO WHAT WE OFFER AS A SYMBOL OF THAT PEACE...

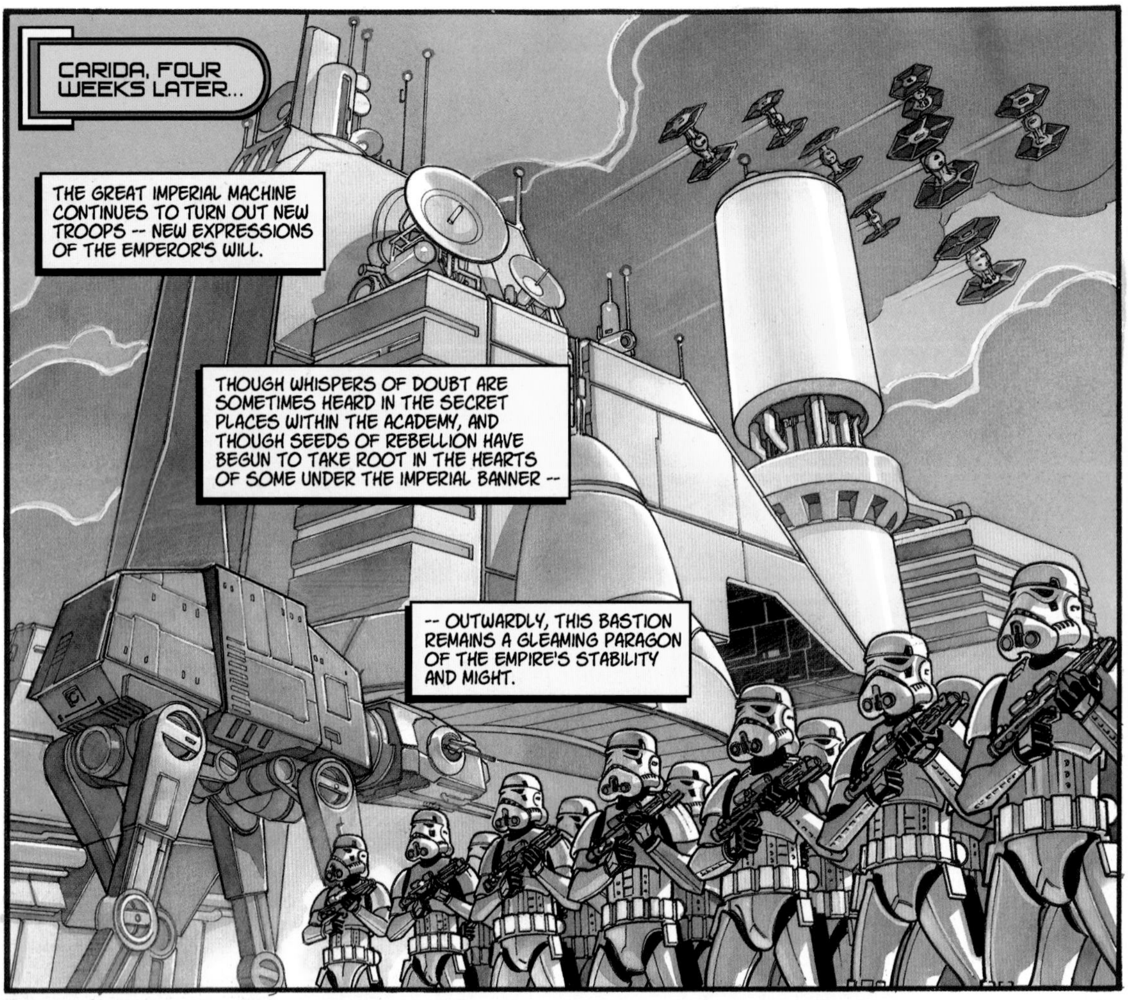
CARIDA, FOUR WEEKS LATER...
THE GREAT IMPERIAL MACHINE CONTINUES TO TURN OUT NEW TROOPS -- NEW EXPRESSIONS OF THE EMPEROR'S WILL.
THOUGH WHISPERS OF DOUBT ARE SOMETIMES HEARD IN THE SECRET PLACES WITHIN THE ACADEMY, AND THOUGH SEEDS OF REBELLION HAVE BEGUN TO TAKE ROOT IN THE HEARTS OF SOME UNDER THE IMPERIAL BANNER --
-- OUTWARDLY, THIS BASTION REMAINS A GLEAMING PARAGON OF THE EMPIRE'S STABILITY AND MIGHT.

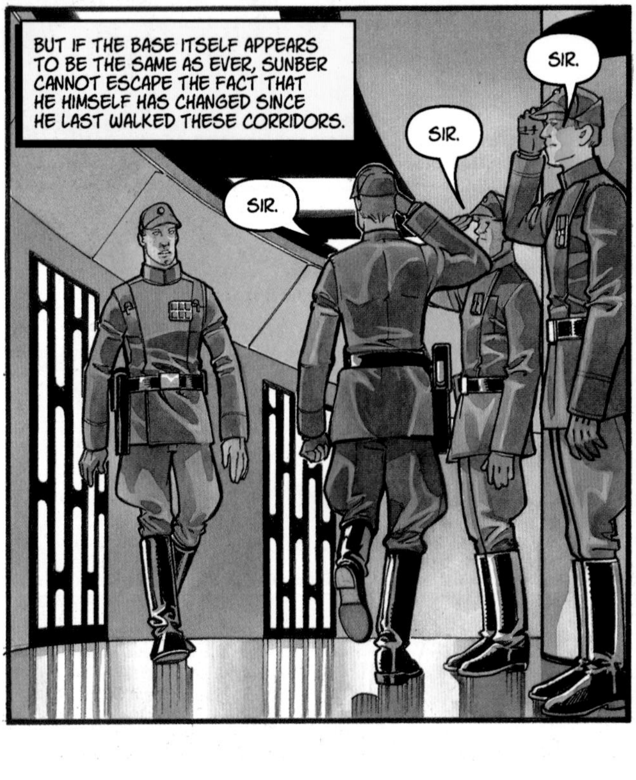
BUT IF THE BASE ITSELF APPEARS TO BE THE SAME AS EVER, SUNBER CANNOT ESCAPE THE FACT THAT HE HIMSELF HAS CHANGED SINCE HE LAST WALKED THESE CORRIDORS.
SIR.
SIR.
SIR.

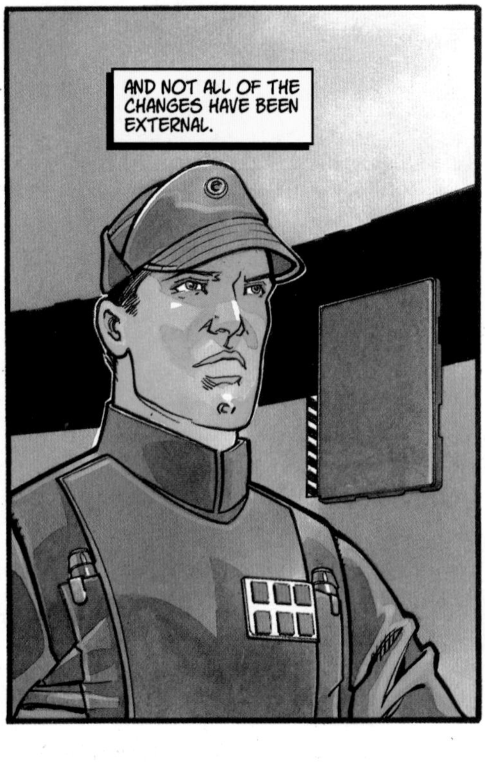
AND NOT ALL OF THE CHANGES HAVE BEEN EXTERNAL.

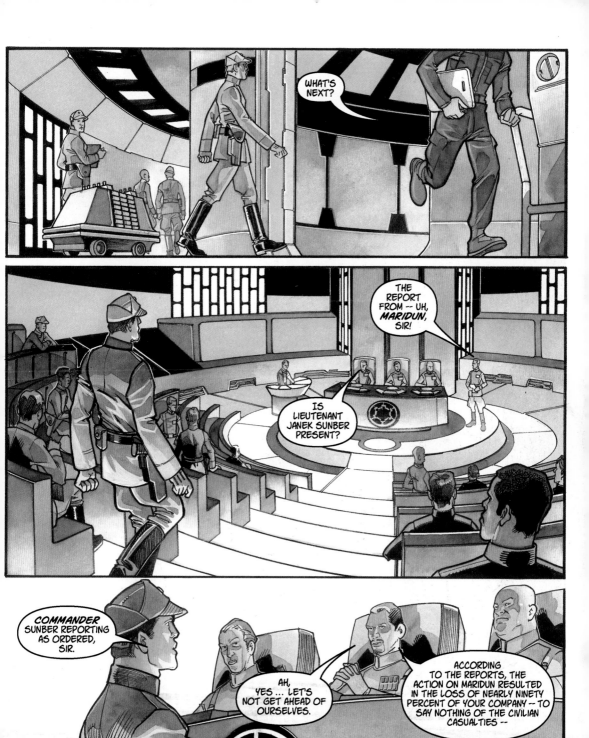

WHAT'S NEXT?

THE REPORT FROM -- UH, *MARIDUN*, SIR!

IS LIEUTENANT JANEK SUNBER PRESENT?

COMMANDER SUNBER REPORTING AS ORDERED, SIR.

AH, YES ... LET'S NOT GET AHEAD OF OURSELVES.

ACCORDING TO THE REPORTS, THE ACTION ON MARIDUN RESULTED IN THE LOSS OF NEARLY NINETY PERCENT OF YOUR COMPANY -- TO SAY NOTHING OF THE CIVILIAN CASUALTIES --

SIR, MY COMPANY WAS OUTNUMBERED *TEN-TO-ONE!* -- YET WE STILL MANAGED TO PREVAIL! AND THE CIVILIANS WERE KILLED *BEFORE* WE ARRIVED ON THE --

RELAX, LIEUTENANT. THIS IS MERELY A BOARD OF *REVIEW* -- NOT A *DISCIPLINARY TRIBUNAL.*

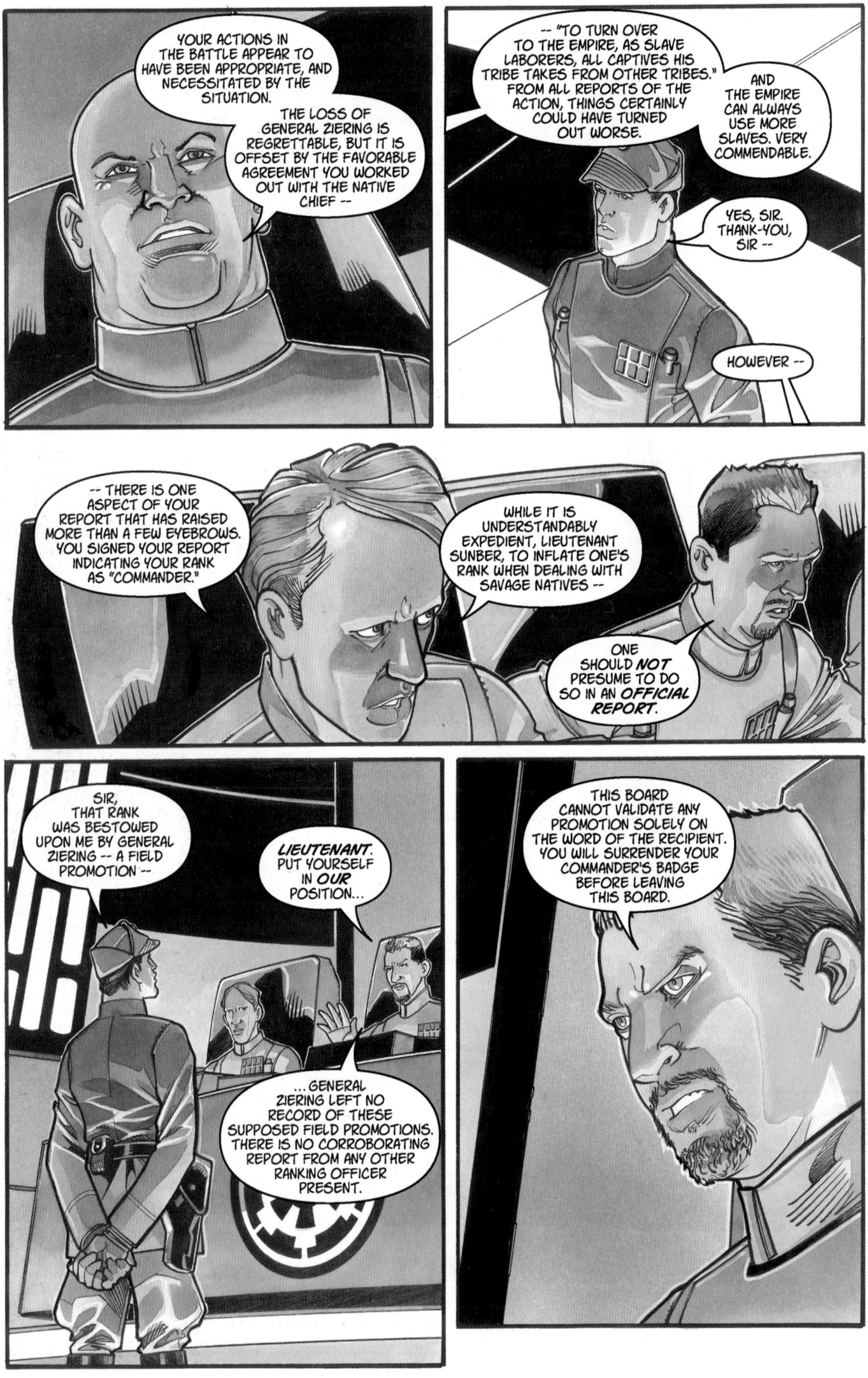

YOUR ACTIONS IN THE BATTLE APPEAR TO HAVE BEEN APPROPRIATE, AND NECESSITATED BY THE SITUATION.
THE LOSS OF GENERAL ZIERING IS REGRETTABLE, BUT IT IS OFFSET BY THE FAVORABLE AGREEMENT YOU WORKED OUT WITH THE NATIVE CHIEF --
-- "TO TURN OVER TO THE EMPIRE, AS SLAVE LABORERS, ALL CAPTIVES HIS TRIBE TAKES FROM OTHER TRIBES." FROM ALL REPORTS OF THE ACTION, THINGS CERTAINLY COULD HAVE TURNED OUT WORSE.
AND THE EMPIRE CAN ALWAYS USE MORE SLAVES. VERY COMMENDABLE.
YES, SIR. THANK-YOU, SIR --
HOWEVER --
-- THERE IS ONE ASPECT OF YOUR REPORT THAT HAS RAISED MORE THAN A FEW EYEBROWS. YOU SIGNED YOUR REPORT INDICATING YOUR RANK AS "COMMANDER."
WHILE IT IS UNDERSTANDABLY EXPEDIENT, LIEUTENANT SUNBER, TO INFLATE ONE'S RANK WHEN DEALING WITH SAVAGE NATIVES --
ONE SHOULD ***NOT*** PRESUME TO DO SO IN AN ***OFFICIAL REPORT***.
SIR, THAT RANK WAS BESTOWED UPON ME BY GENERAL ZIERING -- A FIELD PROMOTION --
LIEUTENANT. PUT YOURSELF IN ***OUR*** POSITION...
...GENERAL ZIERING LEFT NO RECORD OF THESE SUPPOSED FIELD PROMOTIONS. THERE IS NO CORROBORATING REPORT FROM ANY OTHER RANKING OFFICER PRESENT.
THIS BOARD CANNOT VALIDATE ANY PROMOTION SOLELY ON THE WORD OF THE RECIPIENT. YOU WILL SURRENDER YOUR COMMANDER'S BADGE BEFORE LEAVING THIS BOARD.

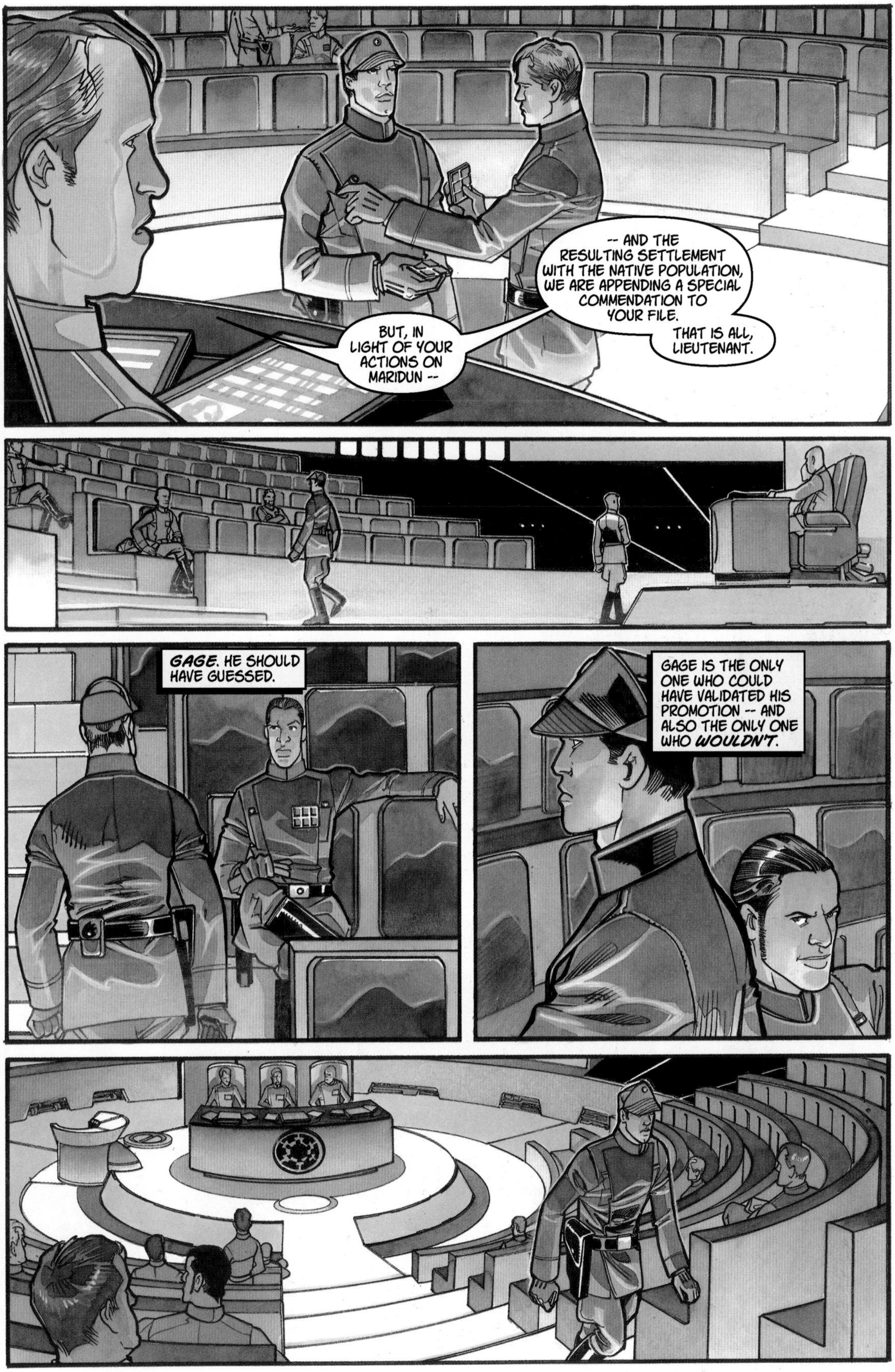
BUT, IN LIGHT OF YOUR ACTIONS ON MARIDUN --
-- AND THE RESULTING SETTLEMENT WITH THE NATIVE POPULATION, WE ARE APPENDING A SPECIAL COMMENDATION TO YOUR FILE.
THAT IS ALL, LIEUTENANT.
GAGE. HE SHOULD HAVE GUESSED.
GAGE IS THE ONLY ONE WHO COULD HAVE VALIDATED HIS PROMOTION -- AND ALSO THE ONLY ONE WHO WOULDN'T.

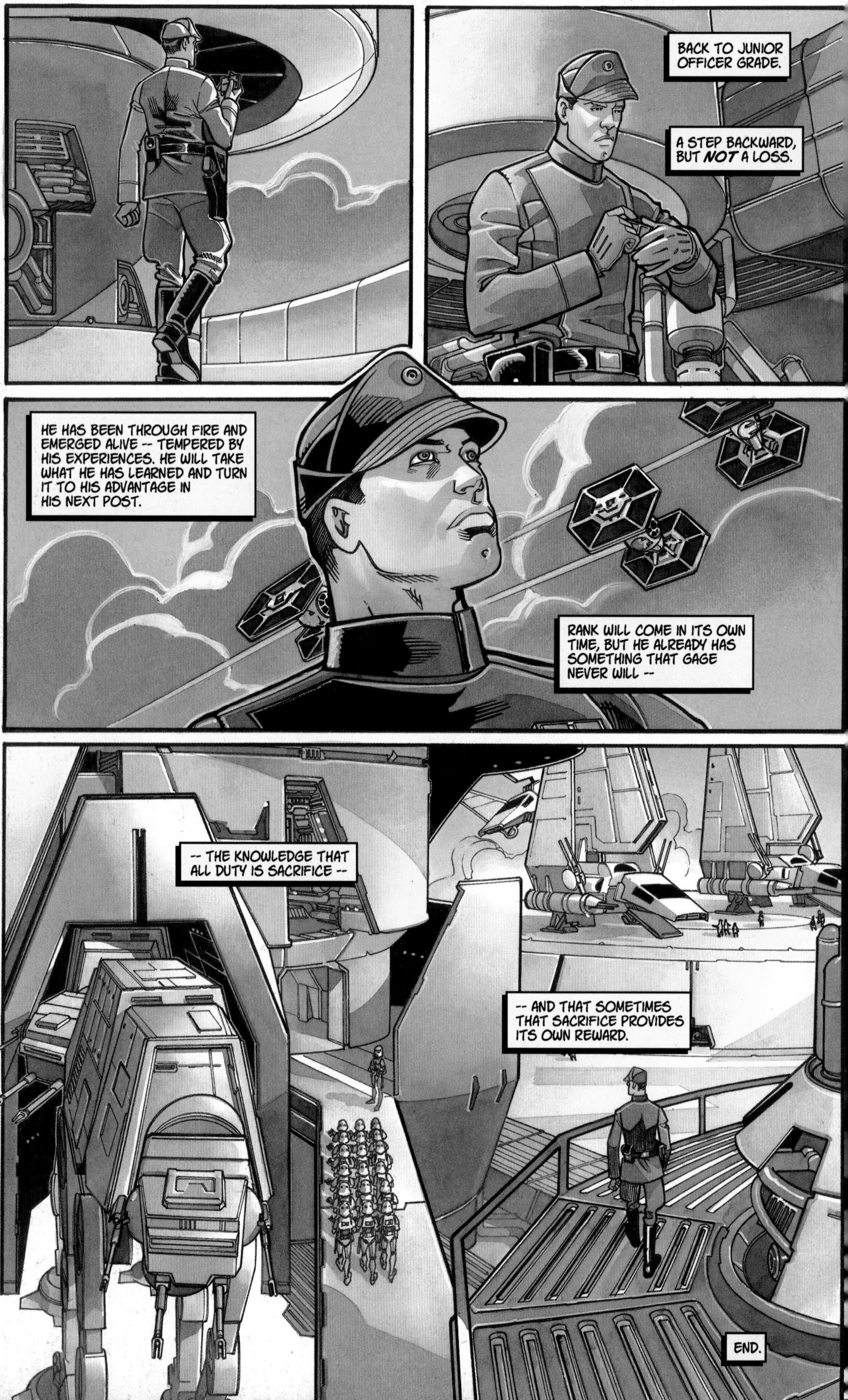
BACK TO JUNIOR OFFICER GRADE.
A STEP BACKWARD, BUT NOT A LOSS.
HE HAS BEEN THROUGH FIRE AND EMERGED ALIVE -- TEMPERED BY HIS EXPERIENCES. HE WILL TAKE WHAT HE HAS LEARNED AND TURN IT TO HIS ADVANTAGE IN HIS NEXT POST.
RANK WILL COME IN ITS OWN TIME, BUT HE ALREADY HAS SOMETHING THAT GAGE NEVER WILL --
-- THE KNOWLEDGE THAT ALL DUTY IS SACRIFICE --
-- AND THAT SOMETIMES THAT SACRIFICE PROVIDES ITS OWN REWARD.
END.

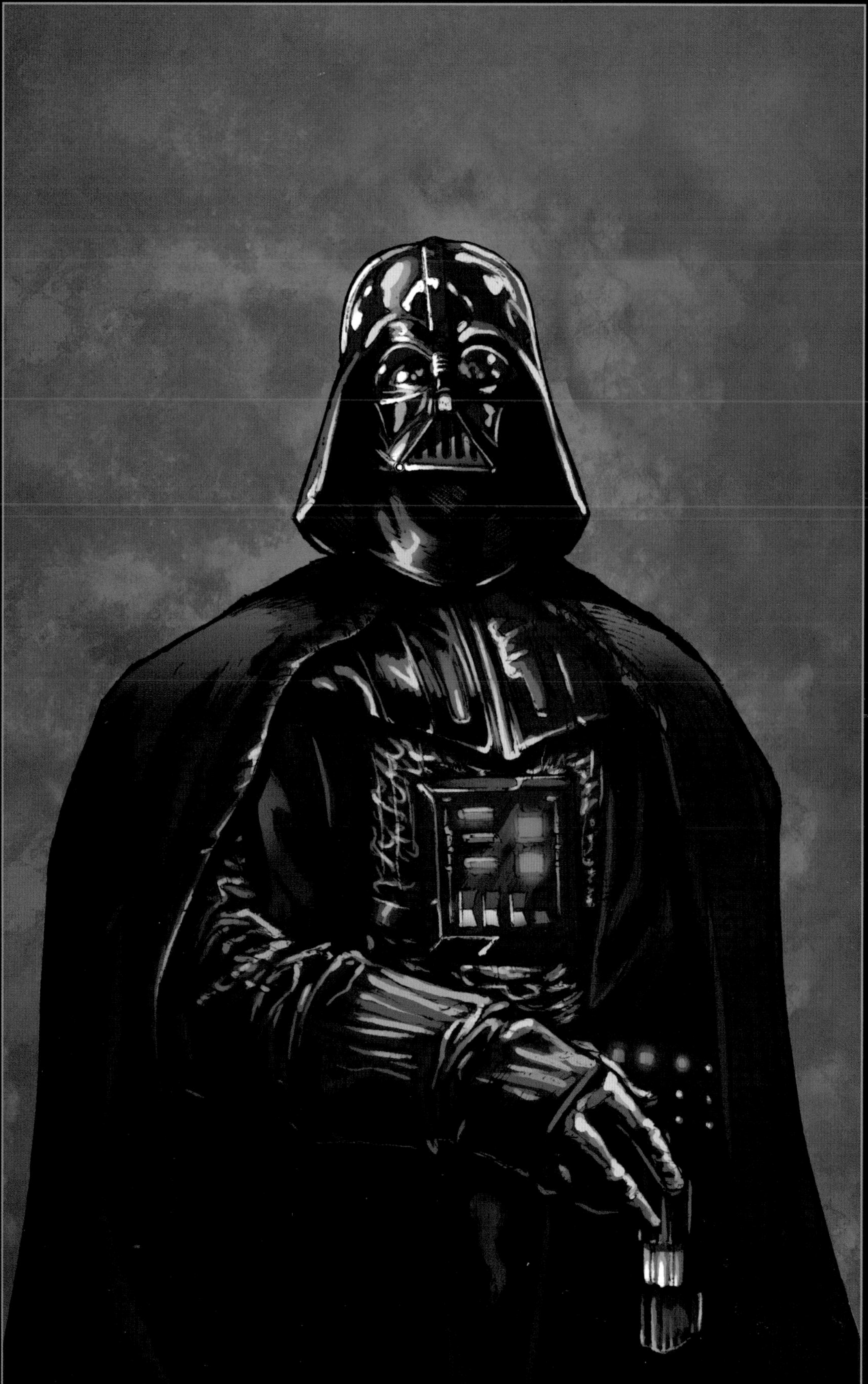

Brian Ching
Colors Michael Atiyeh

TARGET: VADER

Script RON MARZ
art BRIAN CHING
Colors MICHAEL ATIYEH

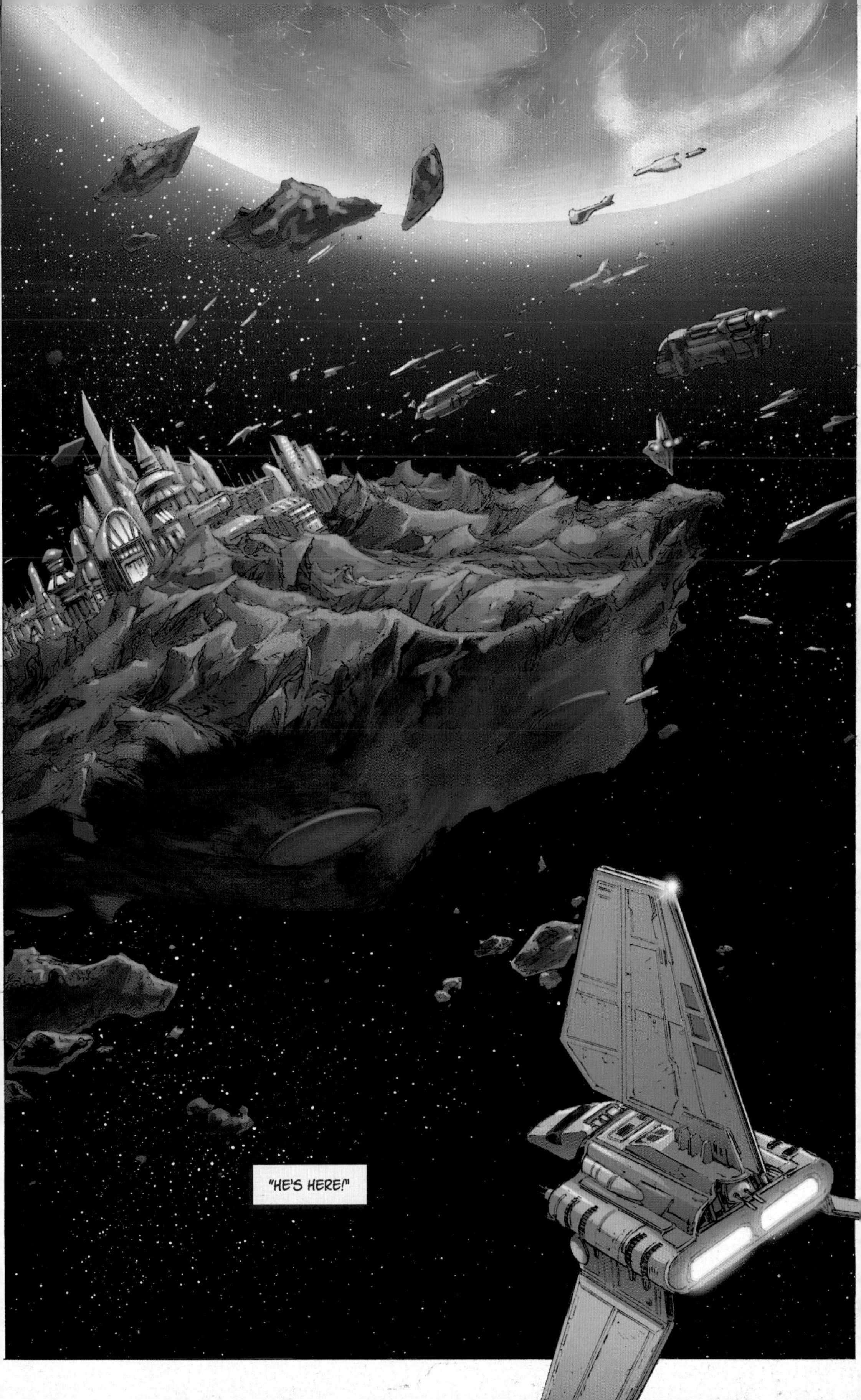
"HE'S HERE!"

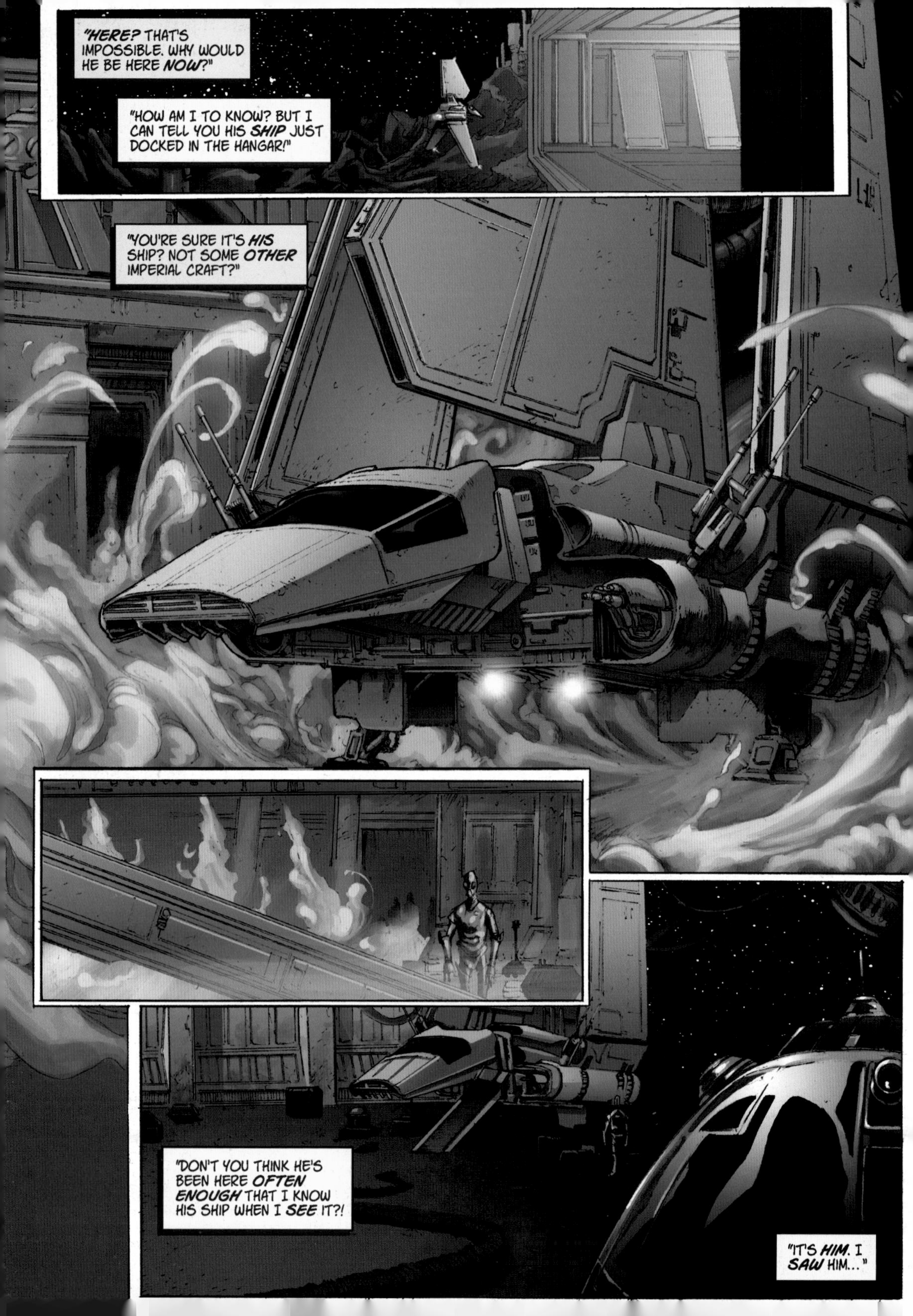
"HERE? THAT'S IMPOSSIBLE. WHY WOULD HE BE HERE NOW?"
"HOW AM I TO KNOW? BUT I CAN TELL YOU HIS SHIP JUST DOCKED IN THE HANGAR!"
"YOU'RE SURE IT'S HIS SHIP? NOT SOME OTHER IMPERIAL CRAFT?"
"DON'T YOU THINK HE'S BEEN HERE OFTEN ENOUGH THAT I KNOW HIS SHIP WHEN I SEE IT?!
"IT'S HIM. I SAW HIM..."

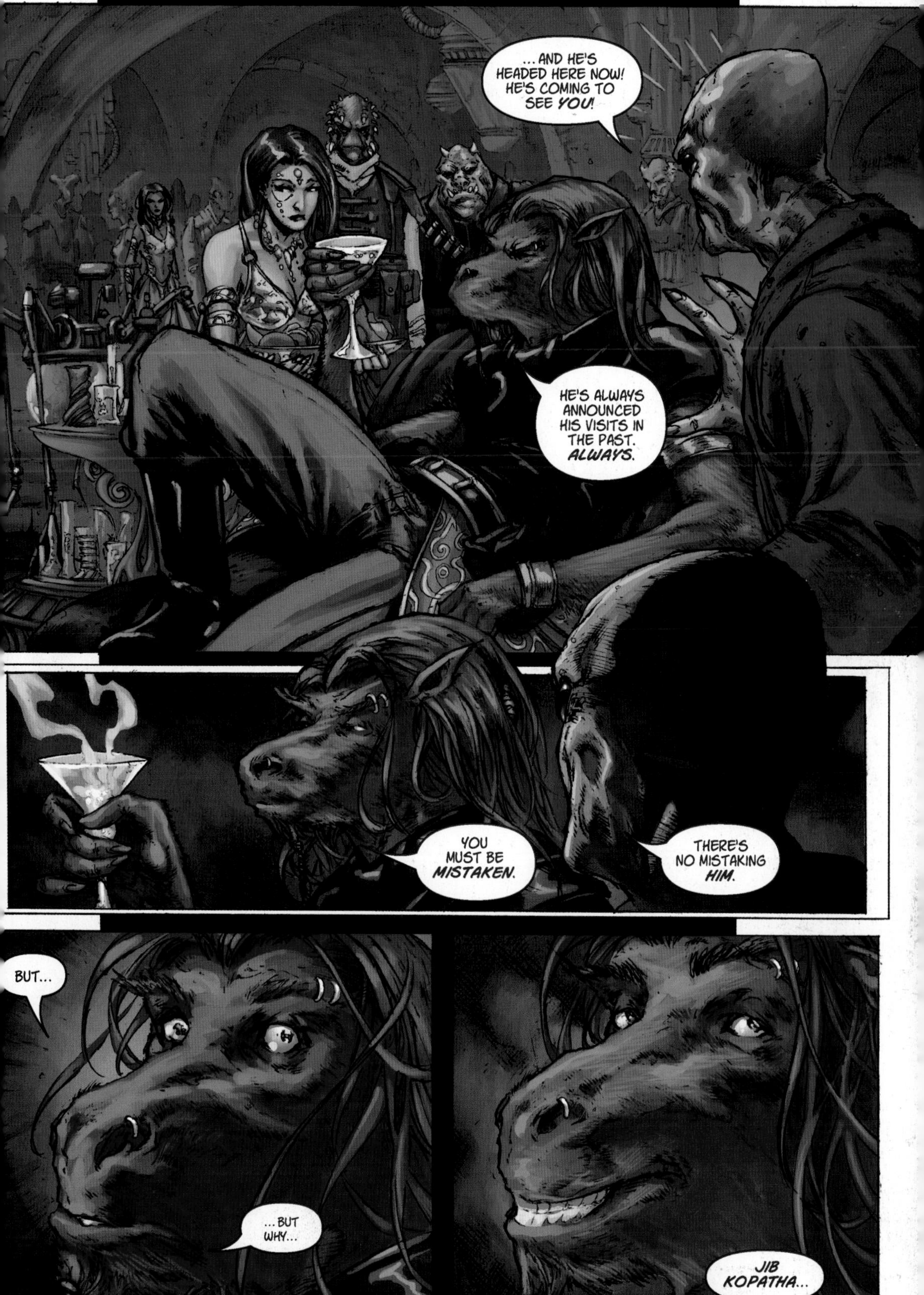

...AND HE'S HEADED HERE NOW! HE'S COMING TO SEE YOU!
HE'S ALWAYS ANNOUNCED HIS VISITS IN THE PAST. ALWAYS.
YOU MUST BE MISTAKEN.
THERE'S NO MISTAKING HIM.
BUT...
...BUT WHY...
JIB KOPATHA...

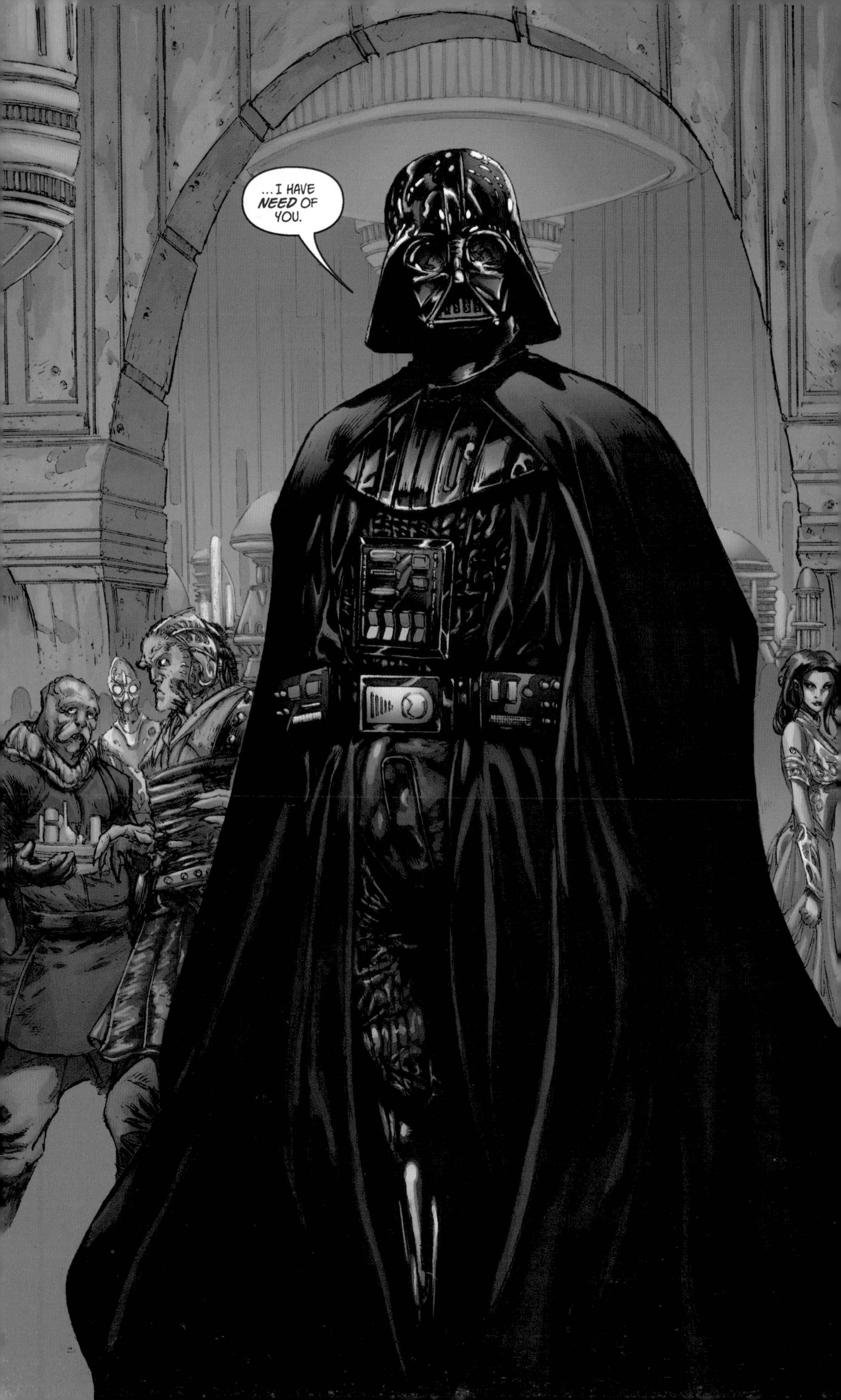
...I HAVE **NEED** OF YOU.

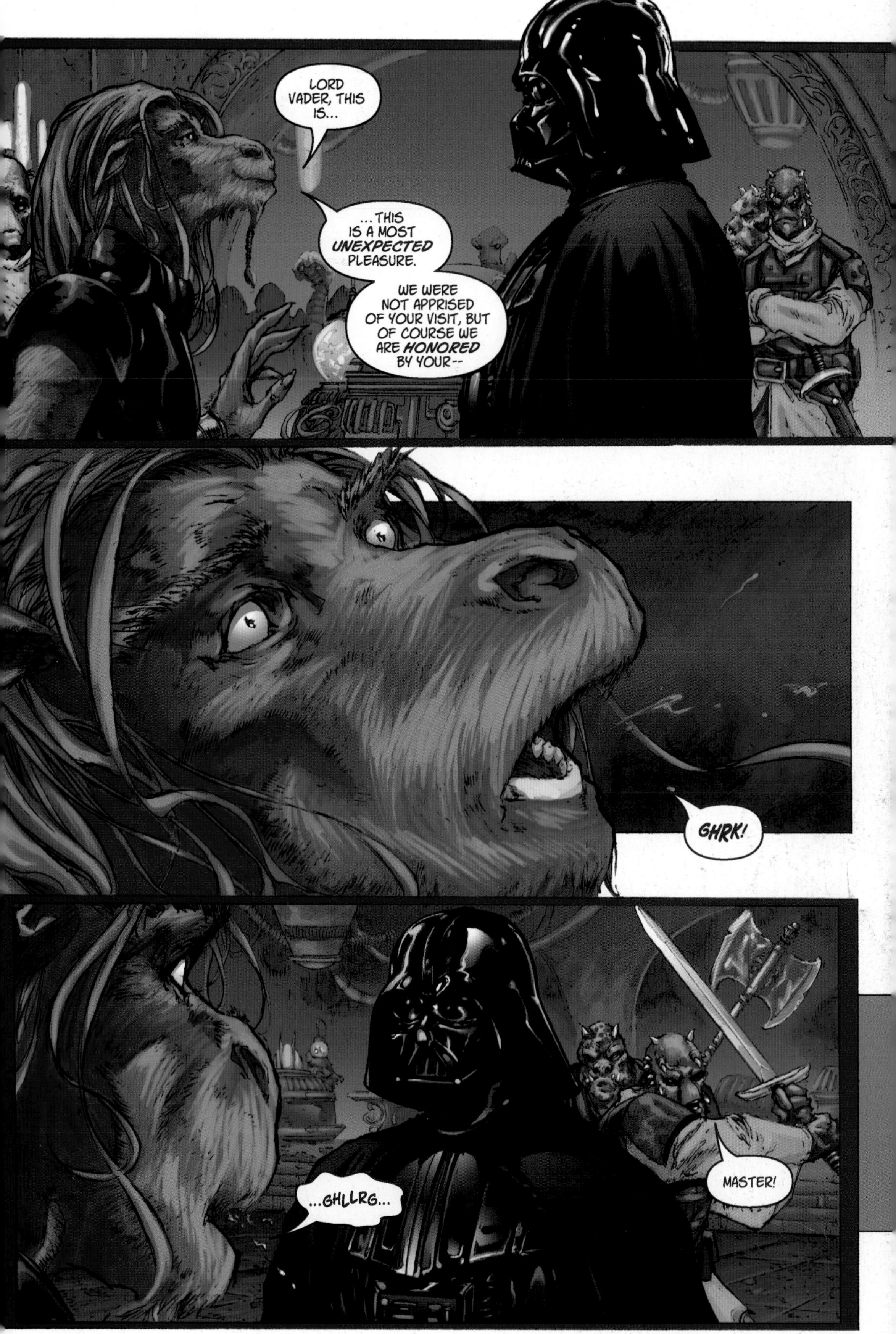
LORD VADER, THIS IS...
...THIS IS A MOST UNEXPECTED PLEASURE.
WE WERE NOT APPRISED OF YOUR VISIT, BUT OF COURSE WE ARE HONORED BY YOUR--
GHRK!
MASTER!
...GHLLRG...

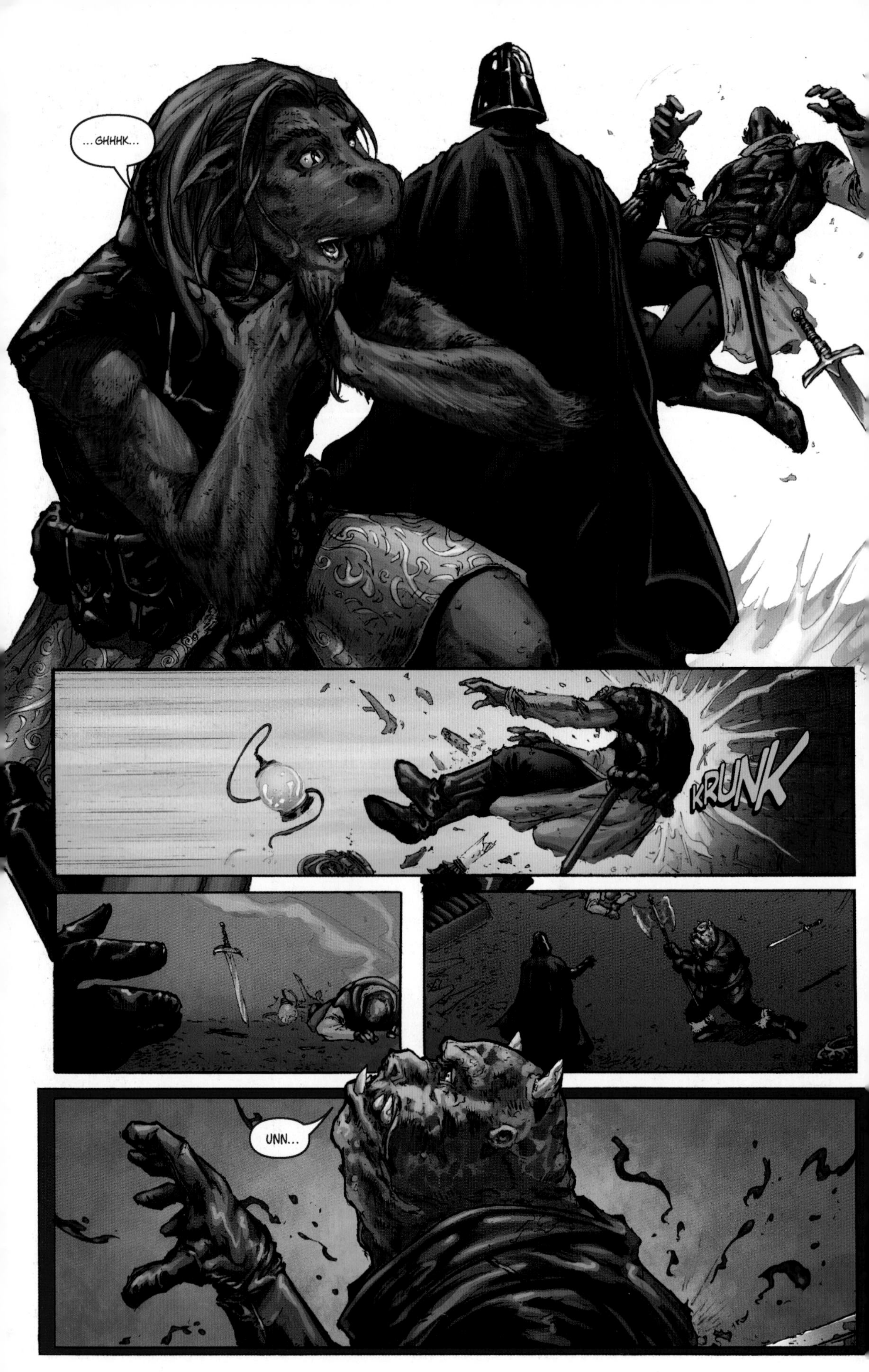
...GHHHK...
KRUNK
UNN...

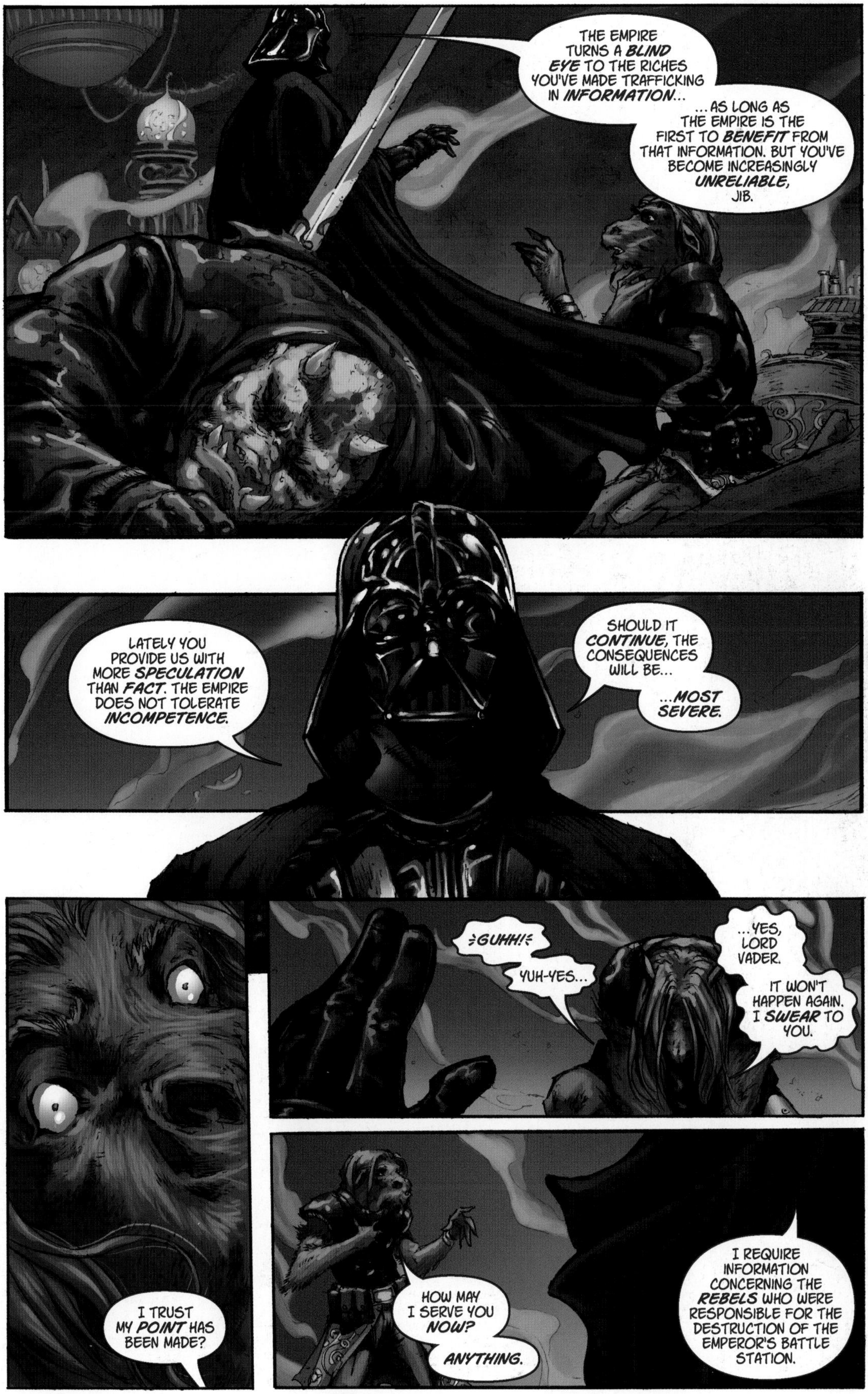
THE EMPIRE TURNS A BLIND EYE TO THE RICHES YOU'VE MADE TRAFFICKING IN INFORMATION...
...AS LONG AS THE EMPIRE IS THE FIRST TO BENEFIT FROM THAT INFORMATION. BUT YOU'VE BECOME INCREASINGLY UNRELIABLE, JIB.
LATELY YOU PROVIDE US WITH MORE SPECULATION THAN FACT. THE EMPIRE DOES NOT TOLERATE INCOMPETENCE.
SHOULD IT CONTINUE, THE CONSEQUENCES WILL BE...
...MOST SEVERE.
I TRUST MY POINT HAS BEEN MADE?
GUHH!
YUH-YES...
...YES, LORD VADER.
IT WON'T HAPPEN AGAIN. I SWEAR TO YOU.
HOW MAY I SERVE YOU NOW?
ANYTHING.
I REQUIRE INFORMATION CONCERNING THE REBELS WHO WERE RESPONSIBLE FOR THE DESTRUCTION OF THE EMPEROR'S BATTLE STATION.

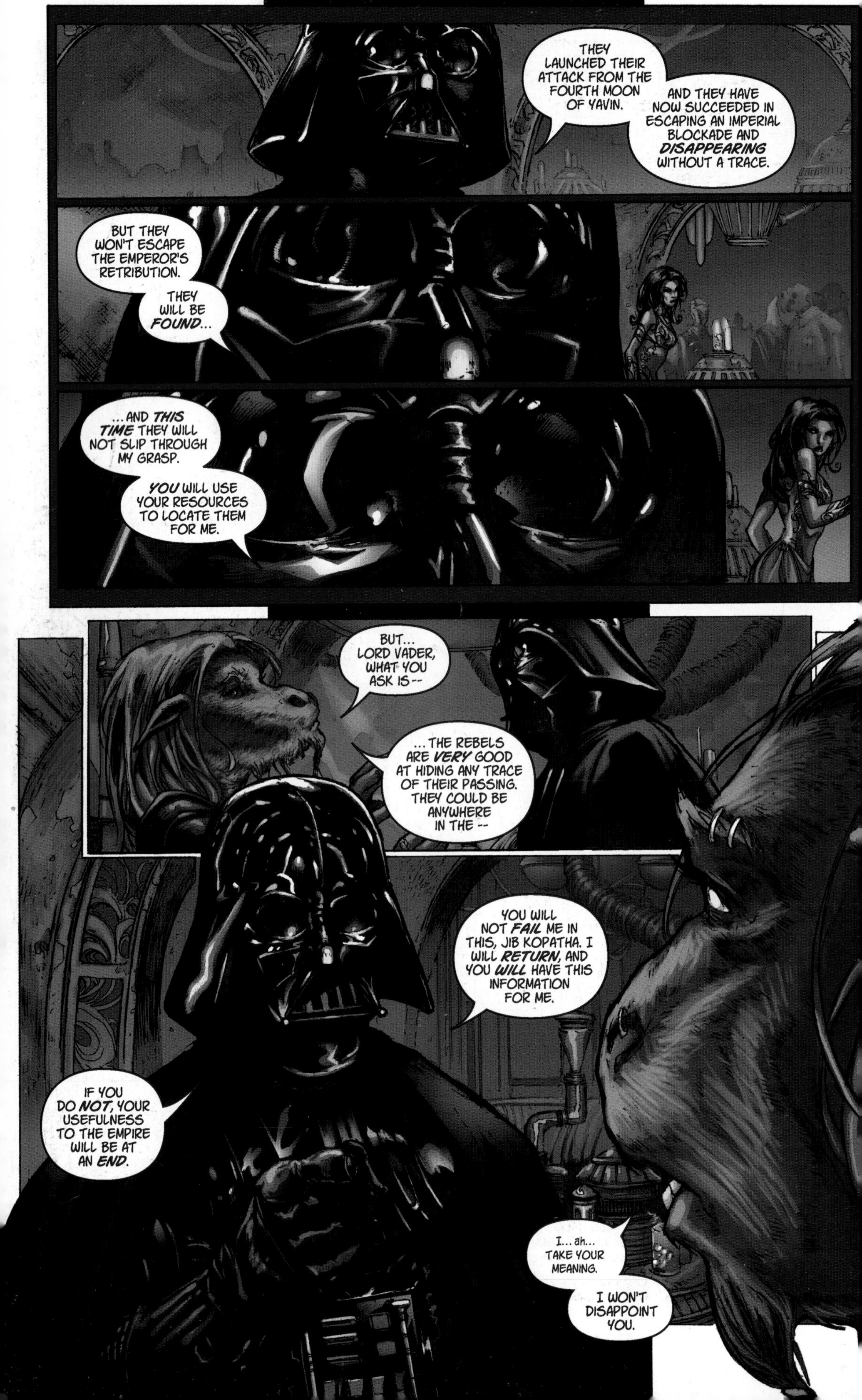
THEY LAUNCHED THEIR ATTACK FROM THE FOURTH MOON OF YAVIN.
AND THEY HAVE NOW SUCCEEDED IN ESCAPING AN IMPERIAL BLOCKADE AND *DISAPPEARING* WITHOUT A TRACE.
BUT THEY WON'T ESCAPE THE EMPEROR'S RETRIBUTION.
THEY WILL BE *FOUND*...
...AND *THIS TIME* THEY WILL NOT SLIP THROUGH MY GRASP.
YOU WILL USE YOUR RESOURCES TO LOCATE THEM FOR ME.
BUT... LORD VADER, WHAT YOU ASK IS --
... THE REBELS ARE *VERY* GOOD AT HIDING ANY TRACE OF THEIR PASSING. THEY COULD BE ANYWHERE IN THE --
YOU WILL NOT *FAIL* ME IN THIS, JIB KOPATHA. I WILL *RETURN*, AND YOU *WILL* HAVE THIS INFORMATION FOR ME.
IF YOU DO *NOT*, YOUR USEFULNESS TO THE EMPIRE WILL BE AT AN *END*.
I... ah... TAKE YOUR MEANING.
I WON'T DISAPPOINT YOU.

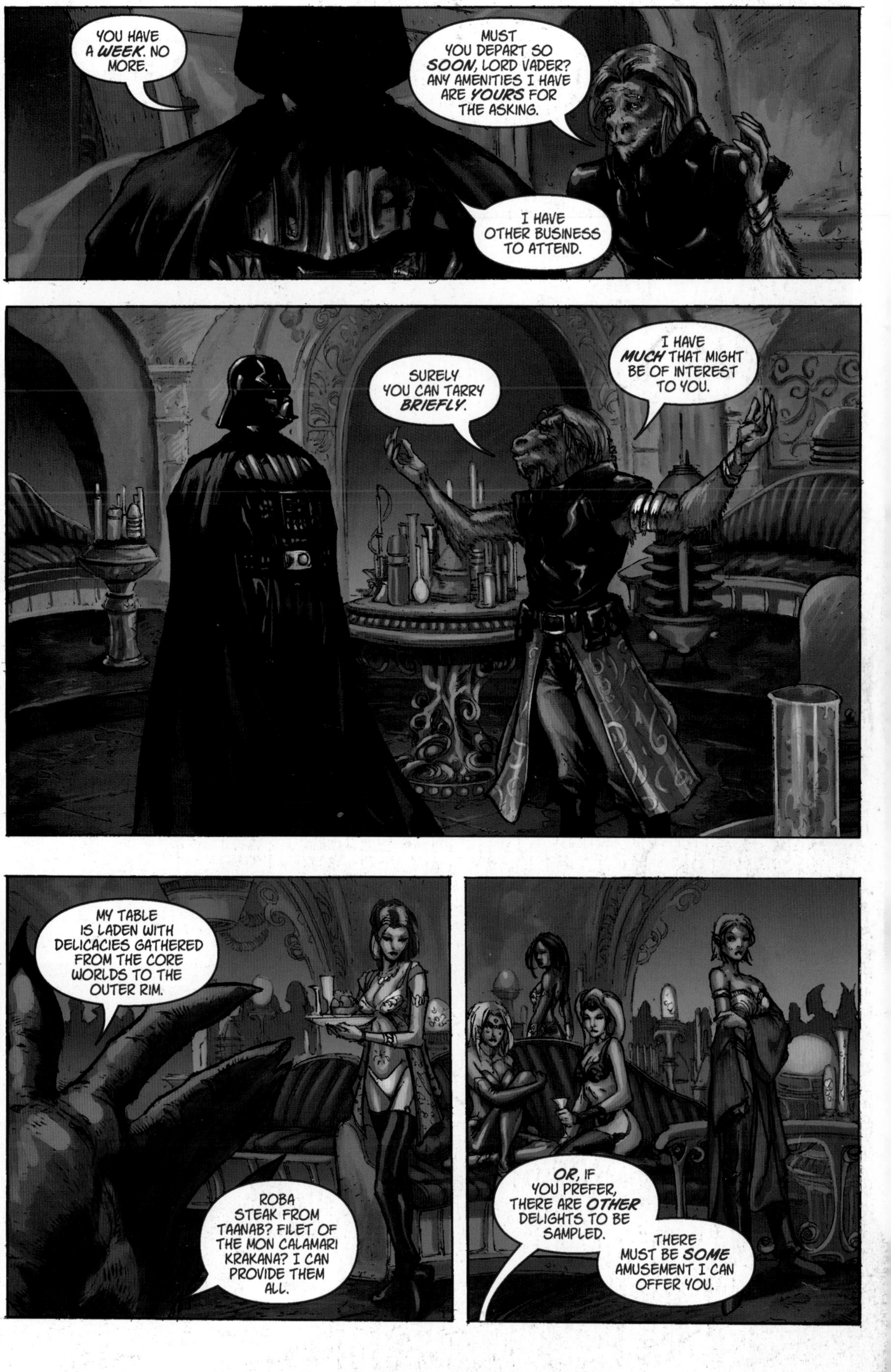
YOU HAVE A WEEK. NO MORE.
MUST YOU DEPART SO SOON, LORD VADER? ANY AMENITIES I HAVE ARE YOURS FOR THE ASKING.
I HAVE OTHER BUSINESS TO ATTEND.
SURELY YOU CAN TARRY BRIEFLY.
I HAVE MUCH THAT MIGHT BE OF INTEREST TO YOU.
MY TABLE IS LADEN WITH DELICACIES GATHERED FROM THE CORE WORLDS TO THE OUTER RIM.
ROBA STEAK FROM TAANAB? FILET OF THE MON CALAMARI KRAKANA? I CAN PROVIDE THEM ALL.
OR, IF YOU PREFER, THERE ARE OTHER DELIGHTS TO BE SAMPLED.
THERE MUST BE SOME AMUSEMENT I CAN OFFER YOU.

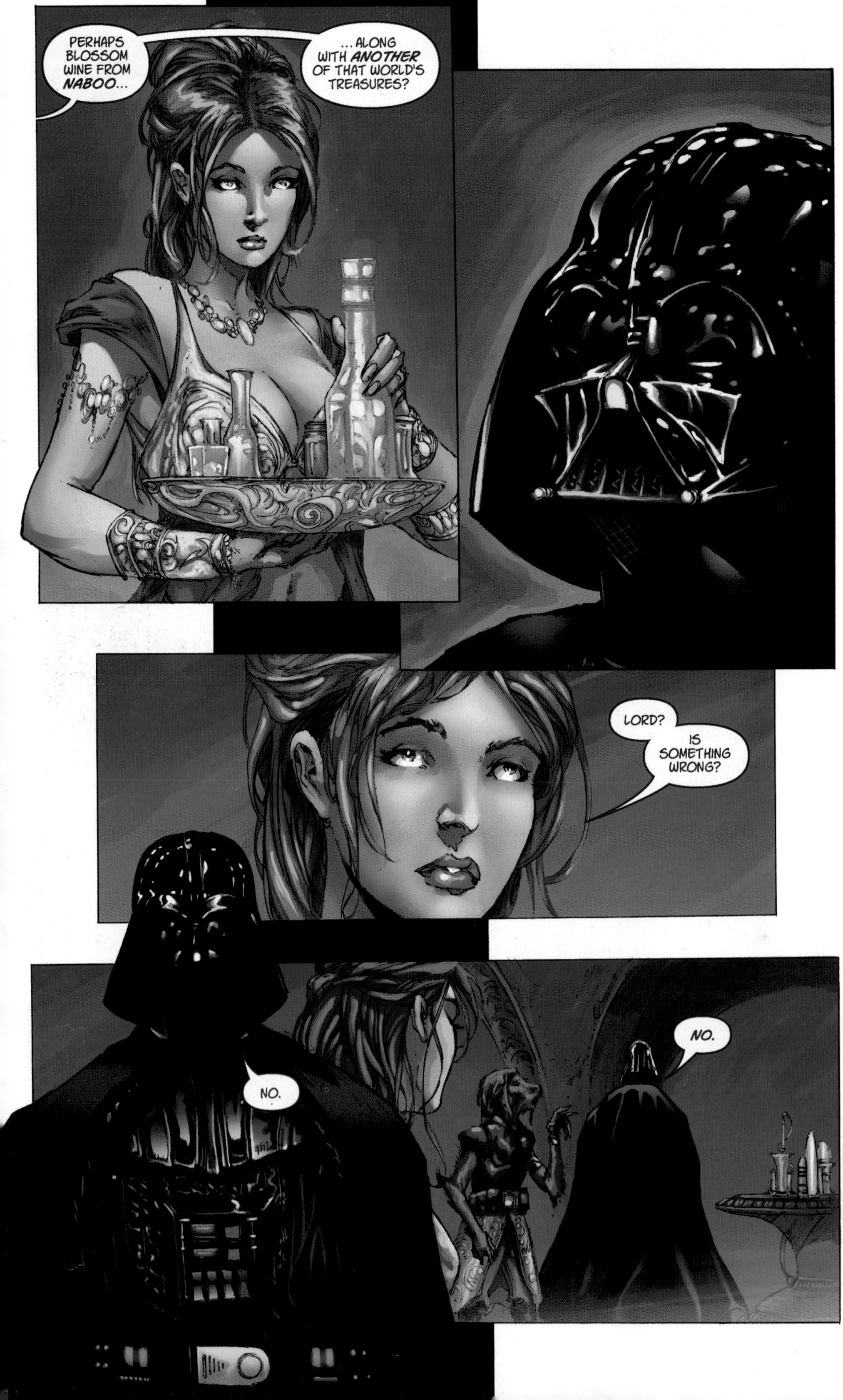
PERHAPS BLOSSOM WINE FROM NABOO...
...ALONG WITH ANOTHER OF THAT WORLD'S TREASURES?
LORD?
IS SOMETHING WRONG?
NO.
NO.

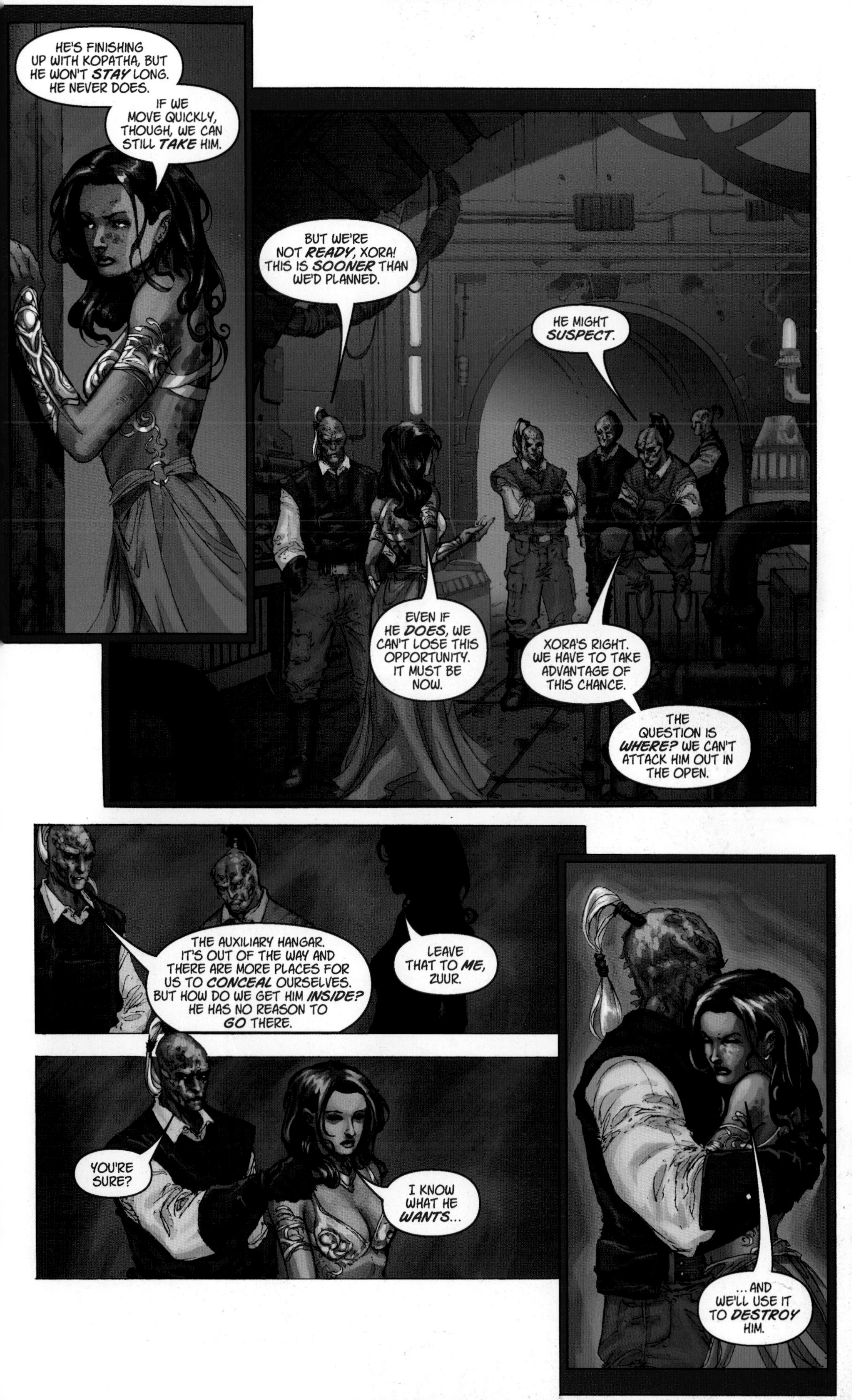
HE'S FINISHING UP WITH KOPATHA, BUT HE WON'T *STAY* LONG. HE NEVER DOES.
IF WE MOVE QUICKLY, THOUGH, WE CAN STILL *TAKE* HIM.
BUT WE'RE NOT *READY*, XORA! THIS IS *SOONER* THAN WE'D PLANNED.
HE MIGHT *SUSPECT*.
EVEN IF HE *DOES*, WE CAN'T LOSE THIS OPPORTUNITY. IT MUST BE NOW.
XORA'S RIGHT. WE HAVE TO TAKE ADVANTAGE OF THIS CHANCE.
THE QUESTION IS *WHERE?* WE CAN'T ATTACK HIM OUT IN THE OPEN.
THE AUXILIARY HANGAR. IT'S OUT OF THE WAY AND THERE ARE MORE PLACES FOR US TO *CONCEAL* OURSELVES. BUT HOW DO WE GET HIM *INSIDE?* HE HAS NO REASON TO *GO* THERE.
LEAVE THAT TO *ME*, ZUUR.
YOU'RE SURE?
I KNOW WHAT HE *WANTS*...
...AND WE'LL USE IT TO *DESTROY* HIM.

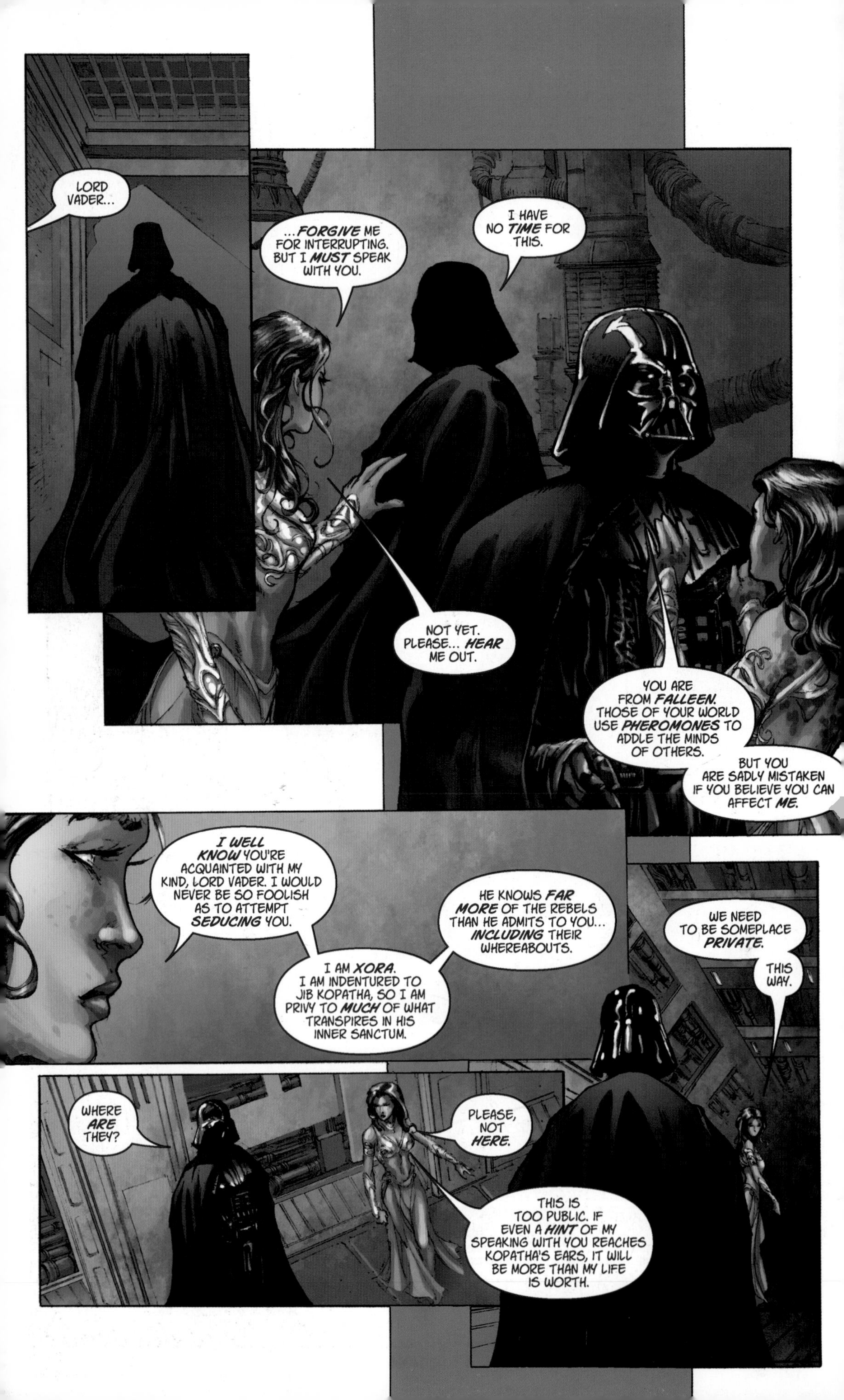
LORD VADER...
...FORGIVE ME FOR INTERRUPTING. BUT I MUST SPEAK WITH YOU.
I HAVE NO TIME FOR THIS.
NOT YET. PLEASE... HEAR ME OUT.
YOU ARE FROM FALLEEN. THOSE OF YOUR WORLD USE PHEROMONES TO ADDLE THE MINDS OF OTHERS.
BUT YOU ARE SADLY MISTAKEN IF YOU BELIEVE YOU CAN AFFECT ME.
I WELL KNOW YOU'RE ACQUAINTED WITH MY KIND, LORD VADER. I WOULD NEVER BE SO FOOLISH AS TO ATTEMPT SEDUCING YOU.
I AM XORA. I AM INDENTURED TO JIB KOPATHA, SO I AM PRIVY TO MUCH OF WHAT TRANSPIRES IN HIS INNER SANCTUM.
HE KNOWS FAR MORE OF THE REBELS THAN HE ADMITS TO YOU... INCLUDING THEIR WHEREABOUTS.
WE NEED TO BE SOMEPLACE PRIVATE.
THIS WAY.
WHERE ARE THEY?
PLEASE, NOT HERE.
THIS IS TOO PUBLIC. IF EVEN A HINT OF MY SPEAKING WITH YOU REACHES KOPATHA'S EARS, IT WILL BE MORE THAN MY LIFE IS WORTH.

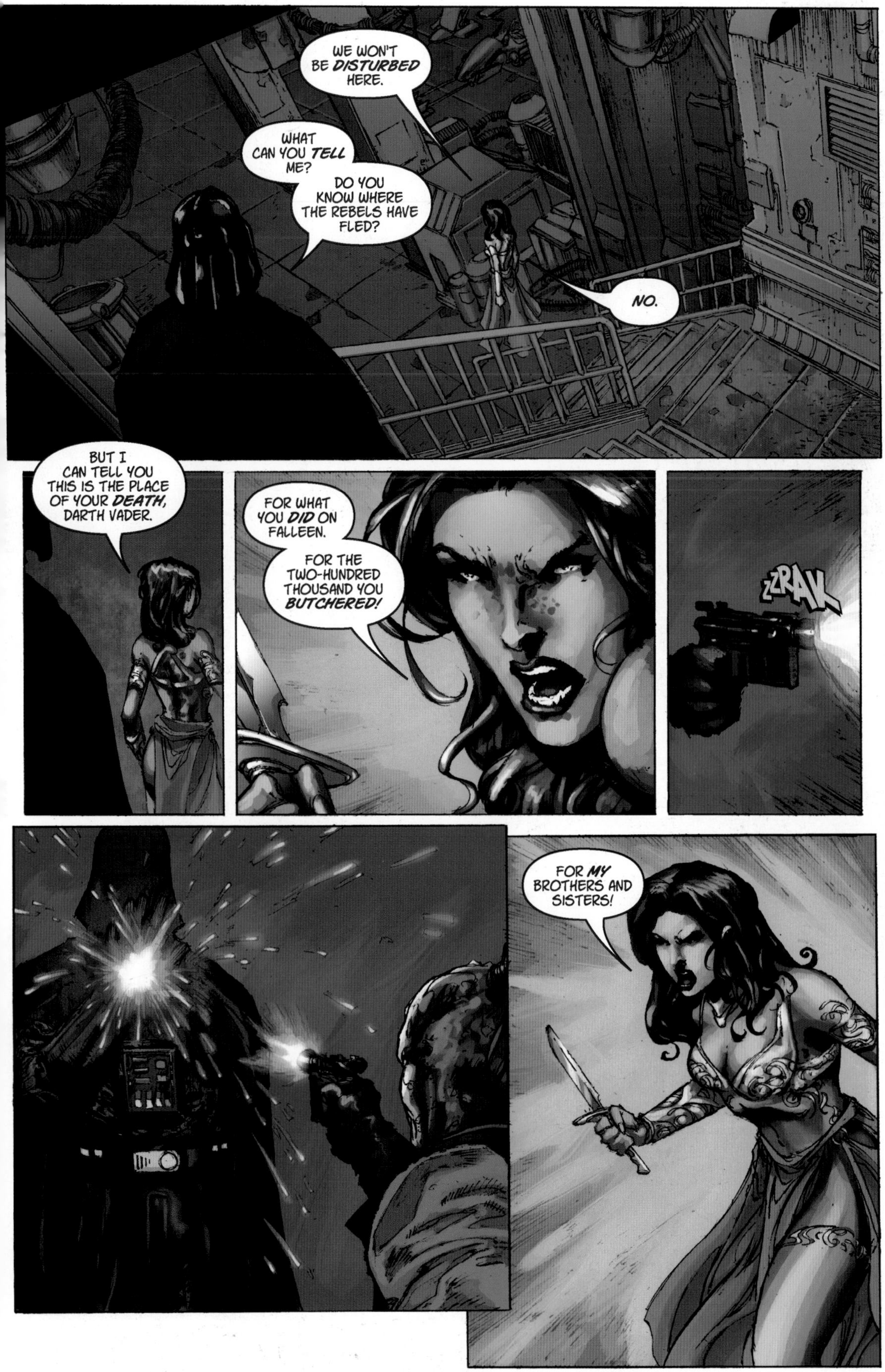
WE WON'T BE DISTURBED HERE.
WHAT CAN YOU TELL ME?
DO YOU KNOW WHERE THE REBELS HAVE FLED?
NO.
BUT I CAN TELL YOU THIS IS THE PLACE OF YOUR DEATH, DARTH VADER.
FOR WHAT YOU DID ON FALLEEN.
FOR THE TWO-HUNDRED THOUSAND YOU BUTCHERED!
ZZRAK
FOR MY BROTHERS AND SISTERS!

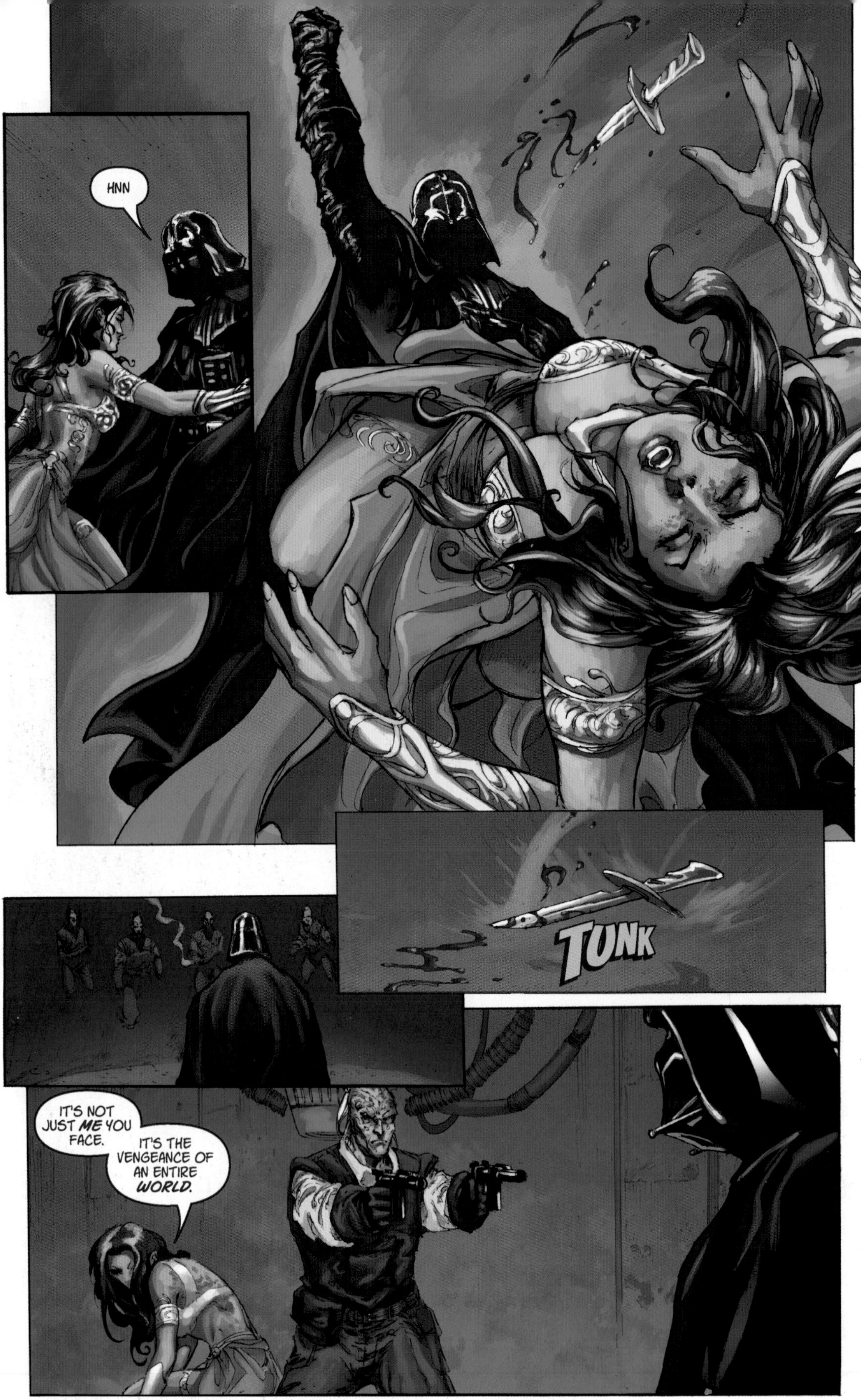
HNN
TUNK
IT'S NOT JUST *ME* YOU FACE.
IT'S THE VENGEANCE OF AN ENTIRE *WORLD*.

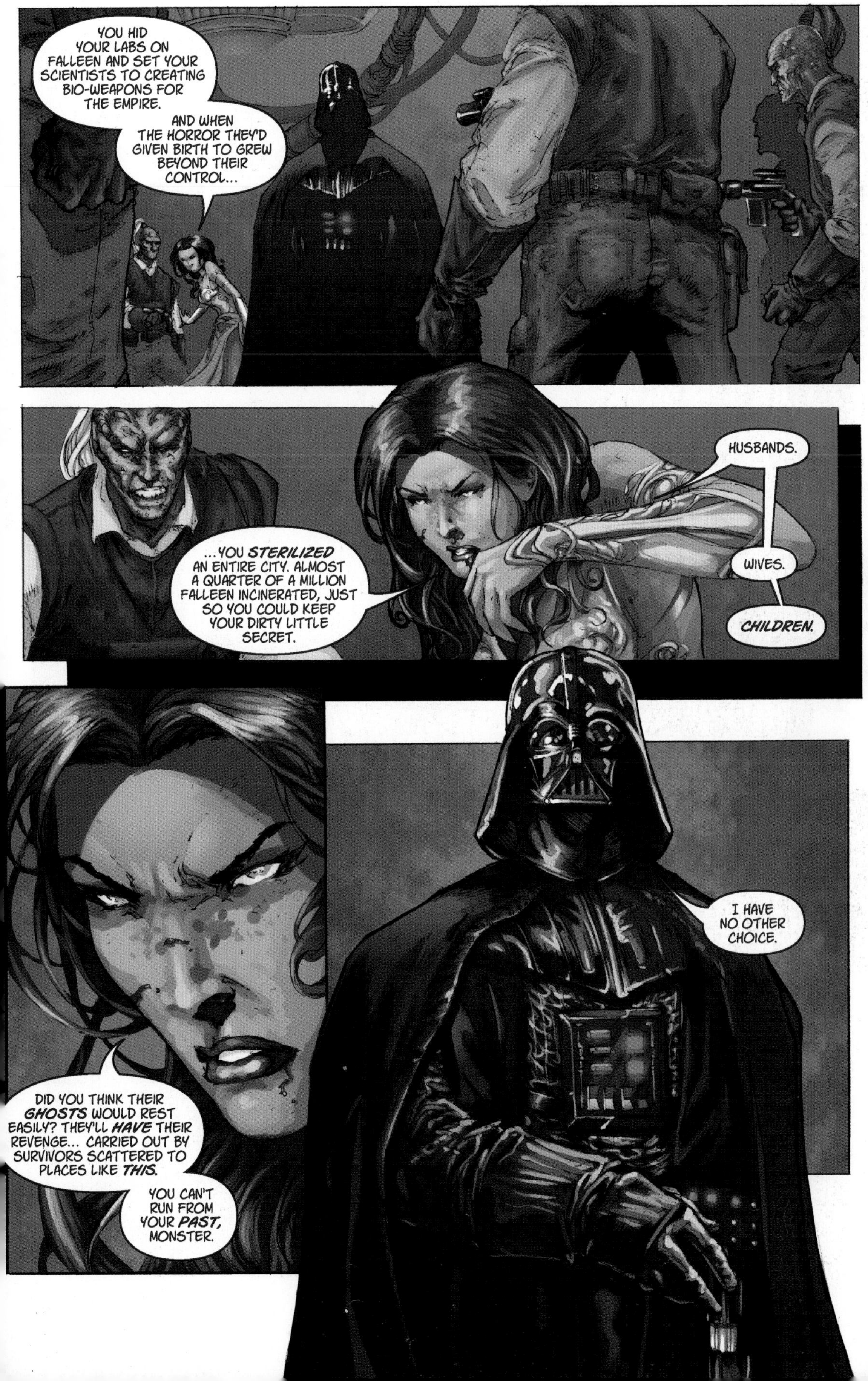
YOU HID YOUR LABS ON FALLEEN AND SET YOUR SCIENTISTS TO CREATING BIO-WEAPONS FOR THE EMPIRE.
AND WHEN THE HORROR THEY'D GIVEN BIRTH TO GREW BEYOND THEIR CONTROL...
...YOU *STERILIZED* AN ENTIRE CITY. ALMOST A QUARTER OF A MILLION FALLEEN INCINERATED, JUST SO YOU COULD KEEP YOUR DIRTY LITTLE SECRET.
HUSBANDS.
WIVES.
CHILDREN.
I HAVE NO OTHER CHOICE.
DID YOU THINK THEIR *GHOSTS* WOULD REST EASILY? THEY'LL *HAVE* THEIR REVENGE... CARRIED OUT BY SURVIVORS SCATTERED TO PLACES LIKE *THIS*.
YOU CAN'T RUN FROM YOUR *PAST,* MONSTER.

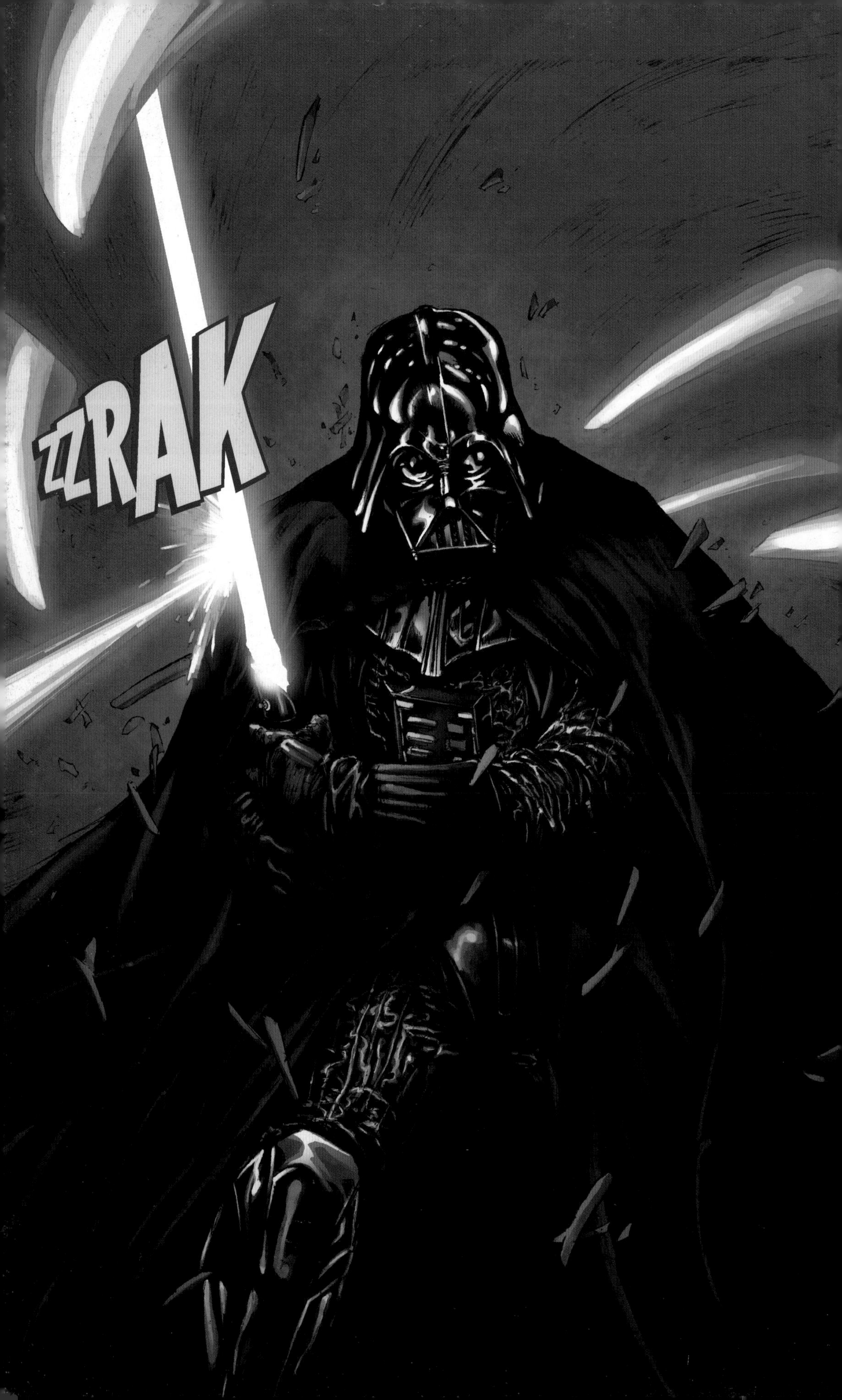
ZZRAK

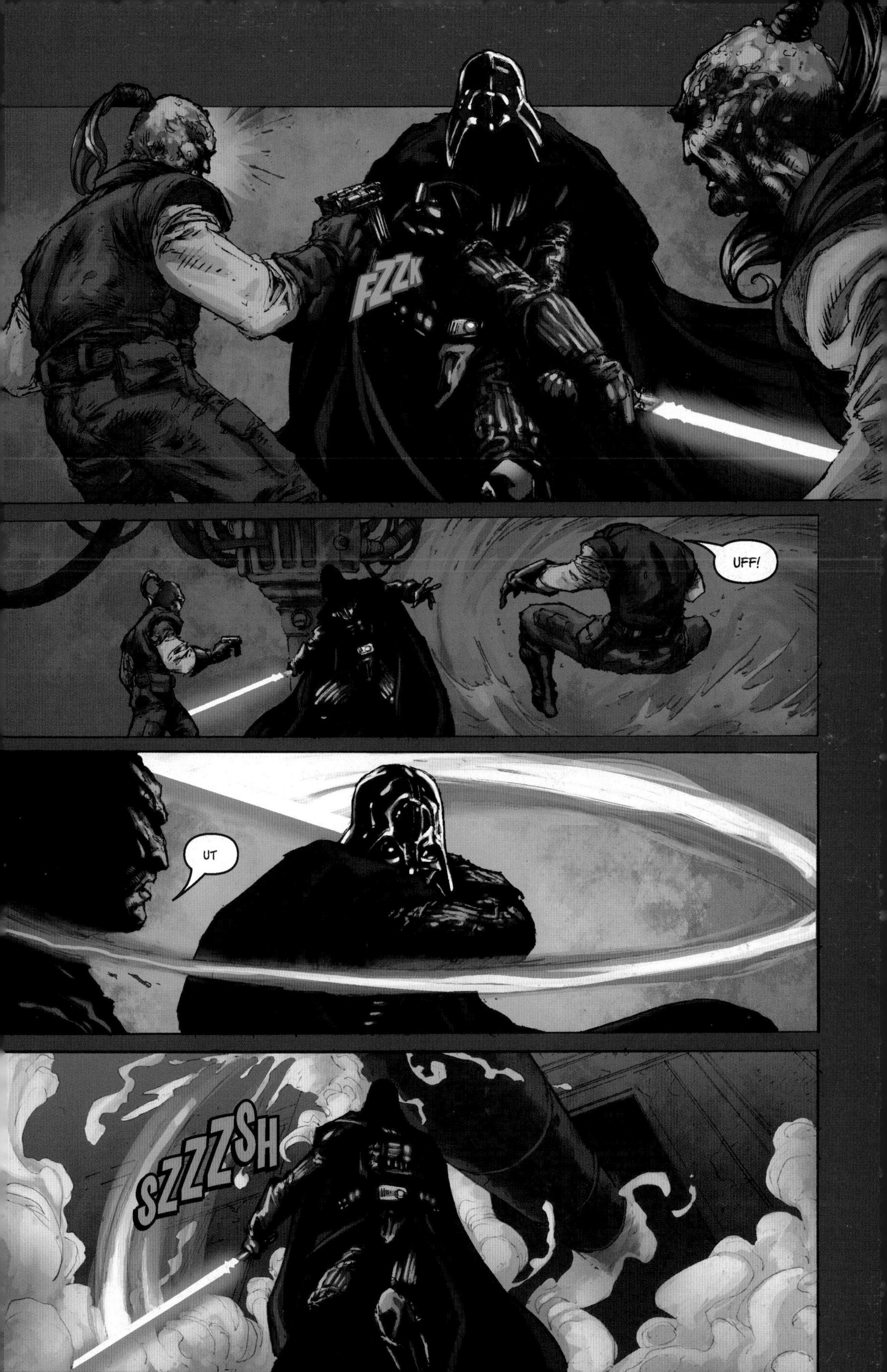
FZZK
UFF!
UT
SZZZSH

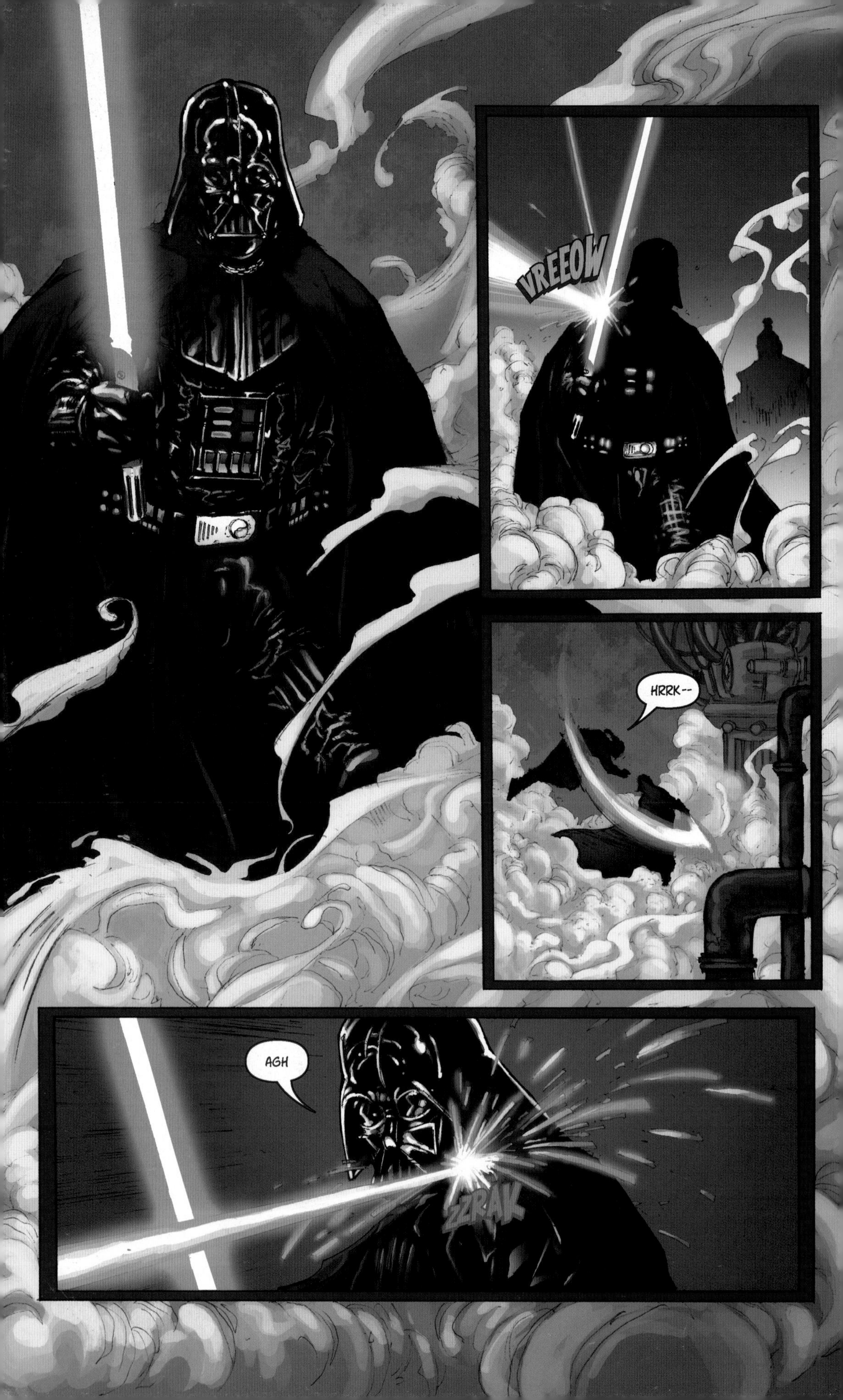
VREEOW
HRRK--
AGH
ZZRAK

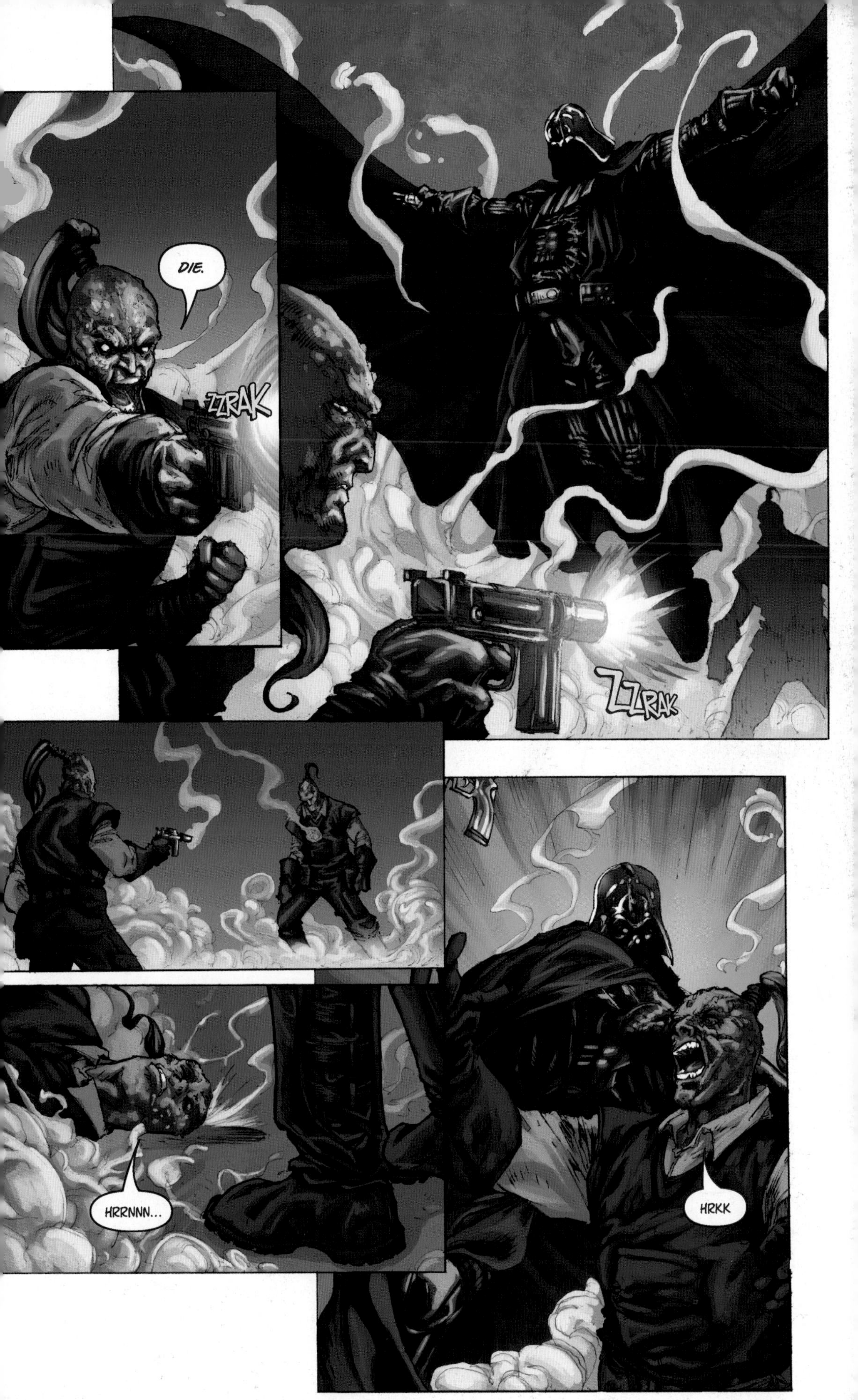

DIE.
ZZRAK
ZZRAK
HRRNNN...
HRKK

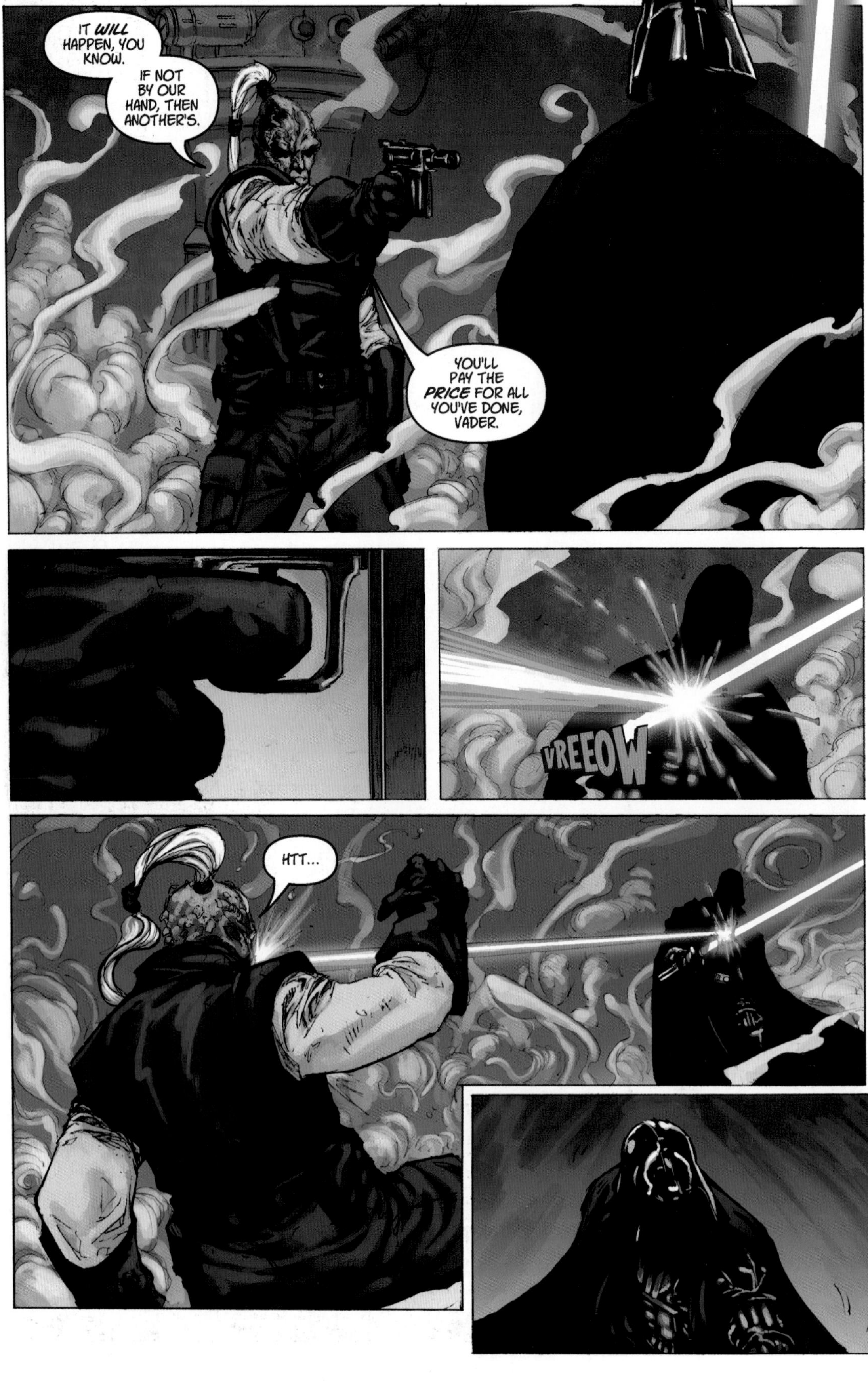

IT WILL HAPPEN, YOU KNOW.
IF NOT BY OUR HAND, THEN ANOTHER'S.
YOU'LL PAY THE PRICE FOR ALL YOU'VE DONE, VADER.
VREEOW
HTT...

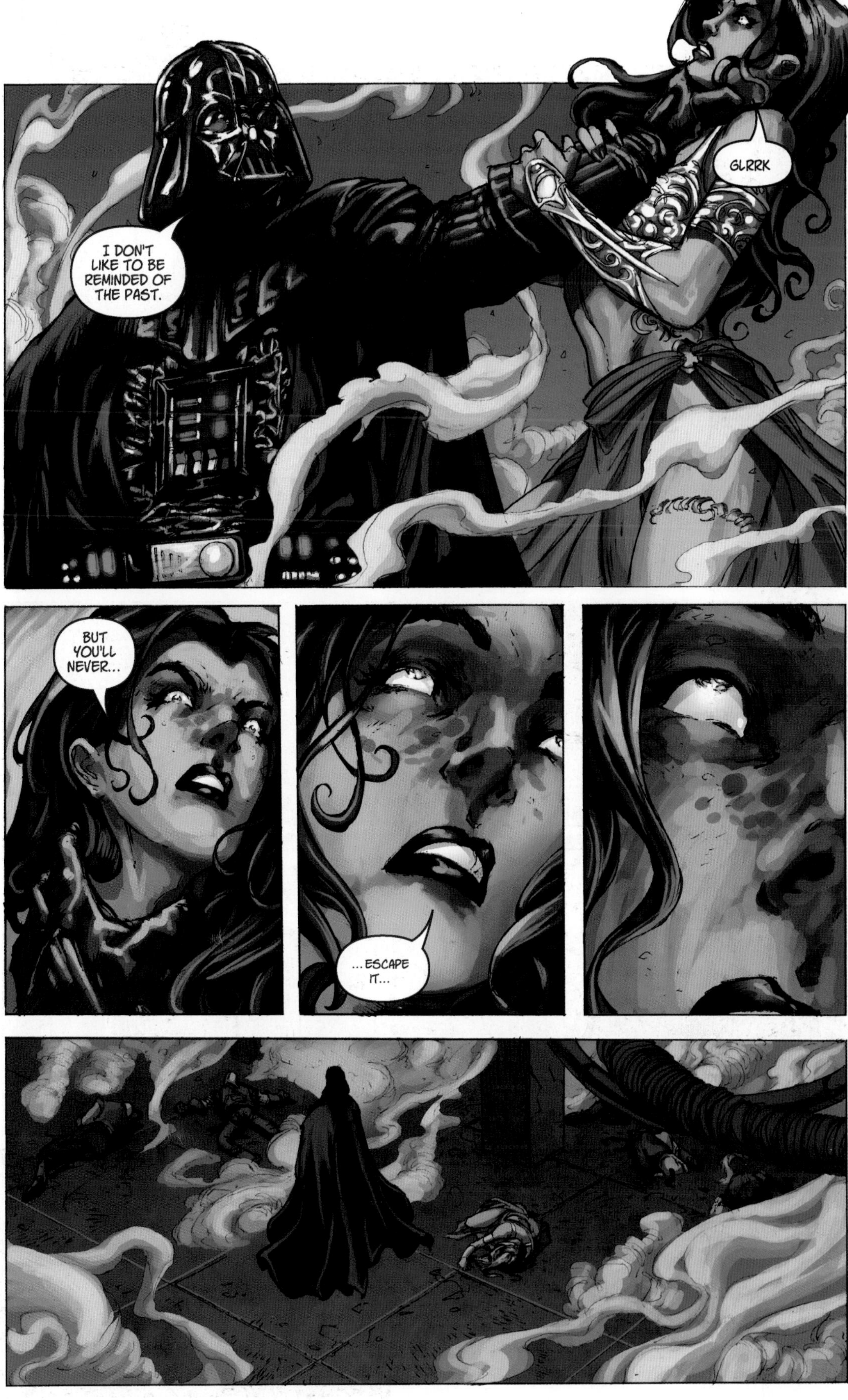
I DON'T LIKE TO BE REMINDED OF THE PAST.
GLRRK
BUT YOU'LL NEVER...
...ESCAPE IT...

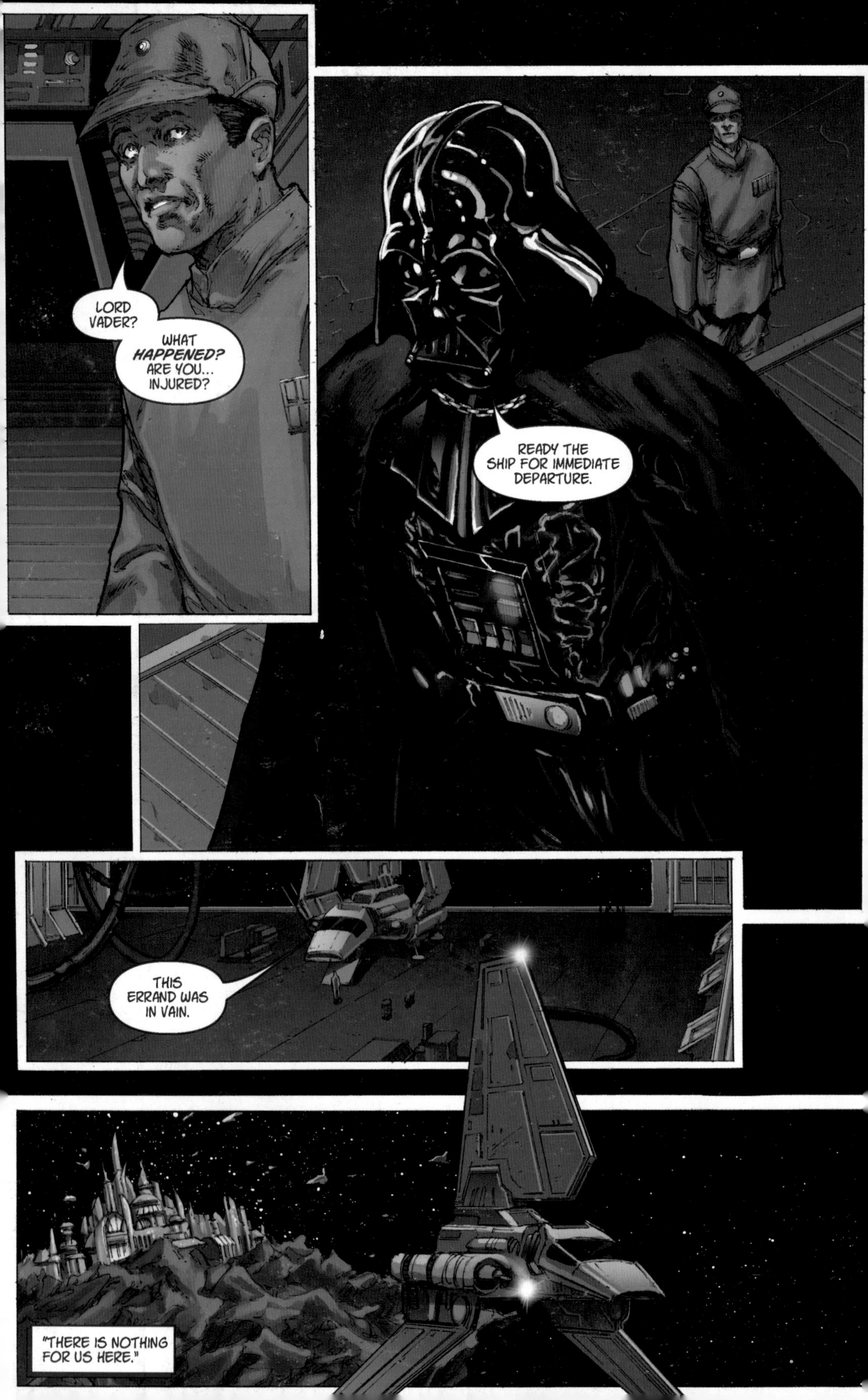
LORD VADER?
WHAT HAPPENED? ARE YOU... INJURED?
READY THE SHIP FOR IMMEDIATE DEPARTURE.
THIS ERRAND WAS IN VAIN.
"THERE IS NOTHING FOR US HERE."